Optimal
Portfolio
Modeling

A PERSONAL NOTE FROM
John McDevitt

Optimal Portfolio Modeling

*Models to Maximize
Return and Control
Risk in Excel and R + CD-ROM*

PHILIP J. McDONNELL

John Wiley & Sons, Inc.

Published by John Wiley & Sons, Inc., Hoboken, New Jersey.

Published simultaneously in Canada.

For general information on our other products and services or for technical support, please contact our Customer Care Department within the United States at (800) 762-2974, outside the United States at (317) 572-3993 or fax (317) 572-4002.

Wiley also publishes its books in a variety of electronic formats. Some content that appears in print may not be available in electronic books. For more information about Wiley products, visit our Web site at www.wiley.com.

Designations used by companies to distinguish their products are often claimed as trademarks. In all instances where John Wiley & Sons, Inc. is aware of a claim, the product names appear in initial capital or all capital letters. Readers, however, should contact the appropriate companies for more complete information regarding trademarks and registration.

Library of Congress Cataloging-in-Publication Data:

McDonnell, Philip J., 1949–
    Optimal portfolio modeling : models to maximize return and control risk in Excel and R + CD-ROM / Philip J. McDonnell.
        p.   cm. – (Wiley trading series)
    Includes bibliographical references and index.
    ISBN 978-0-470-11766-8 (cloth/CD-ROM)
    1. Portfolio management.   2. Risk management.   3. Investments.   4. Microsoft Excel (Computer file)   I. Title.
    HG4529.5.M385   2008
    332.60285′554–dc22

                                                                                2007038105

Printed in the United States of America.

10 9 8 7 6 5 4 3 2 1

Authoring a book is a labor of love coupled with a dash of inspiration and an abundance of hard effort. Needless to say this takes a toll on family life. With these thoughts in mind, this book is dedicated to my wife Pat and my family. Without their patient tolerance this work would not have been possible.

About the Author

Philip J. McDonnell is an active options trader living in Sammamish, Washington. He and his wife have two grown children.

Mr. McDonnell has been trading options since the first listed options exchange was formed. His trading experience spans more than 30 years. The emphasis and focus of his trading have been on quantitative methods.

Formerly, Mr. McDonnell was president of Dollar/Soft Corporation, a financial software company specializing in options and derivatives-related products. He has done consulting for Charles Schwab & Co. and developed risk-management software to allow the firm to perform what-if analyses of its customer margin accounts.

He has also been the president of Accelerated Data Systems, in which he and his team designed a new scientific high-performance minicomputer. Previously, he was vice president of engineering and manufacturing for a microcomputer company and helped turn critical manufacturing problems around. Prior to that, he served as president of Advanced Information Design, a maker of small business computer systems. His experience also includes stints at Stanford Linear Accelerator and a Northern California investment company.

His academic background is centered around the University of California at Berkeley, where he received his B.A. in 1972. His academic credentials include full satisfaction for all the degree requirements in mathematics, computer science, and statistics. His work also included all of the course work in finance and investments at both the undergrad and graduate levels.

He was employed as a researcher by the U.C. Berkeley Business School, where he worked closely with Prof. Victor Niederhoffer.

Contents

Preface

Successful investing is more than just picking the right stock. It is not just about timing the market. It requires two essential ingredients. The first ingredient is having a winning edge. The author's motto is: In order to beat the market, you need an edge. Never let your money leave home without it.

However, that is not enough. Even if one has a winning edge, it is entirely possible to invest too recklessly or too conservatively and not achieve your objectives. Even with a winning system, excessive position sizes can destroy a trade just as surely as lack of an edge. Failure to take adequate risks can also lead to underperformance.

The purpose of this book is to show how to achieve the right balance of position sizing and risk management so as to achieve the investment goals. Many books have covered how to have a winning edge. That is not the purview of this work. Rather, this book focuses on the relatively unexplored realm of money management and portfolio modeling. Managing a portfolio through position sizing is at least as important as finding and maintaining an investment edge.

Optimal Portfolio Modeling provides an introduction to the statistical properties of markets in the early chapters. The book is oriented to intelligent people who may not be full time rocket scientists. The author resisted the very strong temptation to title this work *Rocket Science for Average Folks*. Instead, the seemingly more dignified title was chosen.

Nevertheless, this work is designed to be very accessible to all, even with a limited math background. Only high school algebra is required to understand this book. Readers with an advanced technical degree may be astonished to find that calculus is not required. They may argue that optimization requires the use of calculus. This is true. However, Excel knows how to do the calculus and so does the statistical language R. Users do not need to know the math in order to understand the result. Only basic high school algebra is required.

These tools know how to do the magic. The user merely needs to know how to invoke the magic spell and how to interpret the results. This book assumes the reader has some beginner level of knowledge of Excel. The text fully explains how to use the built-in Solver, which allows the user to optimize models.

For readers interested in the statistical language R, advanced users will find this work to be an augmentation of their knowledge, with special emphasis on portfolio modeling and optimization problems. Beginning users of the open-source language R will appreciate the fact that the appendices and CD offer both a tutorial and introduction to R targeted to the beginning user. Additionally, the text identifies those functions that are appropriate for optimization in the powerful R library.

An important part of setting up a portfolio model is defining the objective or goal that one wishes to achieve. A significant portion of this book is devoted to the question of what is the right goal for the investor to seek. Often, this book refers to this as the utility function. Not all investors will or should choose the same objective function. The text discusses how to choose an appropriate objective function. A manager who is benchmarked to the Sharpe Ratio should choose that as the objective function. However, for more typical investors, the book strongly argues that maximizing long-term compounded growth of wealth should be an important component of the overall model. An innovative formula is provided that optimizes long-term wealth as well as provides a measure of stability not seen in other optimal money management formulas published to date.

Acknowledgments

Any work such as this builds on the advances and ideas of so many previous giants in the field. In particular, this work is based on the breakthroughs and developments of countless researchers in the fields of finance and statistics. Although they are too numerous to name in this space, the author wishes to acknowledge the foundation that they have built in the field. This book would not have been possible without the giants who preceded us, many of whom are named in the text.

Every person owes a debt of gratitude to those who have taught them throughout their lives. In this regard, I wish to acknowledge and thank my parents, who were my first teachers. They encouraged and inspired my endeavors.

The efforts and dedication of the many teachers and even fellow students who have helped in my education must be gratefully acknowledged. Although too numerous to name individually, the cumulative contribution of their efforts and generosity with their knowledge has been of inestimable value in my personal development. Naturally, it has been a requisite foundation, essential to this work.

There is one particular teacher I met as a professor of finance when we were both associated with the University of California at Berkeley. He is Victor Niederhoffer, who has enjoyed a meteoric speculative career. Prior to meeting him, I had the fuzzy notion that the best approach to the markets was through a rigorous quantitative methodology. At that time, the random walk ruled the thinking in finance. So there was little call for eccentric academics who thought they could beat the market, quantitatively or any other way. Professor Niederhoffer was just such a divergent thinker.

His help and guidance taught me to see things at their simplest. That is the essence of his approach. His enlightenment also helped me to learn how to avoid the numerous pitfalls that can arise in quantitative studies. In fact, one of the things he taught me was what *not* to do on a quantitative study. Perhaps more than anything, working with him inspired and motivated me to further my efforts to study the markets from a quantitative perspective. His inspiration has lasted a lifetime.

One must also acknowledge the hundreds of friends known as the *Spec List* who have stimulated my thinking, inspired my work, and helped me in so many ways. Victor was the founder of the group and remains its chair. We all communicate daily to discuss markets with a quantitative focus. Unquestionably, the help and support of this remarkably intelligent but diverse group has been a source of inspiration to me. Many of the ideas herein are amplifications of some of the ideas I have discussed more briefly with the group. Their collective comments, questions, and debate have helped to refine these ideas. Several of my friends in the group have encouraged me to write this book, and certainly this must be acknowledged.

Perhaps most directly, I must acknowledge the very helpful people at Wiley who were directly responsible for helping with this work. Foremost of those is Pamela van Giessen who edited this work. Her experienced guidance and advice were critical in shaping this book. Her encouragement to become an author was the final impetus that helped to launch this project.

Finally, I must thank Kate Wood and Jennifer MacDonald of Wiley, who were so helpful in supporting and editing this book. There are also many other people at Wiley whose names I do not even know who have contributed to this effort. I am very grateful to all of them.

Even though many have contributed to this work, ultimately, any errors are mine.

CHAPTER 1

Modeling Market Microstructure— Randomness in Markets

Traditionally, portfolio modeling has been the domain of highly quantitative people with advanced degrees in math and science. On Wall Street, such people are commonly called *rocket scientists*. *Optimal Portfolio Modeling* was written to provide an easily accessible introduction to portfolio modeling for readers who prefer an intuitive approach. This book can be read by the average intelligent person who has only a modest high school math background. It is designed for people who wish to understand rocket science with a minimum of math.

The focus of this book is on money management. It is not a book about market timing, nor is it designed to help you pick stocks. There are numerous other books that address those subjects. Rather, this work will show the reader how to define models to help manage money and control risk. Stock selection is really just the details. The big picture is actually about achieving your overall portfolio goals.

Included with this book is a CD-ROM that includes numerous examples in both Excel and R, the statistical modeling language. The book assumes the user has a beginner's level knowledge of Excel and focuses mainly on those specific areas that apply to portfolio modeling and optimization. There are many books that offer an introduction to Excel, and the interested reader is encouraged to investigate those.

R is an open-source language that offers powerful graphics and statistics capabilities. Two appendices in this book offer introductory support for users who wish to download R at no cost and learn how to program. Because R is powerful, many functions and graphs can be done with very few command lines. Often, only a single line will create a graph or perform a statistical analysis.

The overriding philosophy of all of the examples is simplicity and ease of understanding. Consequently, each example typically focuses on a single simple problem or calculation. It is the job of the computer to know how to perform the calculations. The user only needs to know how to invoke the right computer function and to understand the results. Understanding and intuition are the primary goals of this book.

This chapter introduces the important background of market microstructure and randomness. This is a foundation for the ideas developed later in this book. The discussion starts with a thorough introduction to the idea of randomness and what a *random walk* is. The topic of randomness is presented as an essential element in understanding how and why a portfolio works. After all, the primary rationale for a portfolio is intelligent diversification.

From there, the book moves to a discussion of market microstructure and how it affects the operation of markets. Later, the reader is introduced to the *efficient market hypothesis*, along with its history and development, starting with early pioneers in the field. Augmenting this is the discussion on *arbitrage pricing theory* and its modern applications. This latter topic shows how the market identifies and eliminates any risk, less arbitrage opportunities.

Trading speculative markets has always been difficult. Over the years, several studies have shown that some 70 to 80 percent of all mutual funds underperform the averages. A study by Professor Terrance Odean of the University of California at Berkeley demonstrated that most individual investors actually lose money. This study analyzed thousands of real-life individual investor brokerage accounts. Thus, it provides a comprehensive look at how real individual traders operate. The inescapable conclusion is that both professional and individual investors find that trading the markets is challenging.

Successful trading is predicated on one thing. Traders must predict the direction of price changes in the future. At a minimum, a successful trader must predict prices so that each trade has an expectation of yielding a profit. This does not mean that each trade must be successful, but, rather, that a succession of trades would usually be expected to result in a profit. This should not be taken to mean that having a positive expectation for each trade is the only thing a successful trader needs. The astute reader will note that the use of words such as *usually*, *average*, and *expectation* naturally implies that the art of forecasting is far from perfect. In fact, it is best studied from a statistical perspective with a view to identifying what is random and what is predictable.

In a recent 500-day period, the stock market as measured by the Standard and Poor's 500 index was generally a modestly up market. A statistical analysis of the daily compounded returns for the period shows:

Average daily return:	.038 percent
Standard deviation:	.640 percent
Probability of rise:	56 percent

The *standard deviation* is simply a measure of the variability of returns around the average. From this simple analysis, we can make some interesting observations:

1. The average daily return is small with respect to the standard deviation.
2. The daily variability is relatively large, at 16 times the return.
3. The market went up 56 percent of the time, or slightly more than half. It also went down the other 44 percent of the days. So even during up markets, the number of up days is only slightly better than 50–50.
4. The variability completely swamps the average return.

Observations such as these have led many early researchers in finance to propose a model for the markets that explicitly embraces randomness at its very core. A cornerstone of this idea is that markets represent all of the knowledge, information, and intelligent analysis that the many participants bring to bear. Thus, the market has already priced itself to correspond with the sum of all human knowledge. In order to outperform the market, a trader must have better information or analysis than the rest of the participants collectively. It would seem the successful trader must be smarter than everyone else in the world put together.

THE RANDOM WALK MODEL

To the typical layman, the *random walk model* is the best-known name for the idea that markets are very good at pricing themselves so as to remove excess profit opportunities. The academic community generally prefers the description the *efficient market hypothesis* (EMH). Either way, the idea is the same—it is very difficult to outperform the market. If someone does outperform, then it is likely only attributable to mere luck and not skill.

The history of the EMH is a rather long one. The first known work was by Louis Bachelier in 1900, in which he posited a normal distribution of price changes and developed the first-known option model based on the idea of a normal random walk (see Figure 1.1). His seminal paper in the field was quickly forgotten for some 60 years. As an interesting side note, the mathematics that Bachelier developed was essentially the same analysis that Albert Einstein reinvented in 1906 in his study of Brownian motion of microscopic particles. Einstein's famous paper was published some six years after Bachelier's work. However Bachelier's paper languished in relative obscurity until its rediscovery in the 1960s.

Prof. Paul Samuelson of the Massachusetts Institute of Technology offered a *Proof that Properly Anticipated Prices Fluctuate Randomly* in the 1960s. This provided a theoretical basis for the EMH idea. However, it fell to M. F. M. Osborne to provide the

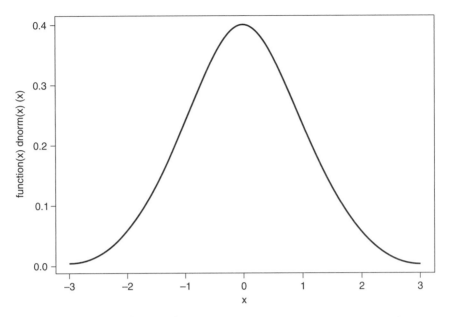

Figure 1.1 Normal Probability Distribution

modern theoretical basis for the efficient market hypothesis. Osborne was the first to posit the idea of a lognormal distribution and provide evidence that the price changes in the market were log normally distributed. Furthermore, he was the first modern researcher to draw the link between the fluctuations of the market and the mathematics of random walks developed by Bachelier and Einstein decades earlier.

Osborne was a physicist by training employed at the U.S. Naval Observatory. As such, he was not an academic, nor did he come from a traditional finance background. Thus, it is not surprising that he is rarely recognized as the father of the efficient market hypothesis in the lognormal form. However, it is very clear that his empirical and theoretical work that described the distribution of stock price changes as log normal and the underlying process of the market as being akin to the process described by Einstein called *Brownian motion* was the first to elucidate both concepts. Osborne deserves the honor of being the father of the EMH.

As so often happens in academia, others who published later and were fully aware of Osborne's work have received much of the credit. Statistician and student of mathematical and statistical history, Stephen M. Stigler has whimsically called the phenomenon his *law of eponymy*. The wrong person is invariably credited with any given discovery.

One aspect of this phenomenon is that when a person is erroneously credited with a discovery for whatever reason, his or her name is attached to that discovery. After much widespread usage, the name tends to stick. So even when it is later discovered by historians that someone else actually discovered the idea first, it is usually just treated as a footnote and rarely adopted into common usage among practitioners in the field.

Such is the case for Osborne's contribution to the efficient market hypothesis. It was partly because he was a physicist working in the field of astronomy. At the time of his publication, he was not really an accepted name in the field of finance.

One form of the EMH defines the relationship between today's price X_t and tomorrow's price X_{t+1} as follows:

$$X_{t+1} = X_t + e \tag{1.1}$$

where e is a random error term. We note that this model is inherently an additive model. The usual academic assumption corresponding to this type of model is the normal distribution. The key concept is that the normal distribution is strongly associated with sums of random variables. In fact, there is a weak convergence theorem in probability theory that states that for *any* sums of independent identically distributed variables with finite variance, their distribution will converge to the normal distribution. This result virtually assures us that the normal distribution will remain ubiquitous in nature.

However, the empirical work of Osborne showed us that the distribution of price changes was log normal. This type of distribution is consistent with a multiplicative model of price changes. In this model, the expression for price changes becomes

$$X_{t+1} = X_t(1 + e) \tag{1.2}$$

WHAT YOU CANNOT PREDICT IS RANDOM TO YOU

Some would argue that the market is not random. Certainly, almost every single participant in the market believes he or she will achieve superior results. Most of these participants are smarter, richer, and better educated than average. Can they all achieve superior returns? Of course, it would be mathematically impossible for everyone to be above average. Can they all be deluded?

To answer this question it is helpful to look at the long-term history of the market. When we fit a regression line through the monthly Standard & Poor's closing prices P_t on the first trading day of each month since 1950 until November 2006, we find the following:

$$\ln P_t = .0059t + 3.06$$

In this case the t values are simply month numbers starting at 1, then 2, and so on for each of the 683 months in the study. The fitted coefficient .0059 can be interpreted as a simple monthly rate of increase in the series. So if we annualize, we get an annual rate of return of about 7.1 percent for the long-term growth rate of the Standard & Poor's 500 average (see Figure 1.2). This is a very respectable long-term upward trend in the

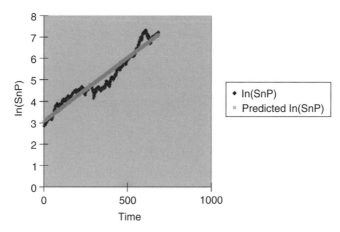

Figure 1.2   Log S&P Regression as Function of Time

market. The R^2 for this regression was 97 percent. Given that 100 percent is a perfect fit, this indicates that the model is a very good one.

The underlying message here is that the market goes up over time. The fact that the natural log model fits well tells us that the growth in the market is compounded and presumably derived from a multiplicative model. But beyond that, it tends to make people think they are financial geniuses who might not be.

> *Bull markets make us all geniuses.*
>
> —Wall Street maxim

From the perspective of the long-term time frame, the market has been in a bull phase for at least the entire last century. Human beings have a natural propensity to attribute good luck to their own innate skill. Psychologists call this the *self-attribution fallacy*. The long-term bull market has created a large group of investors who believe they have some superior gift for investing. Few investors ever stop to critically analyze their own results to verify that they are indeed performing better than the market.

Given that the market exhibits long-term compounded returns over time, it is clear the best model is a multiplicative one. This long-term return is often called the *drift*—the tendency of the market to move inexorably upward over time. However, to understand the shorter-term movements of the market, we must look to a different kind of model in which the short-term fluctuations appear to be more random. The reason for that is simply because the marketplace in general will anticipate all known information, and thus, the current market price is the best price available. Thus, by definition, any news that is material to the market and was not anticipated will appear as random shocks in either direction.

The key idea to understand is that the market will not respond to news that it already knows. Or if it does, that response will be contrary to what a rational analyst might have expected. These contrary movements are caused when a large group of investors was expecting a certain piece of news and thus, holding positions that were previously taken. When the news is announced, the entire group may try to unwind their positions, resulting in a market movement in exactly the opposite direction one might expect. Simply put, the market has already discounted the expected news and adjusted the price well in advance. Because this phenomenon is so prevalent, Wall Street has evolved the maxim, "Buy on the rumor, sell on the news." Although one would never recommend relying on rumors for investment success, certainly buying on the correct anticipation of news is the better strategy.

This leaves us with the realization that, absent informed knowledge of upcoming news, the outcome of such events will be random and unpredictable to us. Some would argue that for most news someone knew the event in advance. Certainly for earnings announcements and government reports, someone did know the information to a certainty. For them, the news was not random but completely predictable. Assuming the information was not widely disclosed, then for the rest of investors, the information remains random and unpredictable.

There is a general principle at work here. *If we cannot predict the news, then it is random to us.* So even if others know the information, then insofar as we do not, and cannot predict it, it remains random for us.

MARKET MICROSTRUCTURE

Generally speaking, the market consists of the interactions between four broad classes of orders. These can be grouped into two categories each. There are market orders and there are limit orders. There are orders to buy and sell. Although there are variations and nuances on each, these characterize the main categories of trading orders.

- *Market order*—A market order is an order to buy or sell that is to be executed immediately at the best available price
- *Limit order*—This is an order to buy or sell that is only to be executed at the specified limit price or better. Limit orders may have an expiration, such as the end of the day or 60 days.

The quote at any given time is essentially based on the best limit order to buy, which is known as the *bid*, and the best limit order to sell, which is the *ask*. When a market order to sell comes in, it is usually crossed with the bid. Therefore, we can expect the price of a market order to sell to be the bid price. We should note that market orders are usually smaller in size than limit orders. Usually, this means that the market order will be executed at the bid and that the remaining size of the limit order(s) at the bid will be reduced by the amount of the market order. In effect, market orders nibble away at the larger limit orders. It is only after enough market orders have consumed the bid that the bid–ask quote will drop to a new lower bid.

The other side of this process is when a market order to buy, say, 200 shares comes in. Assume there are 1,000 shares for sale at the ask price of 50.10. In this case, the market order will be crossed with the limit order, resulting in a transaction of 200 shares at a price of 50.10. After the transaction, the ask side limit order will show the remaining 800 shares offered at 50.10. It is only after the 800 shares have been consumed by market orders that the ask price will move higher.

Because limit orders tend to persist longer than market orders and are larger than market orders, there is a tendency for the last sale price to alternate back and forth between the bid and ask until one or the other price barrier is consumed. Only then does the quote move. For example, when the ask price is extinguished, the ask will move to a new higher price—the next limit order up. Quite often, the old bid will be superceded by a slightly higher bid, either from a market maker or an off-floor limit order. Thus, the entire quote has a tendency to move up. To really understand the current market situation, one must really look beyond simply the last sale and consider the current bid and ask and the relative size of the bid and ask.

Another important aspect of this market microstructure can be understood in the sense of news. We can view the arrival of market orders as news of an investor's decision process. In some cases, orders to sell may simply indicate a need for liquidity. It may be as simple as Aunt Mabel in Peoria sold 100 shares to raise money to buy videogames for all her nieces and nephews this Christmas. Alternatively, the sale may mean that an investor's views on the prospects for the company have changed. This is certainly a different kind of information, but every trade contains information.

The other side of the coin is that predicting and modeling the market at the microstructure level is very difficult. We do not even know who Aunt Mabel is, much less her plans and how many nieces and nephews she has. Thus, her sale of stock for liquidity needs is unpredictable for us. Therefore, any price change it causes is also random to us. So to model this sort of environment we must explicitly allow for a large degree of randomness in the short-term market movements.

The astute reader may have wondered if all market orders are always crossed with limit orders. The answer, of course, is no. Most market orders are crossed with limit orders for the reasons already mentioned, but certainly it is possible for two market orders to arrive at essentially the same time and be crossed with each other. By the same token, it is possible for an aggressive trader to place a large limit order to buy at the ask price or to sell at the bid price. In this case, a limit order will be crossed with a limit order.

There are also stop orders and other contingencies that can be placed on orders. However, for the most part, such as when the stop price is hit, the order becomes a valid market order. Alternatively, for a stop limit order it becomes a valid limit order. Thus, the four-order model just described adequately covers the vast majority of the cases.

It is also worth noting that the market makers effectively act as though they were placing limit orders. Sometimes the bid and ask will both be from a market maker. At other times, one or the other may be an off floor limit order. Nevertheless, the market makers seek to profit from the tendency for the market to trade back and for the several times between the bid and ask prices before moving either higher and lower. This market-maker strategy does not always work, but it works well enough that market makers tend to make a very good profit. A very telling fact is that New York Stock Exchange seats have routinely sold for millions of dollars for quite awhile now.

EFFICIENT MARKET HYPOTHESIS

We are now ready to formalize our efficient market hypothesis as a mathematical model. The general principle is that it is a multiplicative model wherein the near-term price changes are swamped by the short-term variability.

Thus, a good statement of the model is the form expressed earlier:

$$X_{t+1} = X_t(1 + e) \qquad (1.3)$$

Here, we have the price today X_t related to the price tomorrow by a simple random multiplicative term $(1 + e)$, where e is the random variable. In Chapter 2, we will discuss the nature of the random variable e to better understand the structure of the market.

We note that equation 1.3 is the multiplicative form analogous to equation 1.2. This is in contrast to the additive model, which is given by equation 1.1. The multiplicative form is consistent with the log normal distribution put forward by Osborne.

Later in this book, we shall show how the multiplicative and lognormal models are also the most appropriate in order to deal with the compound interest effect known to exist in the equity markets. This forms the foundation for the ideas developed later in this book, which allow an investor to maximize long-term compounded returns on the portfolio.

One of the author's favorite apocryphal stories is that of the finance professor, the economist, and the nimble trader.

One day, a finance professor, who firmly believed in the Efficient Market Hypothesis, was walking along the street. He spotted a one hundred dollar bill lying on the ground. He paused, realized that in an efficient market no one would leave hundred dollar bills lying around. He continued on his walk, confident that it was only a trick of the light.

Minutes later an economist strolled by and saw the hundred dollar bill. He began to calculate to see if picking up the hundred dollar bill would improve his utility of wealth for the day. While he was still calculating, a quick-stepping trader walked past him, picked up the hundred dollar bill and hastily continued on down the street.

The next section has much to do with quick-footed traders.

ARBITRAGE PRICING THEORY

A close cousin of the EMH is a theory called *arbitrage pricing theory* (APT). Essentially, this says that the market will not allow any riskless arbitrage to exist. A simple example of riskless arbitrage is if IBM is selling at $80 per share on the New York Stock Exchange and sells for 79.90 on the Pacific Stock Exchange. A nimble trader can buy shares at 79.90 on the Pacific and sell them for 80 in New York for a quick profit of .10. This trade is essentially riskless if done simultaneously.

Arbitrage pricing theory mandates that such opportunities should not exist, or that if they do, they will be quickly extinguished to the point that they are no longer profitable after expenses. It is easy to see why this should happen. In the case of our arbitrage trader in IBM shares when he buys at 79.90, his buying will tend to increase the price on the Pacific Exchange. When he sells in New York, his selling will tend to drive the price there down. Thus, the two prices will quickly come into line and the arbitrage opportunity will be extinguished.

The ideas of APT have developed largely through the efforts of Stephen Ross and Fisher Black. A broader version of these ideas is the concept that one can arbitrage expectations as well as simple price. So rather than just focusing on price differential, the term can include cross relationships between different assets connected via a common factor.

Suppose the price of oil has risen. Then it might be reasonable to believe that the expectation for the earnings of companies that sell oil would be enhanced as well. They are now able to sell at a higher price. Thus, our expectation for the price of oil stocks is now enhanced and we would buy.

Such buying, if done by many, would tend to force the prices of oil stocks up in response to the rise in the oil commodity itself. It is an example of how one factor can drive many stocks. However, the same factor can have a negative impact on other stocks.

An example of this is obvious as well. Again, assume the price of oil has risen as before. If we consider the impact of this fact on automobile companies, we quickly realize that the impact can only be negative. The effect may vary from company to company, but it is negative. It now costs more to fuel your car and consumers are less likely to purchase new cars or extra cars.

Companies that are heavily into gas-guzzling SUVs will be hurt the most. Consumers have the strongest disincentive with respect to these vehicles. It is much easier for them to defer or cancel any new purchase. However, companies that are strong in the economical car submarkets or in fuel-saving hybrids will likely benefit, relatively speaking.

One might suppose that with the advent and ubiquity of modern computing power, such arbitrage opportunities would vanish. However, it is also the case that there has been an enormous rise in derivative instruments in the last few decades as well. It is now entirely possible to buy a basket of stocks representing some index and to trade a futures contract on the index and to trade an exchange traded fund on the index. The number of arbitrage opportunities increases with the number of combinations of instruments available. So when we add multiple futures contracts to the mix, we have many more combinations. But the real arbitrage opportunities are in the large number of options, both puts and calls, at multiple strike prices and various expiration months. On any given day, the markets will trade over 50,000 equity distinct options. The number of listed options is well into the hundreds of thousands. The number of arbitrage combinations of two, three, or more options on all these stocks is well into the millions.

Thus, even with today's computing power it is still rather difficult for the market to eliminate all arbitrage opportunities. In fact, the market does a remarkably good job, considering the large number of such arbitrages available. The bottom line is that the arbitrage pricing theory is a pretty good model for market efficiency, but not necessarily a perfect one.

At this point the user is encouraged to begin to explore the CD-ROM that came with this book. Each chapter of this work has corresponding examples on the CD-ROM that relate to the topics developed in the chapter. Although using the CD is not required, it is highly recommended as a way to bring the chapter contents to life. The programs and examples provided are generally intended to be as simple as possible and focus only on a particular topic presented in the text.

With that in mind, the user should find it a very worthwhile exercise at the end of each chapter to take a break and review the examples for that chapter. The exercise should take only a few minutes in most cases, but the hands-on experience should prove very helpful in enabling readers to get a feel for the subjects covered.

The reader should start exploring the CD-ROM by reading the appendix, *About the CD-ROM*.

CHAPTER 2

Distribution of Price Changes

In order to discuss the idea of randomness in the markets, it is very helpful to understand some basic statistics. This chapter introduces the essential ideas of that discipline from an intuitive conceptual standpoint. The discussion begins with a definition of what a probability distribution is and proceeds to discuss the well-known normal and lognormal distributions as they relate to the markets. A little of the history of these distributions is provided as well.

In keeping with the practical nature of this book, a handy formula is provided that allows us to approximate the normal distribution with a rational polynomial. Do not be dismayed if you are unfamiliar with rational polynomials. It is just a formula, and your computer knows how to do those very well.

One of the essential topics of this chapter is the discussion of the *reflection principle*. The idea is based on the symmetry and *self-similarity* of the normal distribution. This section should not be skipped, for it is the foundation of several of the ideas presented later in the book.

THE NORMAL DISTRIBUTION

When Maury F. M. Osborne first studied the market, he examined the changes in price for New York Stock Exchange stocks. His research considered both the actual price levels and changes for the stocks in question. His work was the first to scientifically evaluate the distribution of price levels and of changes. This is a good starting point for any research into the nature of market prices.

First we should consider the definition of the word *distribution*. To a statistician, the probability distribution is the probability that the given random variable will be at a certain value level for a given observation. In other words, a distribution associates a range of values and their respective probabilities of occurrence. It is not just one number. For many distributions there is a known formula to calculate the probability that a given observation will be at level x. To calculate the probability, we simply plug x into the formula and calculate. However, for many other distributions there is no known formula or the distribution itself is unknown so the convenience of a closed formula is not available.

Most books on probability and statistics start with a distribution known as the *binomial distribution*. It can be used to model a simple game of coin flipping. For our purposes, the probability of a head will be assumed to be 50 percent as is the probability for tails. If you play this game one time and bet \$1 on heads, then the outcome will be $+1$ half the time and -1 the other half of the time. After only two coin flips, the outcomes and their probabilities are as follows:

Outcome	Probability
-2	.25
0	.50
$+2$	.25

Note that the outcome of zero or breakeven is the most likely event after only two flips. The more extreme outcomes of plus or minus two are less likely. So even after two flips we see that the outcomes tend to pile up in the middle. The reason for this effect is clear if we examine the four possible paths in getting to these outcomes:

$$- \; -$$
$$- \; +$$
$$+ \; -$$
$$+ \; +$$

There are only these four paths possible, and each is equally likely. An inspection of the paths $-+$ and $+-$ shows that these two will both result in the zero outcome. Even though the order is different, the outcome is the same. However, to arrive at plus or minus two, there is only one available path. Both must lose or both must win. Intuitively, we can see that the number of paths to arrive at the center is greater than the number of paths to arrive at extreme values. This principle will generalize to more coin flips. It is easier for a random process to arrive near the center than it is to arrive near an extreme value simply because there are more paths to the center and fewer to the extremes.

Another property to note in this discussion is that the distribution of outcomes is *symmetric* about the midpoint. This results partly from the fact that the game outcomes are symmetric. At each stage the participant is equally likely to win equally large amounts. It is also the case that each stage is composed of another similar bet. Thus, this distribution over many outcomes will be *self-similar*.

It is well known in statistics that the binomial distribution will eventually converge to the normal distribution. The mathematical proof of this convergence will not concern us here. Rather, we shall focus on the underlying intuition of the result and try to gain an understanding of the properties of the normal distribution from that. The important point is, that if we play the game long enough, the binomial will eventually result in a distribution of outcomes that is very close to the normal distribution.

In Figure 2.1 we see a graph of the probability distribution for the normal distribution. The obvious bell shape of the curve naturally inspired the nickname *bell-shaped curve* for this distribution.

We immediately note three properties:

1. *The height of the curve represents the probability of that event occurring.* The center of the curve is the highest. This means that the greatest probability is for the next random outcome from a normal distribution to come from the center.

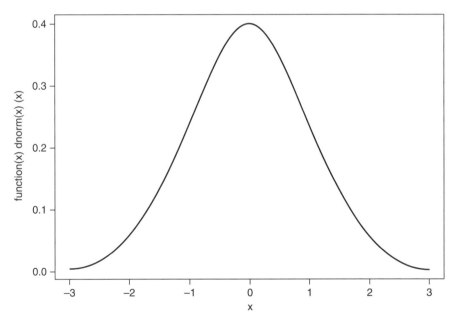

Figure 2.1 Normal Probability Distribution

2. *The extremes of the distribution are the least likely.* It is less likely that the next outcome will come from the extremes.

3. *The distribution is symmetric.* The left half is the mirror image of the right half.

From our discussion of the simple binomial distribution, we saw that the binomial is self-similar in the sense that each added outcome looks like the previous ones but adds more paths. Knowing that the binomial converges to the normal distribution given large enough *sample size,* then we have an intuitive basis to understand that the normal distribution is self-similar as well. The reason is the same. At each added stage the normal adds more similar paths to the resulting outcomes. Thus, we have the important result that any given normal distribution is simply the outcome of a succession of similar normal distributions.

The cumulative density function (cdf) for the normal distribution is given by Figure 2.2. The cumulative distribution function is obtained by starting at the left side

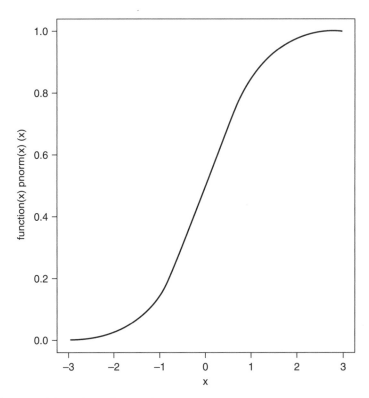

Figure 2.2 Normal Cumulative Density Function

of the normal bell-shaped curve and adding up each probability. This is simply the calculus concept of adding up the area under the probability curve. Thus, the cdf always starts at zero and moves monotonically upward to the right to a final value of one. The fact that the value is one simply means that the probability is 100 percent that a given value from the normal distribution will lie somewhere on that curve.

REFLECTION PRINCIPLE

The self-similar symmetry of the normal distribution results in another well-known and important property of the normal distribution. It is the *reflection principle.*

> **reflection principle**—*The normal distribution is a mirror image of itself-reflected through its central axis.*

The mean is equal to the median for a normal distribution. Because the mean of the normal distribution is the central axis, it is also true that the normal distribution is reflected through the mean and median as well.

Although there are several proofs of the reflection principle in statistics that involve advanced mathematics, the result has been proved using elementary concepts as well. In a similar fashion, the reflection principle can be used to prove concepts in a very elegant and intuitive manner. The important concept here is that the reflection principle arises in any self-similar, symmetric distribution and specifically applies to the normal distribution. We shall use the reflection principle later to prove several important modeling concepts that are of general importance to investors.

We should consider that the normal distribution naturally arises in conjunction with the additive model for market prices. Thus, the appropriate model is of this form:

$$X_{t+1} = X_t + e \tag{2.1}$$

where X_t is the price at time t, and e is a normally distributed random *innovation*. Here the word innovation simply implies new information that presumably contributed to the change in price.

We should also note that the normal distribution is completely characterized if we know the mean and standard deviation for the distribution. The usual notation to precisely denote a normal distribution is something like:

$$N(\mu, \sigma)$$

where μ is the mean and σ is the standard deviation.

The probability function for the normal distribution is given by:

$$p(x) = \frac{1}{\sigma\sqrt{2\pi}} \exp[-(x-u)^2/(2\sigma^2)]$$ (2.2)

Equation 2.2 gives us the probability that a random variable drawn from a normal distribution with mean u and standard deviation σ will take on value x. In essence, it defines the height of the bell curve at any given point.

The complete formula for the cumulative probability of the standardized normal distribution is

$$\Phi(z) = \frac{1}{\sqrt{2\pi}} \int_0^z e^{-1/2z^2} dz$$ (2.3)

where z is a standardized transform of the random variable x given by:

$$z = (x-u)/\sigma.$$

We note in passing that the terms of the formula are greatly simplified by using the transformed z variable. Thus, the mean and standard deviation terms need not appear because they are zero and one, respectively.

Although the formula may look intimidating to some, in fact one rarely needs to deal with the actual formula for practical modeling. Most computing platforms that one might use for financial modeling include simple methods to calculate the probabilities of the normal distribution. In particular, the open source statistical language R and Excel both include such library functions.

APPROXIMATION OF THE NORMAL DISTRIBUTION BY RATIONAL POLYNOMIAL

For situations in which the computing platform does not offer a method to compute the normal distribution, one can use the following rational polynomial to evaluate the function for any given x:

$$N(x) = 1 - p(x)(ak + bk^2 + ck^3 + dk^4 + fk^5) \quad \text{for} \quad x \geq 0$$ (2.4)

where

$$k = 1/(1 + .2316419x)$$
$$p(x) = 1/\sqrt{2\pi} \, e^{-x^2/2}$$

And the constants are

$$a = .319381530$$
$$b = -.356563782$$
$$c = 1.781477937$$
$$d = -1.821255978$$
$$f = 1.330274429$$

Note that this formula applies to a standardized variable from an $N(0, 1)$ distribution. This means that the variable has been transformed by subtracting the mean of the distribution and dividing by the standard deviation. Equation 2.4 applies only to values for x that are greater than or equal to zero. However, by the reflection principle we can use the formula for negative values of x simply by taking it as:

$$N(x) = 1 - N(x) \quad \text{for} \quad x < 0 \tag{2.5}$$

LOGNORMAL DISTRIBUTION

Earlier, we discussed the idea that the lognormal distribution was the more appropriate model for modeling stock prices. This result springs directly from the fact that the markets offer a continuously compounded return that appears to be relatively constant over long spans of time. Thus, the underlying time series model is a multiplicative one of the form:

$$P_{t+1} = PP_t(1 + r + e) \tag{2.6}$$

Where P_t is the price at time t, r is the rate of return, and e is the random variation around the *mean r*. Here e is drawn from $N(0, \sigma)$ because we have already extracted the mean r explicitly.

The above formula could also be expressed as

$$P_{t+1}/P_t = (1 + r + e) \tag{2.7}$$

and trivially

$$\ln P_{t+1}/P_t = \ln(1 + r + e) \tag{2.8}$$

From the latter form, we see that on the right-hand side, the $1 + r$ part is constant for all t. Thus, at each time t, the entire random variation is due to the e term. The systematic variation is associated with the r term.

A lognormal distribution is a distribution of a variable X whose log is normally distributed. Generally speaking, sums of independent identically distributed random variables tend to converge to a normal distribution. In a similar fashion, products of independent randomly distributed variables tend to converge to a lognormal distribution. The phrase *independent identically distributed* is such an important concept in statistics that it is often abbreviated as IID.

All of the preceding properties of the normal distribution hold with respect to the lognormal if we look at the properties from the perspective of the logarithmic transformation. Essentially, this means nothing more than if we graph the lognormal distribution on an arithmetic scale, it appears to have a skewed (long) right tail such as in Figure 2.3. But if we graph it using a log scale, the graph appears to be indistinguishable from the normal distribution. Therefore, considered from the perspective of a log scale, the lognormal follows the properties of the normal as well.

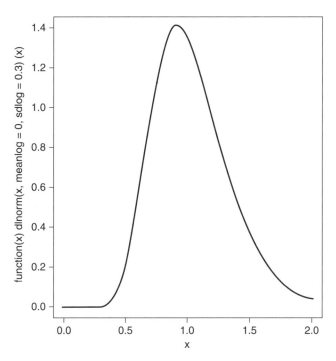

Figure 2.3 Log Normal Probability Distribution

Logarithms can take several forms. Most of us are familiar with logs base 10 in which the log of 10 is 1, log of 100 is 2, and so on. These are common for scientific notation and some everyday uses. For computers, communications, and information theory, the most natural base is base 2. In each of these fields, the basic unit of information is the *bit* that can have only two values—zero or one. These values naturally correspond to the on or off state of an electronic switch.

For finance, the natural log base is base e. This is the base used for the math of continuous compounding. Here the base e is Euler's constant e, which is approximately equal to 2.718281828 ... Most scientific calculators have this built in as a standard function. Often, one will see e raised to a power. Also, e to a power is sometimes written as the exp( ) function. The exp notation is very common in computing languages. From this we have the following:

$$e^x = \exp(x) \tag{2.9}$$

So that e to the power of x is the same as $\exp(x)$ (see Figure 2.4).

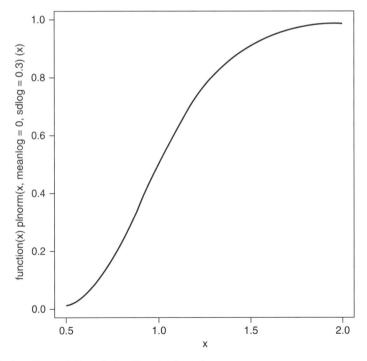

Figure 2.4 Log Normal Cumulative Density Function

SYMMETRY OF THE NORMAL AND LOGNORMAL

From this discussion we can now summarize the symmetry properties of the normal and lognormal distributions. For this purpose, we should remember that we will consider the symmetry of the lognormal only in the transformed log space.

Many people have argued that the distribution of stock market prices is not strictly lognormal. On the face of it, there would appear to be some truth to this assertion. Central to the arguments against the lognormal is the fact that there appears to be a slight discrepancy in the tails of the distribution. The tails of the distribution are defined as the outlying edges—the low-probability extreme areas of the distribution. What researchers have found is that there are a few too many observations in the tails to be perfectly consistent with the normal or lognormal models. B. Mandelbrot has even argued that the variance of price changes in speculative markets is infinite. This author has studied the complete price history of the top 6,000 stocks currently traded and has failed to find a single instance of an infinite price. Absent even a single observation of an infinite price actually being recorded, we must look elsewhere for a reasonable explanation of the *fat tails* phenomenon.

Fortunately, there is a better explanation available. During the 1990s, a number of researchers developed a branch of time series analysis that looked at the variance and standard deviation of price changes as a function of time. The studies started with a model called *GARCH* (generalized auto regressive conditional heteroskedasticity). At the core of the model is the concept of *auto regression (AR)*. Auto regressive models attempt to capture any innate serial correlation in the time series in order to predict the future values of the series. Such models assume a process of the form

$$X_{t+1} = a_0 X_t + \cdots + a_d X_{t-d} + e \tag{2.10}$$

Where X_t is the realization of the time series at time t and e is the random innovation to arrive at X_{t+1}. GARCH models expand on this concept by focusing on and trying to model the variance of the price series. The word *heteroskedasticity* simply means *different variances*. In other words, the GARCH models do not assume a constant variance, but rather, an ever-changing one that can be modeled by identifying regime changes. That is the meaning of the word *conditional* in the GARCH acronym.

The GARCH models have proved quite successful at modeling the changing cycles in the variance of stock prices, as well as other markets. But perhaps the most interesting observation is that these models can be shown both mathematically and empirically to predict the fat tail phenomenon with considerable accuracy. Thus, we have a model that predicts the variance with reasonable accuracy, as well as provides a theoretical basis for the observed distribution of price changes. This stands in stark contrast to those who claim that a few too many outliers can only mean the variance is infinite.

Fundamentally, the claim of infinite variance is fatally pessimistic. Assuming infinite variance obviates any sort of statistical testing because one can never trust the results. Infinite variance dictates that no predictions would ever be possible, simply because any prediction would likely be in error by an infinite amount. Needless to say, such a theory is untestable and inherently incapable of being falsified. In order to be validated by the scientific method, a theory must be both testable and capable of being falsified. Theories that assume an infinite variance as an axiom cannot be tested, nor can they be falsified. Thus, they are not amenable to the scientific method. It is fair to say that they are not even scientific theories at all, but really mere philosophical arguments or just raw opinions.

Fortunately, the GARCH models and their close kin, the EGARCH and other models, provide a perfectly acceptable alternative. More importantly, they provide a sound and scientific explanation for the fat tails. So from the practical point of view of the investor or finance professional, these models are ideal and offer the added benefit of the ability to predict the volatility as well. Another often-overlooked aspect is the fact that the empirical distribution of stock price changes, and those of most other markets as well, also exhibit a larger-than-expected number of small price changes. The GARCH models also explained this phenomenon well as a low-volatility regime.

WHY PICK A DISTRIBUTION AT ALL?

In the early days of finance, computing power was expensive, memory was at a premium, and data was expensive. It was incumbent upon all researchers and practitioners to conserve computer resources. Today, the equivalent of a super computer sits on everyone's desktop. It is no longer unthinkable to analyze the detailed numbers from the actual distribution of price changes. Thus, the computational obstacle has been forever removed. But there is still a very important place for studying the markets as a lognormal distribution with perhaps the variance changing regimes of a GARCH model added to create a better fit between the empirical data and the theoretical concept. Studying the distributions can yield insights and formulas that would be impossible to see from merely studying the data. By studying these well-known distributions, we can gain understanding.

> *The purpose of computing is insight, not numbers.*
> —Richard W. Hamming, one of the greatest mathematicians
> of the twentieth century

So we can gain an intuitive understanding from the theoretical distributions and achieve insights not obtainable elsewhere, but we should also be aware that the empirical distribution may tell a different story. Each is important in its own way. The theoretical can be used for insight and intuition where appropriate but should always be cross checked against the empirical as a kind of reality check.

THE EMPIRICAL DISTRIBUTION

The *empirical distribution* is simply the distribution of price changes that actually occurred in the market. A conditional distribution is the distribution that actually resulted after a certain condition or event was observed. Suppose the condition that we propose to study is, "The market makes a new high." Our trading system should study the time after the market makes a new high and simulate what happens when we buy the Standard & Poor's 500 stocks. For practical purposes, it is always best to use data from actual market trading, as opposed to data from large calculated indices.

One reason for this is a phenomenon known as *bid–ask bounce*. When a market is rallying, there is a tendency for the last actual price to occur on the ask price. When the market is falling, the last reported price will tend to be at the bid. Thus, the short-term direction of the market tends to appear slightly exaggerated during sharp moves. It is noisy.

Another reason to focus on heavily traded vehicles is called *stale pricing*. For an average such as the Standard & Poor's 500, not all stocks trade all the time. Some stocks may not trade for a half hour or more. Thus, any sharp market movement near the close may only be partially reflected in the final index closing price. To that extent, the index represents a lagging poor-quality measure of the true level of the underlying stocks. A better measure would be to use the S&P futures or the exchange traded fund (ETF) called *Spyders* with ticker symbol SPY. Each of these is more likely to reflect the true level of the market at any given time.

An example might illustrate the need to consider the empirical distribution. Per our previous discussion, suppose our goal is to find the conditional empirical distribution of SPY price changes after the market makes a new high. We simply make a list of all such changes in the SPY the day or week after a new high event and exclude all the observations for which the new high condition did not apply. The remaining compiled list is our conditional empirical distribution. However, we do not wish to assume a normal or lognormal distribution because we have added a condition into the mix. We cannot safely assume that the market will behave at new highs in the same manner as it would at other times. Thus, choosing the empirical distribution represents the safest choice from the standpoint of the researcher.

To compile a probability density function for our empirical distribution, we simply sort the list of values in order. If we had say, 1,000 values, the first 10 would represent the top 1 percent of the distribution, the next 10 would be the second percentile, and so on.

The 500th value by rank is the median, midpoint, and fiftieth percentile of the distribution. Note that there are no advanced mathematical formulas for the empirical distribution. It is what it is. We are implicitly saying that we do not know what the theoretical shape of the distribution really is. We accept merely that it seems to repeat—which is to say, it is stable over time. When the empirical distribution is used, one is *not* assuming a normal or lognormal distribution with its underlying process. Rather, we are working in an environment that statisticians term *nonparametric*. In this sense, the expression *nonparametric* means that we are not assuming the parameters of the normal distribution, or even that the distribution is normal.

A very strong case can be made to only look at the empirical distribution. It offers the advantage of no prior assumptions other than a stable distribution with finite variability. However, sometimes knowing the properties of the underlying distribution and the math behind it, can allow us to make powerful leaps that would otherwise not be possible. The normal distribution is the most studied and well understood distribution of all. By extension, the lognormal is well understood, also. So, before we throw these distributions out for our modeling purposes, we should at least ask how close they are to the real empirical distribution of the market. Figure 2.5 shows a histogram of the empirical distribution of the S&P 500 on a monthly basis.

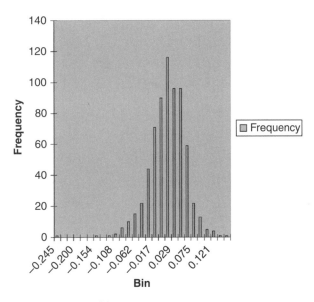

Figure 2.5 Histogram in S&P Monthly

THE LOGNORMAL AS AN APPROXIMATION

In order to compare the lognormal to the empirical distribution, we need only graph the two side by side. Figure 2.6 and Figure 2.7 show the relationship between the theoretical distributions and the empirical distribution for the SPY exchange traded fund that tracks the trading of the S&P 500 index.

These are QQ plots performed in R. The idea of a QQ plot is to match up the quantiles of the two distributions that we would like to compare. We can then see where the two distributions differ. In particular, we should note where the tails diverge and look for the presence of outliers. As a general policy, looking at a QQ plot of one's data is always advisable. In a QQ plot we usually draw a straight line through the central quantile of the distribution. It is then easy to see by eye whether the empirical distribution fits the expected normal distribution. Deviations from the straight line indicate deviations from the expected underlying distribution.

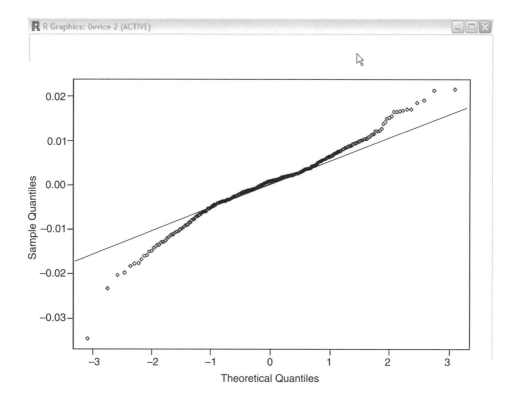

Figure 2.6 QQ Plot SP vs. Normal

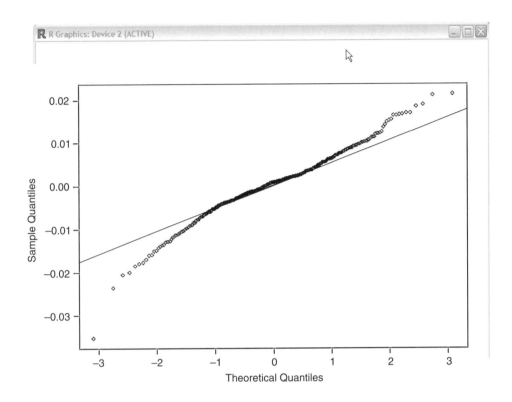

Figure 2.7 QQ Plot Ln SP vs. Normal

From Figure 2.6 we see that the normal is rather inadequate to describe the behavior of the markets. The two figures differ in the tails far too much. From Figure 2.7 one might reasonably conclude that the lognormal is an adequate model for the underlying data for most purposes. However, as has often been noted, the tails of the empirical distribution are too fat. In other words, the probability of arriving in one of the tails in the empirical distribution is greater than that for the lognormal.

For reference purposes, it is always helpful to compare our results to those achieved at random. This is often good as a reference point or a reality check. In this case, the appropriate reality check is given by Figure 2.8. In this figure, we see the results of a QQ plot of the normal distribution versus some normally distributed random numbers. The results seem to show a fairly good agreement with a few minor discrepancies in the tails of the distribution.

Thus, we conclude that for most purposes the lognormal is a good approximation to the empirical distribution for stock prices. However, it is not perfect. Subsequent

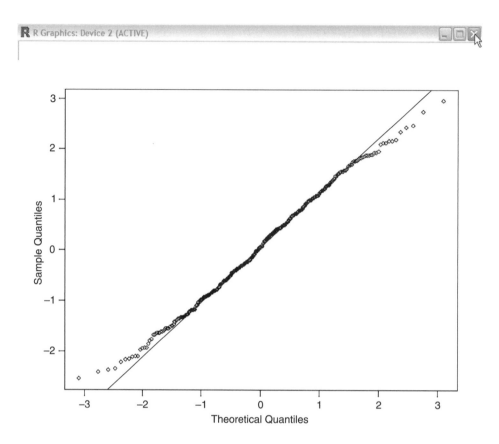

Figure 2.8   Normal Q-Q Plot

chapters will deal with both the lognormal and the empirical distribution where appropriate. Both have their place, and we shall identify where each can make a contribution to our understanding. In particular, the lognormal has well-understood theoretical and mathematical properties that can permit powerful insights into the nature of the market process. For prediction and statistical work, the empirical distribution is generally to be preferred. We shall give each its due.

CHAPTER 3

Investment Objectives

A key element in any investment program is defining our investment objectives. At a superficial level, it is clear that investment objectives should include a measure of return, a risk metric, and perhaps some consideration of personal preferences. Each of these issues is a difficult topic on its own and worthy of individual discussion.

Another important consideration is the correlation between returns on different investments. When two assets are positively correlated, both tend to be up at the same time or both down at the same time. The variability of return is increased without necessarily yielding added return. When assets are uncorrelated, the returns often tend to cancel out, thus reducing variability without decreasing average return. The best scenario for an investor is when assets are negatively correlated. When one asset is up, the other tends to be down. In this case, we obtain the greatest reduction in variability without adversely impacting return, because the expected combined return is simply the weighted average of the two investments.

STATISTICIAN'S FAIR GAME

In statistics, the formula for the expectation of some random variable X is

$$E(X) = \frac{\sum\limits_{i=1}^{n} X_i}{n} \qquad (3.1)$$

In common parlance, we would call this an *average*. It is the mean of the distribution in statistical language. It is calculated as the sum of all the observed instances of X_i

divided by the number of such observations. If the random variable in question is the return on investment during various periods, the expectation is of critical import to the investor. The expectation is the investor's return looking forward. It must be positive and better than alternative investments at the same risk level.

A FAIR GAME IS A LOSER!

In virtually every introductory statistics book ever written, the presumption is that a simple game with an expectation of zero is a *fair game*. This idea is patently absurd! One of the strong themes of this book is that one should never play a game or make an investment unless it has a positive expectation. An investor should always have an edge.

The author's motto:
Always have an edge. Never let your money leave home without it.

An expectation of zero means that the player has no expected return but is exposing himself to risk—and even the risk of ruin—if the game is played indefinitely with a finite bankroll. Certainly, that is a rather bad choice for anyone. No one who is risk averse should ever choose to play such a game.

In all fairness, what the authors of these books really mean by *fair* is that the game is equally bad for both sides. Nevertheless, the correct strategy for each player is not to play the game!

CRITERIA FOR A FAVORABLE GAME

The question of a fair game naturally raises the question: "What game should we be willing to play?" Part of the answer lies in the reason why the zero expectation game is flawed. In a zero expectation game, we are not compensated for assuming risk. Thus, we can conclude that a worthwhile game for us must be one in which there is an expected gain. This is because an intelligent and rational investor requires return as compensation for bearing risk.

Next, we should consider available alternatives. If there is a game available to us that offers the same risk level but a higher return, we would always want to play that to the exclusion of a game with a lower expected return. Thus, any game must be at least as good as available alternatives.

Finally, we should consider each game as a long-run sequence of games. This aspect of the analysis is especially relevant in the investment world. We presume there will always be stocks, bonds, and derivatives to buy. Investment opportunities are not going away any time soon. So this principle requires that we prefer games or investments in which the return from repeated plays is favorable.

This latter point may not seem obvious to most, but is at the heart of the subject of this book. In statistics, there is a well-known principle that the expected sum of n independent identically distributed variables is simply n times the expectation of one variable. Hence, if a game has a positive expectation of r for one play, then the expected return for n plays with equal bet sizes is simply n times r. So why is this third criterion necessary? It would seem redundant.

GAMBLER'S RUIN

The key to this mystery lies in understanding the idea of gambler's ruin. Simply expressed, this is the chance of going broke after repeated plays of a game. It depends on the bet size, payoff amounts, and the probability of wins and losses. But more than that, it depends as well, on the size of one's bankroll. This is an important point that is often overlooked.

The relationship with the bet size and bankroll can be seen intuitively. Suppose we have the traditional fair game of flipping an unbiased coin. Each time, we bet 1 and win an amount equal to our bet if it is heads and lose our bet if it comes up tails. Starting with a bankroll of 10, it takes an initial run of 10 losses in a row to lose our bankroll. The odds against this initial run of bad luck are 1 in 1,024. So it would seem unlikely.

But what if we played the game 1,024 times? What if we played indefinitely, betting 10 percent of our bankroll each time? What are the chances that at some point we would experience a net downswing of only 10 and be ruined? For an investor, these are the realities of life. Investors should be and are in the game for life, whether they realize it or not. Thus, one critically important goal of investing is to stay in the game. Any strategy or money management scheme that jeopardizes this goal is unacceptable.

Let us consider the same coin-flipping game, but this time we have a bankroll of 1,000. Now it takes a net cumulative loss of 1,000 to break us. It is much more likely that we can play for a long time, and perhaps even indefinitely, simply because we have a larger bankroll. From this we see that a larger bankroll reduces the risk of ruin.

Suppose we change the rules of the game one more time to require that the bet size be 10, and go back to our original bankroll of 10. Under this scenario, even a single loss in the beginning will break us, with no chance of recovery. So, we see that our chance of going broke on the first play is 50 percent.

But there are other ways we can bust on subsequent plays. In fact, if our cumulative winnings ever fall to zero, we are out of the game forever. This shows in an intuitive fashion that increasing the bet size relative to our bankroll increases the risk of ruin.

OPTIMAL RETURN MODELS

From our discussion of iterated plays of a game, it is clear that the investor needs to take a long-term view of things. Even though each play itself may seem to be an isolated event, it is actually an instance of a series of events that are sequential in time.

It makes no difference if the investor is an individual or a professional money manager. For an individual managing his life savings or retirement account, by definition his actions are part of a lifetime of such investment choices. Each choice is made in sequence.

For a professional money manager, his investment choices are part of a career-long series of such choices. As such, they heavily influence his income bonuses and job security. No matter who you are, the right viewpoint is that of a lifetime series of investment decisions.

The importance of this can be seen no more clearly than in the preceding discussion of ruin. If one goes bankrupt first, all subsequent plays are precluded. The sequence terminates. So, even if a game has a positive expectation, such as the stock market, that expectation is excluded if one becomes ruined. In such a situation, the secret is to stay in the game. Any putative positive expectation is rendered meaningless if the investor is knocked out of the game.

Another important consideration is to maximize one's long-term return from repeated plays of the game. In investments, this means maximizing the compounded rate of return. The compounded rate of return depends on the return per period.

In the simplest model, this return is then reinvested at the presumed same rate. The essence is that the total bankroll or account value is rolled forward and reinvested into the next period. Thus, returns multiply, not add. Each period's returns are multiplied times the rate of return in the next period.

The math behind this is simpler than most believe. If we invest $1 in an investment for a year and it returns 10 percent the end-of-year value of the investment is 1.10. After two years at the same rate, it is 1.21. The value increases at a multiplicative rate faster than simple addition of the return would suggest. Thus, after two years the accumulated balance is $1.10 \times 1.10 = 1.21$. It is not just $1.10 + 1.10 = 1.20$, because the reinvestment of the first .10 increases the second year's value to 1.21.

One way to calculate this is just to multiply all the factors out for as many years as needed. Another is to add the natural logarithms of the factors. This function is abbreviated as ln( ). After we get the total of the logs, we need to calculate the exponential function exp( ) to return the number to its usual format. In order to use logs, we need to be sure that the parameters that we input to the log function are in the neighborhood of one (1). Another investing term for this is *relative return*. If one invests in a stock that goes up 10 percent by year end, then the relative return is 1.10, not .10. If our stock goes down 10 percent, then the relative return is .90. Note that both numbers .90 and 1.10 are in the neighborhood of one. The formula for the log of the relative return is

$$\ln(1+r) \tag{3.2}$$

where r is the total return. Alternatively, we may say:

$$\ln((P_{t+1} + D)/P_t) \tag{3.3}$$

where P_t is the stock price at time t and D is the value of any distributions that accrued to the shareholders during the period.

Usually this means the value of dividends or stock splits. However, academics have counted more than 300 different kinds of distributions that been given to shareholders, so the value of each must be included to be truly accurate. Undoubtedly, more exotic distributions will be created in the future, so there can be no final and definitive catalog of what is included in D. Generally speaking, it is the value of anything that the shareholder receives as a result of owning his shares during the time period.

So, then we have the formula for average compound return:

$$\text{Avg. compound return} = \exp\left\langle \frac{\sum \ln(P_{t+1} + D)/P_t}{n} \right\rangle \tag{3.4}$$

It can be understood as the average of the logs converted back to regular numbers by using exp( ), which is the inverse of the ln function. The key thing to understand about logs and the exp function is that you add the logs to figure and average log and then take the inverse. Adding the logs is just another way to do compound arithmetic without doing the multiplications. The exp( ) is simply the transcendental number e raised to the power of what is inside the parentheses. The famous eighteenth-century mathematician Leonhard Euler is credited with the discovery of some of the properties of e, and it is often called Euler's constant. The now-standard choice of the letter e stems directly from Euler's last name.

The important point here is that the average of the logs of the relative returns gives us a scientific metric for looking at the value of compounding in a given investment. The relationship between the logs and the value of the exp( ) function is monotonically increasing.

The higher the sum of the logs, the higher the ultimate value will be when the logs are converted back to real values. So any model that tries to achieve maximum return will need to maximize the sum of the logs of the relative returns for each period.

MARKETS ARE RATIONAL, PSYCHOLOGISTS ARE NOT

In a rather famous paper, Professors Daniel Kahnemann and Amos Tversky argued that test subjects made irrational and biased choices when presented with gambling game opportunities. The paper was titled "Prospect Theory: Decision Making under Uncertainty" and was published in 1979 in *Econometrica*. Essentially, the methodology of the paper was to enlist a group of university-based test subjects that included both faculty and students. Presumably due to simple economics, the students formed the bulk of the test subjects. The subjects were presented with simple gambling games and asked to pick the one they preferred. The experimenters evaluated the games on a strictly statistical expectation basis. Essentially, the study found that in several very interesting situations, the test subjects did not choose the game with the best expectation (in the classic but flawed statistical sense) but seemed to prefer alternate choices with seemingly worse expected gain.

The criteria used by the experimenters was simply:

$$E(x) = \sum_i p_i r_i \tag{3.5}$$

where the product of the probability p_i times the return r_i, which is summed over all outcomes i.

No consideration was given to the relatively impecunious economic profile of the students. In fact, net worth or wealth was not even known or considered by the experimenters, as evidenced by the fact that the paper is moot on the subject.

We saw in the foregoing discussion the importance to investors of maximizing the log of the relative returns. It would be enlightening to see how the results might differ if evaluated from a log return standpoint. The experimenters never considered the possibility of their subjects having a logarithmic preference for money or seeking to maximize their long-run compounded return. Implicitly, the experimenters defined a logarithmic preference toward money as irrational.

In one of the applications in the R language at the end of this chapter, we consider the effect of applying a logarithmic utility function to the anomalous problems presented in the Kahnemann and Tversky paper. We shall consider Problem 1 here, as well as the accompanying R code.

Subjects were asked to choose between two gambles, A and B. The returns and probabilities for gamble A are shown in Table 3.1. In gamble A, there were three possible outcomes with their associated probability, as indicated in the second column.

We note that gamble B is a single outcome of 2,400, which is certain, as indicated by the probability of 1.00. This is shown in Table 3.2. Gamble A is a .66 probability of the 2,400 plus two other outcomes. There is a .33 chance to improve the result from 2,400 to 2,500. The expected value of that improvement is .33 × 100 = 33. There is also the small

TABLE 3.1	Gamble A
Return	**Probability**
2,500	.33
2,400	.66
0	.01

TABLE 3.2	Gamble B
Return	**Probability**
2,400	1.00

chance of .01 to lose the entire 2,400 and wind up at zero. The relative loss of $2,400 \times .01$ gives us a negative value of -24. Thus, viewed on an arithmetic expectation frame of reference, we see that gamble A has an expected value that is 8 more than gamble B. It should thus rationally be preferred, or so the professors would presumably argue.

In the experiment, the paper reports that an overwhelming 82 percent of the subjects selected gamble B, which has an expected value of 2,400. Only 18 percent chose gamble A with its slightly higher 2,408 expected value.

In order to analyze these choices from a log utility standpoint, we need to make an assumption about the net worth of the typical student of the era. First, most students only have part-time jobs and most of that money goes to tuition and room and board. There is little left over for most, in that pretty much all the income is earmarked for future educational expenses. Thus, the typical student of the era probably has just enough left over for beer and pizza on the weekends. For our purposes, we shall assume that the discretionary wealth of our students is $100 as an arbitrary estimate.

We can now write some simple code that basically uses R as a calculator. Our goal is to calculate the value of the various gambles from the perspective of a logarithmic utility function based on our relatively impecunious student subjects and their putative wealth. Because this is essentially a financial exercise, we shall use the natural logs as our base. Following is the R code to calculate the desired arithmetic and logarithmic utilities of the various gambles offered to the students.

Problem 1: Kahnemann-Tversky Problem A

```
xa  < −c(2,500, 2,400, 0)
pa  < −c(.33, .66, .01)
w   < −100
u   < −log((xa + w)/w)
    sum(pa × u)
```

TABLE 3.3	Comparison of Kahnemann–Tversky to Log Expectation		
Problem	**KT Expectation**	**Log Expectation**	**Subjects Choice**
A	2,408	3.20	18 percent
B	2,400	3.22	82

In this code, the variable xa is assigned a vector of numerical returns corresponding to the returns for gamble A. The vector pa is the probabilities and w is the assumed wealth of 100. Then the calculation of the utility u is straightforward:

$$u < -\log((xa + w)/w)$$

This simply takes the effect of each outcome in vector xa and adds the constant w to it and then divides by w to express it as a wealth relative. Then the log of each outcome is taken and the results are placed in vector u. The final line sums the product of the probabilities times the utility to give us an expected utility. When the code for Problems A and B is run, we get the comparison shown in Table 3.3.

Viewed from the standpoint of expected log utility, it is clear that the subjects made better choices than the experimenters. The code on the CD-ROM associated with this chapter shows five of the problem choices presented in the paper on prospect theory that were deemed anomalous. In each case the test subjects chose a gambling choice that was inferior to the one dictated by a simple arithmetic expectation theory. Using traditional statistical fair game logic the professors naturally deemed these answers *wrong* and therefore irrational.

However, in each case, the test subjects chose the one that had the highest expected log utility. Clearly, the simplest, most straightforward interpretation of the data is that the test subjects are quite good at evaluating their log utility functions. In contrast, the conclusions of the study broke the analysis down to several anomalous cases that each required its own divergent explanation. Together, the complex of these anomalies and rationalizations is called *prospect theory*. For their work Kahnemann and Tversky received a Nobel Prize in 2002.

The author asks, were the students truly irrational because they consistently selected optimal logarithmic choices or were the professors the irrational ones? Let the reader decide.

THE ST. PETERSBURG PARADOX

It would be understandable if modern researchers had overlooked the idea of logarithmic utility because it had never been discovered. However, that is not the case. The idea has been known for a very long time—more than 200 years!

In September 1713, Nicolas Bernoulli had first formulated a problem of the following form. A casino pays $1 on the first coin flip that is heads and $2 on the second head and continues to double the payoff each time a head is tossed. However, if any single tail is thrown, the game is over and the player keeps the amount won up to that point. The question is, how much should one wager on such a game?

Using expectation analysis we see that each flip has a 1/2 probability of turning up heads. So the sequence of probabilities is 1/2, 1/4, 1/8, 1/16 and so on. The expected payoffs are 1,2,4,8,16, ... So the payoff after 1 toss is $1 \times 1/2 = .50$, after the second it is $2 \times .25 = .50$, and so on. Each toss is worth an added .50, and there are *infinitely* many such tosses possible. So, expectation analysis tells us we should rationally be willing to bet an infinite amount. But common sense tells us that is just plain silly.

Fortunately, Nicolas Bernoulli had a cousin by the name of Daniel Bernoulli who was a noted mathematician and statistician at the University of St. Petersburg in then czarist Russia. Daniel Bernoulli had already proposed the idea of a decreasing marginal utility of money, arguing, for example, that twice as much money is not necessarily twice as useful. Bernoulli had also recognized the importance of one's wealth in the analysis. A given fixed gain might be a small increment in total wealth to a rich man, but might make a huge difference in the circumstances of a poor man. Consideration of one's wealth was critically important.

So when Bernoulli published his analysis of the *St. Petersburg Paradox*, it included his idea that money should be valued using the utility function concept. It should come as no surprise that the utility function he settled upon was the natural log, or ln( ) function. This, of course, has the base e and is the natural base for compound interest calculations in finance, as discussed previously. Readers may recall that the constant e was discovered and thoroughly analyzed by Leonhard Euler. So perhaps we should not be too surprised to learn that Euler and Daniel Bernoulli boarded together while they were both associated with the University of St. Petersburg. The results achieved when great minds work closely can be astounding.

COMPOUNDED RETURN IS THE REAL OBJECTIVE

In the preceding discussion, we have seen that compounded growth is governed by the log function and preferably the natural log ln. We have also seen how maximizing the average log maximizes long-term compounded growth for our investments. From the results of Kahnemann and Tversky, we learned that their subjects tended to operate using a natural log utility function based on their supposed wealth. The log model was clearly consistent with the preferences of the test subjects and comprises a simpler model than does the arcane rule based complexity of prospect theory. Finally, we discussed the ground-breaking work of Daniel Bernoulli more than 200 years ago when he first proposed using the natural log as the appropriate utility function for the solution to the St. Petersburg paradox.

For the remainder of this book, we shall accept the premise that one part of our investment objective should be to maximize our expected ln of the wealth of our portfolio at each point in time. In doing so, we keep in mind that the simple arithmetic average of our portfolio returns is our end of period average portfolio return. However, the ultimate long-term value of the portfolio return to us is its contribution to our ln weighted wealth. Thus, any metric we use must include in it an explicit measure of the log weighted return. This latter is essentially equivalent to the long-run compound return.

In this discussion, we have ignored the variability of returns. It seems clear that a return that is certain to always yield a given amount is preferable to an identical return that is highly variable. If a minimum return is assured, it is possible to budget the return for future use. However, if the return is so variable that a loss is a significant possibility, no budgeting is possible. In other situations, a return that has little or no variability may allow the use of leverage, whereas a more variable return would preclude such an option because of the risk of ruin.

DEFINING RISK

The definition of risk has always been a bit controversial in the finance world. Certainly part of the idea of any risk measurement is to evaluate the chance of losing. Along this line, one might be tempted to simply let risk be the probability that a given investment will lose money. Clearly, this is an interesting number, but falls short because it does not measure how much money is made or lost.

Another measure of risk might be to look at the average loss. By itself, this metric has limited value as well. The trouble is that it contains no probability measure. Considered alone, it cannot be evaluated relative to how likely the loss is relative to the gain.

Investors primarily make or lose money through changes in market value. Although interest earned and dividends collected all contribute to investment return, most of the higher returns and variability are due to market changes. As we discussed, the market seems to resemble a lognormal distribution arguably with fat tails. Because the attributes of the normal distribution family are well understood, most people in finance have settled on the variance and standard deviation as the best measures of the variability of returns.

Any normal distribution is characterized by only two parameters—the mean and variance. Clearly, the mean is always relevant to investors, and thus, it seems natural to look to the variance as a reasonable measure of the variability of returns. We should remember that the standard deviation is simply the square root of the variance, so if we know one, we know the other by a simple calculation. For most financial work, the standard deviation is the preferred unit of measure because it relates to units that are naturally familiar. For example, if we had an expected return of +10 percent and a standard deviation of 15 percent, then we can use the well-known properties of the normal distribution to aid our intuition. We can look at the standard deviation as a simple plus or minus measure of variability. For the previous example, we would expect our distribution to be centered at +10 percent, but with a variation of plus or minus 15 percent about two thirds of the time. This means we would expect returns as low as −5 percent to as high as +25 percent some two thirds of the time. About one sixth of the time, we would expect returns greater than 25 percent, and the other one sixth we should get returns worse than −5 percent.

Using the properties of the normal distribution, we can make similar statements with 95 percent confidence as well. For this, we simply make our plus or minus bands to be two standard deviations. Thus, the return of +10 percent plus or minus 40 percent ($= 2 \times 20$ percent) is a range that we would expect to occur about 95 percent of the time. Only about 5 percent of the time would we expect the outcome to lie outside that range.

It is clear that the normal family of distributions can be very useful for analyzing variability of returns. In particular, the standard deviation is pretty much the accepted simple measure of risk. However, it does have its detractors who have legitimate arguments.

One common objection to the standard deviation as a measure of risk is that it includes both upside price changes and downside changes. One can make the very reasonable argument that only downside changes should be included, because those are the only ones that actually result in loss for a long-only investor. There can be little question that this is a valid claim with respect to the narrowly focused question of losses alone.

One can carry that argument to extremes. Suppose a given portfolio gained 6 percent during a year. However, it was subject to wide swings during the intervening months. Because the portfolio lost no money at the end of the year, does that mean it was riskless? Does that mean it had no more risk than investing in 6 percent Treasury bills during the same time? Common sense would say no.

However, there is really a bigger issue. That issue is *estimation*. We use measures of risk to estimate how much variability there is in a given return. If we want to evaluate the merits of a given trading system via historical backtesting, we need the best estimate of variability we can find. We also often wish to measure the performance of a portfolio manager. Again, the best measure of variability is needed. Sometimes we wish to estimate the volatility of a given stock. For that, we need the best measure of variability we can find.

A different but related requirement is to measure significance. We often wish to know if a trading system is significantly better than average, or did its backtested results come about merely through chance? It is a statistical fact that systems that show high variability have a better chance of *getting lucky* than systems that are more stable. A confluence of just a few large outliers can sometimes make a system or portfolio manager look much better than is the case. This is especially true if the number of observations is limited.

Fortunately, there is a solution to both the estimation and the significance issues. Serendipitously, it turns out that the answer is to use the standard deviation as the measure of choice. Again, based on the well-understood properties of the normal family, the standard deviation is the best estimator of variability possible under the criterion of maximum likelihood. In other words, the variability of the distribution is most likely to be well measured by the standard deviation. This is a very powerful argument in favor of the standard deviation as our preferred risk metric.

To measure significance, one only needs the mean and standard deviation to perform a t test. The t statistic is given by this formula:

$$t = \frac{(\bar{X} - \mu)}{\sigma \sqrt{n}} \tag{3.6}$$

Where $\bar{X}$ is the average of the data points X, μ is the population mean, σ is the standard deviation of the Xs and n is the number of observations in the sample. This statistic is governed by the t distribution that is also commonly called the *Student distribution*.

The story behind the name *Student* is a rather interesting one. William Sealy Gosset (1876–1937) was the master brewer at the Dublin Guinness factory. Presumably, because of his daytime occupation, he felt compelled to write his statistical papers under the pseudonym *Student*. Another theory has it that his employer considered the use of Statistics to be a trade secret and forbade him to reveal his techniques. In any event, Gosset developed what is now known as the Student distribution. By all rights, perhaps, it should be called the Gosset distribution. This case is yet another example of Stigler's *law of eponymy*, which essentially says that great breakthroughs are rarely named after their original inventor. Perhaps Gosset's own modesty in writing under a pseudonym is much to blame as well.

In any event, the understanding of Gosset's distribution was augmented by his contemporary and correspondent R. A. Fisher into the full-blown t test. The t test provides us with an excellent and well-understood means of testing for significant results, either in backtesting or in evaluation of portfolio management.

Alternative ideas such as semi-variance and semi-standard deviation have been proposed. These metrics measure risk using only losses, but are otherwise similar to the usual standard deviation formula. The key difference is that the usual standard deviation formula includes all of the data. It simply has more information. By contrast, measures such as the semi-standard deviation defenestrate the winning portion of the data. Given the positive long-term upward drift of the market, the market usually rises 60 percent of the time in any given month. Consequently, these alternative measures wind up ignoring as much as 60 percent of their data. In particular, they completely ignore all lucky upside outliers. There is simply no way for such metrics to evaluate when luck associated with high variability has been the underlying factor. They have systematically removed all information regarding such luck.

MINIMUM RISK MODELS

Given a rational choice of a risk metric, it is now possible to define another type of investment goal. Specifically, this is the goal of minimizing risk. This arises in scenarios where an investor has a certain goal with respect to return but little incentive to exceed that goal. Rather, for this type of investor it may be more important to reduce the risk of not achieving the desired goal.

A good example of this situation is a defined-benefit pension plan. Under this, the employer has defined a fixed benefit payable to the employees. It is important that the capital of the fund is able to achieve the desired return goal so as to meet the benefit obligations.

If the fund does not meet the return goal, the corporation or governmental employer will have to dip into current income to make up the difference. So, in this case, the employer may wish to use a strategy that targets a given acceptable return goal and seeks to minimize the risk of not achieving that goal.

Clearly, the use of standard deviation is still the best way to measure the variability of returns around the projected mean. The well-understood statistics of the normal family also facilitate the development of models that can minimize risk or alternatively minimize the probability of falling below a given level of return.

CORRELATION OF ASSETS

When statisticians speak of sampling real-world events, inevitably words like *independent identically distributed* (IID) variables are used. Critical to this is the concept of *independence*. This means that each new observation has no relationship to any previous observation. In other words, the variables have no memory, in much the same way that a coin has no memory. Whatever the last result was in no way influences future outcomes.

If the IID assumption is true, we have some very interesting results:

1. The expected sum of n IID variables X is given by

$$n\,E(X) \tag{3.7}$$

2. The variance (VAR) of n IID variable X is given by

$$VAR\,(X_1 + X_{2+} + \ldots X_n) = VARX_1 + VARX_2 + \ldots VARX_n \tag{3.8}$$

However, when the assumption of independence is violated, we have a different result. Variables that are not independent are said to be correlated. One measure of the correlation is the covariance between two random variables X and Y. The covariance (COV) is given by

$$COV(XY) = E(X - E(X))(E(Y - E(Y))) \qquad (3.9)$$

When two assets are correlated the overall variance is given by

$$VAR(X, Y) = VAR(X) + VAR(Y) + 2 \times COV(XY) \qquad (3.10)$$

If two assets move together, they are said to be positively correlated. If two assets tend to move with positive correlation, then the covariance will be positive. If they move in opposite directions, the COV will be negative. If the assets are independent, the covariance will be zero or near zero.

We should also observe that positively correlated assets tend to *increase* the resulting variance and hence the risk. But negatively correlated assets will tend to reduce the overall variance and hence the risk. So, to the extent that we can identify negatively correlated assets, we can help to reduce the overall portfolio's level of risk.

SUMMARY OF CORRELATION RELATIONSHIPS

Table 3.4 summarizes the effect on risk that will be achieved for different correlation regimes. For example, if two assets are positively correlated, then diversification will yield only a minimal decrease in risk.

A close relative of the covariance is the correlation coefficient, r. Essentially, the idea is to scale the covariance to a simple and intuitive number that will characterize

TABLE 3.4 How Correlation Effects Comovement and Risk

Correlation	Comovement	Effect on Risk (°)
Positive	Together	Minimal decrease
Negative	Opposite	Large decrease
Zero	Independent movements	Moderate decrease

*Effect on risk is for fixed position sizes as additional positions are added. Note that as diversification is increased using uncorrelated assets, the risk is reduced approximately as a function of the square root of n, where n is the number of equally weighted positions. Diversification with positively correlated assets, as is typical for most stocks, reduces risk at a rate less than the square root of n. Use of negatively correlated assets such as call options, written on a portfolio, will reduce risk at a rate faster than the square root of n.

the correlation relationship. So the correlation coefficient, r, is defined as the covariance divided by the product of the two variances. The formula is

$$r = \mathrm{COV}(XY)/\mathrm{VAR}(X)^*\mathrm{VAR}(Y) \tag{3.11}$$

This effectively rescales the correlation coefficient to a range from -1.0 to $+1.0$. A correlation near $+1$ indicates strong positive correlation while a number near -1 shows a strong negative correlation. A near-zero correlation tells us that the two variables are independent of each other.

BETA AND ALPHA

Modern portfolio theory (MPT) has defined various measures to evaluate the relationship and correlations between stocks. Beginning with Harry M. Markowitz's seminal paper in the *Journal of Finance* in 1952, modern portfolio theory has a long and rich history. Markowitz was the first to understand how to put measures of expected return, risk, and correlation together to select an optimal portfolio, given his set of assumptions.

The Markowitz model optimized the expected mean and variance using a standard arithmetic return model. One key realization was that the variance covariance matrix was critical to solving the problem in a multiasset environment where most assets are highly correlated. The model could be used to define an efficient frontier line of portfolios. Each point on the line corresponded to a portfolio that was the highest return for a given risk level. Alternately, one could view each point as the lowest risk for the given return.

The initial Markowitz model would require an estimate of the expected arithmetic mean and variance for each stock. The model itself is moot as to how such estimates should be developed. The two usual sources are an analyst's estimate or an historical estimate. The other required information is either the correlation matrix or the variance-covariance matrix.

Essentially, the latter requirement means that the covariance or correlation between each pair of stocks must be estimated. The problem grows quadratically as the number of stocks grows. Thus, for 20 stocks we would require a table of 400 entries. Each entry is simply the pairwise covariance for each pair of stocks. We note that the main diagonal in which row i equals column j is simply the covariance of the stock with itself. This can be shown to be simply the variance of the stock itself. The number 20 squared gives us the 400 entries.

However, to design an optimal portfolio for some 2,000 stocks on the New York Stock Exchange is a more daunting task. It would require a matrix of 4 million entries. During the 1950s and 1960s, this was beyond the main memory capacity of all computers. As a result, Markowitz's work was proclaimed as a great theoretical breakthrough but inspired little in the way of practical applications.

In 1959, James Tobin extended the work of Markowitz to include the idea of a cash position. This allowed the portfolio manager to explicitly use cash as a way to manage risk and return. It also allowed a means by which one could add leverage to the overall portfolio optimization problem.

It was not until the work of William F. Sharpe in 1964 that the science of modern portfolio theory became practical. Modern portfolio theory is often abbreviated MPT. Sharpe's innovation was to realize that all stocks tended to be positively correlated (with some exceptions). Realizing this, he proceeded to devise a surrogate for the market that could reduce the number of correlations down from potentially millions to just the single correlation with the market. The usual market index at the time was the Standard & Poor's 500 index. The key enabling insight was the realization that essentially all investment assets were correlated with the market.

Sharpe's new theory became known as *capital asset pricing model* (CAPM). At the time it was a marvelous breakthrough because it allowed investment managers to optimize their portfolios on the limited memory of the computers of that era.

Essentially, the idea of CAPM is that each security has a correlation with the overall market and has a separate intrinsic variability that is not correlated with the market. Sharpe used a simple regression of this form:

$$\text{Stock change} = \beta\,(\text{market change}) + \alpha + u \tag{3.12}$$

where u is the uncorrelated error term.

More highly correlated and presumably more volatile stocks might have a beta of 2.0. This would mean that the stock moves twice a fast as the underlying market change. An average stock might move 1.0 times as much as the market, percentagewise. It would essentially move with the market. Very stable stocks might only move .50 times as much, or half as much.

It has been shown that betas tend to persist. Using decile analysis, it was found that the highest-decile stocks generally tended to stay in the highest deciles in subsequent periods and that low-decile stocks stayed in the low deciles.

The alpha coefficient is a different story. Alpha is a measure of how the stock tended to perform against the market. A positive alpha means the stock performed better than the market after its correlation with the market index had been factored out. A negative alpha means it underperformed. If alpha is near zero, the stock performed in line with the market. The trouble with alpha is that it does not persist. High-decile alphas in one period appear to be randomly distributed throughout all the deciles in subsequent periods. Unlike beta, alpha does not appear to be a good predictor of future risk-adjusted behavior of the stock.

One important concept to understand is that the CAPM model decomposes the risk associated with stock ownership into two broad classifications. The first is the part of the risk that is directly correlated with the market. This is represented by the beta coefficient in equation 3.12. The underlying rationale is that this part is not diversifiable. Each stock is correlated with the market to some degree. Thus, each stock is correlated with one another. Therefore, this is the correlated portion of the risk that all stocks share in common with one another. It cannot be diversified away. However, the portion of the variance that is attributed to the u term in the above regression model is uncorrelated with the overall market. It can be diversified so as to reduce risk.

We recall that things are linear in the variance and that we can decompose the total risk into its constituent components as follows:

$$\begin{array}{c} \text{Correlated risk as measured by beta} \\ + \text{ Uncorrelated risk as measured by squared errors } (u) \\ \hline \text{Total risk of the stock} \end{array}$$

For example, a typical stock might have something like 65 percent of its total variance explained by its relationship with the market. So, the calculation might look something like this:

$$\begin{array}{ll} 65 \text{ percent} & \text{Correlated risk explained by beta} \\ +35 \text{ percent} & \text{Uncorrelated risk (Unexplained risk)} \\ \hline 100 \text{ percent} & \text{Total risk of the stock} \end{array}$$

Of course, these percentages are merely representative and can vary significantly from stock to stock and from one time period to the next. The correlated risk is that fraction of the variance, expressed by R squared, which results from the regression calculation. The uncorrelated portion is based on the sum of the squared residuals, or the errors in which the regression did not quite fit the data precisely.

The key understanding that Sharpe had was that the correlations between stocks could be neatly summarized by their correlation with the overall market. Thus, the beta represents that correlation with a single term. This can greatly economize the CAPM model as compared to the older Markowitz model where each covariance was required. The other key insight that Sharpe propounded was that the uncorrelated risk intrinsic to each stock was also largely uncorrelated with other stocks as well. The uncorrelated risk could be substantially eliminated through diversification.

Thus, the beta term that relates to the correlated risk expressed the risk that was associated with the market. It is commonly called *systematic risk* or *market risk*. According to the theories of CAPM, this risk cannot be reduced through diversification because all the assets are correlated with the overall market. Because it cannot be eliminated, this risk is the only risk for which the investor will be rewarded for bearing risk.

Several large cross-sectional studies have looked at this question from the standpoint of beta and the subsequent returns. Generally speaking, the theory holds up well.

Higher beta stocks do perform better than lower beta stocks, but at the price of greater correlated risk.

Betas were also found to persist from one period to the next. Generally, the stocks that were in the highest deciles were in the highest deciles in later periods. From this, we can conclude that beta is a reasonable measure of correlated market return and of nondiversifiable risk.

However, it was a different story for alphas. Alpha represents the excess return a given stock had over and above its expected level of market return. If alpha is negative, the stock underperformed the market during the regression period. The large sample studies found that alphas did not persist. A high alpha in one period did not enable one to predict whether the next period's alpha would be high or low. Thus, it was not possible to simply invest in stocks with high past alphas and expect them to continue to perform well. CAPM did not offer any free lunch to investors. Nor does it offer much of predictive value. Rather, it is a methodology that defines what diversification can do for the investor and what it cannot do.

THE EFFICIENT FRONTIER AND THE MARKET PORTFOLIO

One important result from CAPM was that the Markowitz efficient frontier was now calculable and still intact. The efficient frontier is that set of portfolios that is the best combination of risk and return for any given level of risk or for any given level of return. Thus, an investor could select a point on the efficient frontier and have a realistic expectation that his or her portfolio was optimal, given the expectations and assumptions that were made. Further, the theory provided the assurance that portfolio was optimal for the given risk and reward level.

Another important conclusion was that one could pick a point on the efficient frontier and simply vary cash and leverage to adjust the risk and return along a straight line passing through any given point on the frontier. Thus, it was possible by choosing an appropriate tangent line, to find the optimal portfolio that would allow one to perform better than all others (see Figure 3.1). Not too surprisingly, the CAPM proponents argued that this portfolio was none other than the market portfolio weighted by capitalization. By holding some cash, one could reduce the risk of the market portfolio to any given level. Alternatively, through the use of leverage, the return could be increased at a corresponding increase in risk.

These findings of CAPM came into wide acceptance as added numbers of MBAs were trained in the approach. As a result, by the 1990s many new index funds were coming into vogue. It was argued that investing in widely diversified portfolios was nearly impossible for the average investor, and thus, owning the optimal market portfolio could not be done. Another, perhaps more persuasive argument was that the market portfolio *is the*

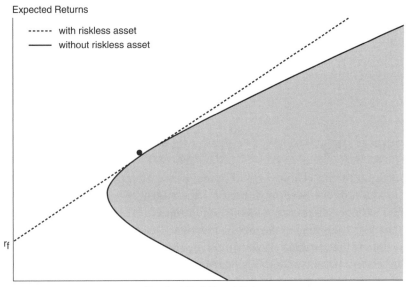

Standard Deviation of Returns

Figure 3.1 Efficient Portfolio Frontier

optimal portfolio. Thus, investing in the entire market gave one the best possible portfolio. With the advent of the new index funds and even newer *exchange traded funds* (ETFs), the individual investor could now own the market portfolio with relative ease.

THE SHARPE RATIO

Essentially, CAPM had boiled portfolio theory down to a simple ratio between the mean expected return and the expected variance. This ratio defined the slope of the capital market line. However, given that it was now possible to measure return and risk as variance and the nondiversifiable market correlation as beta, there soon arose ideas concerning how to measure the management skills of portfolio managers.

For this purpose, Sharpe developed the Sharpe Ratio. It is simply expressed as the following formula:

$$\text{Sharpe ratio} = (u - r)/\sigma \qquad (3.13)$$

where:

u is the mean portfolio return
r is the riskless rate of return
σ is the standard deviation of the portfolio

The mean less the riskless short-term Treasury bill rate is known as the *excess return*. Short-term T-bills are considered a riskless asset. Thus, the excess return is the excess return that a portfolio manager received for bearing risk. The excess return is divided by the amount of risk taken, which is measured by the standard deviation. Therefore, we can interpret the Sharpe ratio as the amount of excess return per unit of risk taken.

LIMITATIONS OF MODERN PORTFOLIO THEORY

Modern portfolio theory is an excellent model to enable one to find efficient portfolios. It can help to identify the best portfolio for a given level of risk and reward as measured by mean and variance. However it has its limitations.

In particular, it assumes a normal or lognormal distribution. Although the markets appear to exhibit distributions similar to those, this assumption may break down in the limit. To the extent that the underlying distribution is fat tailed, then the optimal portfolio may well depend on higher moments of the underlying distribution, as some have argued.

The variance only incorporates the second moment. It is based on the sum of the squares of price changes in the underlying security. Higher moments may be necessary to adequately describe risk and return with respect to the preferences of real investors. Alternatively, better models may explicitly assume an underlying empirical distribution that has no closed form description.

Some of the more recent GARCH models and their many variations have been introduced to explain the fact that the variance does not seem to be stationary. In fact, the variance can often double from one period to the next. The GARCH models attempt to deal with this phenomenon.

In a sense, the variance of the variance may be a very interesting statistic in its own right. Since the variance is a squared variable, the variance of the variance would be an X to the fourth power variable. However, we already have the well-understood kurtosis statistic based on fourth-power calculations.

Others have attempted to model the markets using the skew—a third-power statistic. These attempts are probably misguided in the sense that using the lognormal distribution adequately accounts for the skew because the lognormal distribution appears skewed when viewed from arithmetic space. The symmetrical bell-shaped distribution only appears when the data is presented on a logarithmic scale. Nevertheless, the study of the relationship of the markets with respect to the skew of the underlying distribution continues to be an active field.

Another possible flaw in modern portfolio theory is that it does not directly accommodate an investor's logarithmic utility function. Instead, it presupposes a utility based on mean and variance. In effect, the intersection of the capital market line and the investor's presumed linear utility for risk return is taken as the optimal portfolio for that particular investor. However, this flaw can be handled to some extent by incorporating a logarithmic function directly into the portfolio model.

Although modern portfolio theory has a few flaws, it still represents the framework of the best attempt to deal with the challenges of building an optimal portfolio in a rational and intelligent fashion.

CHAPTER 4

Modeling Risk Management and Stop-loss Myths

*"Play the game for more than you can afford to lose. . .
only then will you learn the game."*
—Winston Churchill (1874–1965)

Many authors, brokers, and market commentators espouse the use of stop-loss orders as a kind of free lunch. It is often billed as a technique that allows one to control risk without any associated cost. Some even claim that it increases returns. This chapter explores the myths associated with this technique and debunks many of the claims made by supporters.

To the author's knowledge, these results have never appeared in book form before. The author does not wish the reader to simply take his word for it that the concept of stop-losses has been largely oversold to investors. Because the results are quite innovative, this chapter offers mathematical proofs of the results. In keeping with the minimum math theme of this book, the proofs can be understood with only an understanding of the reflection principle and simple high school algebra.

The section discusses and shows how stops affect the mean return, probability of a win or loss, and the variance of returns. The effect on the more esoteric skew and the kurtosis is also demonstrated for completeness of exposition. A mid-chapter summary of these results serves as a convenient refresher for the latter part of the chapter.

Using the results concerning stop-losses naturally leads to a discussion of the important practical considerations when modeling stops, as well as knowing when to use them and when they should be avoided. The results for stop-losses naturally can be extended to the concept of stop profits and fixed-profit targets as well. Finally, the discussion considers how the use of stops of either variety creates a return distribution that is very similar to the returns from using puts and calls.

Winston Churchill was a famous political leader but not particularly noted as an investor. However, there is much to be learned from the quote at the beginning of this chapter with respect to balancing risk and reward. For him to lay it all on the table was the only way to play the political game.

In politics, in which an election is either won or lost, there is no middle ground. In that arena, perhaps Churchill's advice makes sense. From the perspective of the global power struggle of World War II, again his wisdom seems true. It seems unlikely that Allies and the Axis could have negotiated a lasting peace. After all, that had already failed after World War I. His genius was that he had the moral fortitude to bet his nation on the outcome of the war.

But in the investment arena, the investor has more choices. It is eminently possible to invest part of your portfolio in one stock and even to spread it out over many stocks and different asset classes. Part of this idea of balancing risk and reward can be described as using stop-loss orders to control risk. Much of this chapter deals with the question of whether stop-loss orders work.

STOP-LOSS ORDERS

A stop-loss is an order placed with a broker that is used to exit a trade if a certain adverse price is hit. For example, a trader may buy a stock at 50 and simultaneously place a stop order to sell at market if a price of 48 or lower is seen. His goal is to protect himself from a loss of larger than 2 points. Most frequently, this type of trading tactic is used as a form of risk management.

There is a considerable lore of stock market literature that advocates the use of stop-losses as a sort of free lunch money management system. This school of thought argues that stop-losses will cut your losses but allow your profits to run. On its face, it seems as though such tactics are a foolproof way to reduce losses and retain all of one's profits.

However, stop-loss orders have their drawbacks. When the price target is hit, the stop sell at market order becomes executable immediately. However, there is no guarantee that the order will be executed at or even near the 48 price. Sometimes there are gaps in trading that can mean that the sell stop 48 is triggered when a price of 46 is hit, because no trading occurred from 49 through 46. Thus, the hapless trader may be left with an execution at 46 or so, instead of the putative 48 price target.

The goal of this book is to present the ideas and concepts of portfolio modeling in an easily accessible intuitive manner. Wherever possible, the use of higher mathematics has been avoided. In particular, proofs are generally omitted in this work in the dual belief that they have been adequately covered elsewhere and tend to obscure the essence of the idea itself. However, to the best of the author's knowledge, the following sections discuss ideas pertaining to stop-losses that have not been derived elsewhere. Thus, it was not possible to omit the proofs. Otherwise, the earnest reader would be left in the hapless position of taking the author's word for the results in the face of so many market experts who espouse divergent opinions. Fortunately, the proofs offered are based solely on the very intuitive reflection principle augmented by nothing more than simple high school algebra. Hopefully, even nonmathematical readers will find the arguments and proofs understandable and intuitive.

STOPS: EFFECT ON THE MEAN RETURN

Once a stop-loss order is executed, one of two things can happen. The stock can go up or it can go down. Naturally, this begs the question as to whether it was a good idea to enter the stop order in the first place. Suppose we make the naïve but neutral assumption that it is equally likely for the stock to go up or down. Then half the time the investor would have recovered some or all of his losses. The other half of the time, the losses would continue to mount. Thus, there is no clear advantage to the investor. Nor is there any obvious augmentation to the expected average amount to be won or lost by using a stop-loss.

In Figure 4.1, we see a plot of the normal distribution with the stop-loss point *s* defined. The region to the left of the stop-loss point is the region that the investor hopes to avoid through the use of his stop-loss order.

The lack of increased expectation is predicted by the reflection principle and the self-similar properties of the normal distribution. Suppose a random walk with a symmetric distribution is currently at a loss point that we shall call *s*. Then the number of paths that go up from *s* is exactly equal to the number of paths that go down from that point. The downside distribution is an exact mirror image of the upside distribution from that point on. If we recall the picture of the normal distribution and a loss point *s* that is below the mean, then the tail to the left of point *s* represents the distribution that results from all of the paths that continue downward.

But the reflection principle says there is another equal and opposite set of paths that were reflected in the upward direction. The upside distribution is an exact mirror image of the avoided downside distribution.

In Figure 4.2, we see the avoided upside recovery area as well. It is shown as the reflected area to the right of the stop-loss point. In accordance with the reflection principle, we see that it represents an exact mirror image of the distribution that was avoided via the stop-loss order.

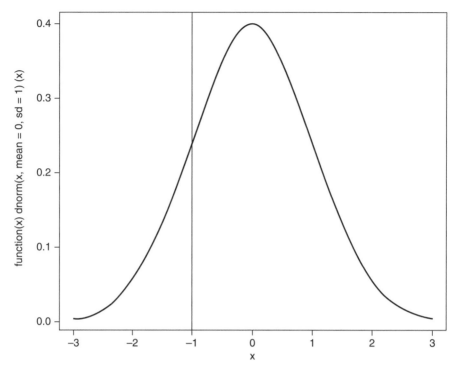

Figure 4.1 Normal Probability Distribution

For each point in the downside distribution, there is an equal and opposite point in the reflected upside distribution. The probability of each point occurring is equal. Each point is equally distant from point s, the original stop-loss point. Suppose we were to pair each resulting point in the downside distribution that went down, x, with its mirror image in the upside distribution that went up by the same amount. The avoided loss on the downside would be

$$s - x$$

The avoided more favorable result in the upside portion would be

$$s + x$$

Thus, the combined total for each matched pair is given by

$$s - x + s + x = 2s \qquad (4.1)$$

The result is always $2s$ because the x terms always cancel each other out. But we are dealing with point pairs composed of two points. So we must divide by 2 to find the

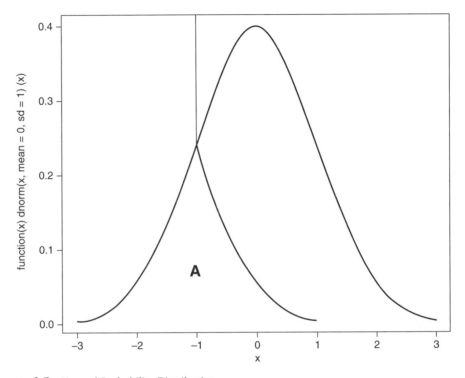

Figure 4.2 Normal Probability Distribution

result per trade. After dividing by two, the average result is simply a loss of *s* per path. This is the same result that would have been achieved without the use of a stop-loss.

Therefore, we can say that there is no net contribution to expected or average return by adding a stop-loss. This probably comes as a surprise, if not an outright shock to most traders. It is certainly at odds with the conventional wisdom of Wall Street.

However, it is good to remember that much of the lore of Wall Street has been popularized by sell-side brokers. Such so-called wisdom has often served to generate the commissions and trading volume that the Street needs for its very life blood. After all, buy and hold is bad for a commission-based business. The only strategies that the average broker is likely to espouse without cutting his own throat are those that will increase the level of active trading by his customers.

For this purpose, a stop-loss is perfect. Not only does it appear to make sense, but it actually generates two commissions. The first commission is the obvious one, when the position is sold through the stop-loss. The second is the commission that is generated when the money is reinvested in a new position.

There is another hidden cost, as well. Over time, the equity market tends to rise. The phenomenon is often termed the long term upward drift of the market. Thus, in the absence of any superior timing ability, the time out of the market represents lost return. As an unintended consequence of using stop-loss orders, the investor typically is also out of the market and thus loses out to some extent on the long-term upward drift, while a new investment is being evaluated.

STOPS: EFFECT ON THE PROBABILITY OF GAIN

Another consideration in the use of stop-loss orders is how stops mutate the probability of a gain or a loss. We shall see that adding a stop-loss always *increases* the probability of a loss and *reduces* the probability of a gain.

At its simplest we can see that when a stop-loss is executed, it is a loss. Thus, no loss events are avoided by a stop-loss strategy. Only the size of the largest losses can be reasonably argued to be reduced. Conversely, a stop-loss strategy causes possible profitable recovery events to be avoided. Thus, qualitatively, the probability of a loss can only increase through the use of stop-loss tactics. In the following discussion, we will attempt to address this idea in a quantitative manner as well.

Again, we shall invoke the reflection principle. The reader is referred to Figure 4.2. For a given stop-loss s it is easy to see that the tail to the left of s represents the avoided downside outcomes. The area under the curve represents the probability of being below s if the stop-loss had not been placed. However, again the reflection principle assures us that there is an equal mirror image distribution to the right, as well. Theoretically, the tails of the normal distribution go off to infinity. However, the tails become vanishingly small as they do so. But the point to understand is that some part of the right tail that is avoided by a stop-loss would have allowed the trader to recover back into profitable territory. Thus, the amount of the tail area under the curve that stretches back into profit territory is the amount by which the probability of a gain will be reduced, and the chance of loss increased. If the trader uses stops that are close to the current market price, this adverse effect on probability is considerable. If the stop-loss point is very distant, the effect on probability may be quite negligible. However, there is always an effect, and it always reduces the probability of a gain.

STOPS: PROBABILITY OF BEING STOPPED OUT

Suppose we have a stop-loss at price s. From our handy tables of the normal distribution contained in Appendix 1, we can tell that the probability of the price being in the tail anywhere below point s is given by some number p if there is no stop-loss order in place. It

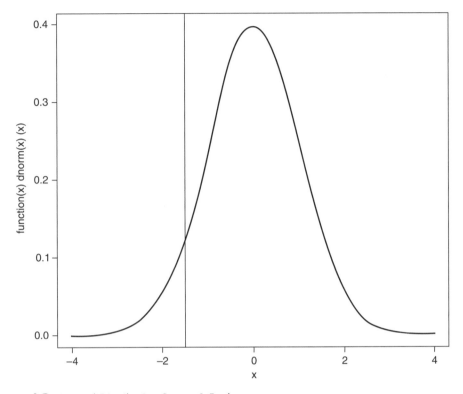

Figure 4.3 Normal Distribution Stop = 1.5 sd

is simply given by the cumulative probability density function of the normal distribution up to price *s*. In this case, we would treat *s* as a normalized value or *Z* score. For example, if *s* is placed at one standard deviation below the starting level, the normal tables would tell us that about 16 percent of the distribution lies below the 1 standard deviation level.

At first blush, it would seem that this is the probability of being stopped out. But that reasoning is not correct. Once again, we recall the reflection principle. For each of the paths that wound up in the leftmost tail, an equal and opposite path came back above the stop-loss point *s*. According to the reflection principle, the area under that curve must be equal. The reader is referred to Figure 4.3 for a visual illustration. In our example, this would represent another 16 percent of the total probability distribution. Thus, we have 16 percent in the leftmost tail lower than point *s* and we have another 16 percent in the reflected mirror image of that tail. This gives us a total of 32 percent of the time that the trade will be stopped out with a loss of *s*.

Again, the reflection principle assures us that if the probability of being at or below s without a stop is given by p, then the probability of being stopped out is exactly double that, or $2p$. Placing a stop-loss order exactly doubles a trader's odds of being at or below the stop-loss point. This is a profound result that traders should consider carefully.

STOPS: EFFECT ON VARIANCE AND STANDARD DEVIATION

To examine the effect of stop-loss orders upon the variance and therefore, also its close cousin, the standard deviation, we will once again invoke an analysis based on the reflection principle. For a given stop-loss level s we again analyze the distribution based on the matched pairs of reflected points. Again, the reflection principle assures us that there is an equal number of matched points above and below the stop-loss point. Thus, for a stop-loss at s and a given displacement x above and below that point we have:

$$\text{Downside avoided loss} : s - x$$

$$\text{Upside avoided gain} : s + x$$

The variance and standard deviation formulas are based on the sum of the squares of the returns values. So the only thing we need to consider is the contribution to the sum of the squares.

Assuming no stop: We set s to a minus value, reflecting that it is a loss. Then taking squares, we have

$$(-s - x)^2 + (x - s)^2$$

$$(s^2 + 2sx + x^2) + (s^2 - 2sx + x^2)$$

Combining we have

$$2(s^2 + x^2) \tag{4.2}$$

Assuming a stop is in place, the sum of the squares for the two paths is simply given by

$$2s^2 \tag{4.3}$$

Clearly, the difference between equation 4.2 with no stop and equation 4.3 with a stop, will be

$$2x^2 \tag{4.4}$$

Because x^2 is always a positive number, we have the important result that:

The variance and standard deviation will always be reduced as a function of that amount for each set of matched pair points. Trivially, the sum of all the matched pairs will always show a *positive reduction.*

EFFECT ON SKEW

To evaluate the impact of a stop-loss order on the skew of the return distribution, we shall use a similar technique. We first decompose the problem into the two cases. They are the case in which no stop is used and the case in which a stop-loss is employed. We compare the difference in the skew between these two cases.

For the Case of No Stop-loss

We can derive the effect on skew with a similar matched pair calculation based on the cubes of the matched points. Here we have the cubes of the avoided loss and avoided gain:

$$\text{Part}\,1 + \text{Part}\,2$$

$$(-s - x)^3 + (x - s)^3$$

Expanding, we get
Part 1:

$$-s^3 - 3s^2x - 3sx^2 - x^3 \tag{4.5}$$

Part 2:

$$-s^3 + 3s^2x - 3sx^2 + x^3 \tag{4.6}$$

Combining the two parts yields

$$-2s^3 - 6sx^2 \tag{4.7}$$

For the Stop-loss Case of Stop-loss

We have a loss of $-s$ and the skew is based on the contribution of the cubes of the deviations from the mean. The resulting skew for both sides is

$$-2s^3 \tag{4.8}$$

Clearly the difference is $-6sx^2$. Given that x^2 is always a positive number, we see that $-6s$ is always negative. Thus, the skew is always reduced by the addition of a stop-loss order to the strategy. Many traders consider a positive skew to be a desirable attribute of a distribution of returns.

EFFECT ON THE KURTOSIS

Using our usual definitions for avoided loss points and avoided gain, we can calculate the kurtosis or fourth moment of the normal distribution. Starting with the expanded form of equation 4.2 from the variance proof, we proceed as follows:

$$(s^2 + 2sx + x^2)^2 = s^4 + 4s^3x + 4s^2x^2 + 4sx^3 + x^4 \tag{4.9}$$

and

$$s^2 - 2sx + x^2 + s^4 - 4s^3x + 6s^2x^2 - 4sx^3 + x^4 \tag{4.10}$$

Combining equations 4.9 and 4.10 we get

$$2s^4 + 12s^2x^2 + x^4 \tag{4.11}$$

For the trade with a stop-loss, the fourth moment contribution for both sides is:

$$2s^4$$

Clearly, the difference between equations (4.11) and (4.12) is

$$12s^2x^2 + x^4 \tag{4.12}$$

Because all of the signs and terms of the difference are positive, it is clear that the effect of adding a stop-loss is to *reduce* the kurtosis.

STOP-LOSS: SUMMARY

In the foregoing discussion, we see that stops are not all they are supposed to be. They have some benefits and some drawbacks. There are still many who prefer stops. They should remember that for a random walk, based on a normal distribution, five points are true on a per-trade basis:

1. Stops will neither help nor hurt your expected (average) return.
2. Stop-losses will double the probability of being at or below the stop value. Your probability of loss will invariably increase with stop-losses.
3. The reduction in probability of wins will result in more runs of losses, and thus, overall, drawdowns over a succession of trades will tend toward the original value.
4. The variance and standard deviation will decrease. This represents a real reduction in risk.
5. The skew of the returns will become more negative resulting in approximately the same number of large gains with more numerous but limited losses.

Using a stop will mutate the distribution of returns. The resulting distribution will tend to somewhat like a normal but with many losses piled up at the stop loss point.

There is a tendency to return to the original normal distribution when the trades are considered collectively over time. Under reasonable assumptions, all distributions tend to return to a normal distribution in the limit. If the underlying process is additive, then it will tend to return to the normal distribution. If the native process is multiplicative, it will tend to return to the lognormal distribution in the limit. In other words, the stops make little difference in the long run, but do alter the shape of the distribution in the short run.

MODELING STOPS

When modeling stops, it is important to remember that the process is very path dependent. Thus, the model must accurately duplicate and include the entire path. In the foregoing, we have assumed the normal distribution as our theoretical model. As we know, the normal distribution conforms to an additive model of the price formation process. However, the results also apply to a lognormal distribution if viewed from logarithmic space.

When modeling stops, one must be careful to include highs and lows for the day in the model. It is never sufficient to simply use closing prices and assume the stops were or were not executed. In addition, some estimate must be made to account for slippage.

Slippage is always caused by the fact that there is a gap between the bid and the ask on the exchange at any given time. Thus, it is a rarity that, after a price of 48 is hit, one could actually get out at 48. It will usually be somewhat lower. The analyst must also take into account gap openings.

All things considered, stops are hardly the foolproof free lunch that some have made them out to be. It is quite clear that stops involve trade-offs in the short term and have only a modest impact on the distribution of returns in the long-term scheme of things.

In this chapter, we have focused on the theoretical distributions in order to derive some properties concerning how stops will change the distribution. Naturally, the focus is on intuition. Readers who wish to use the empirical distribution will probably prefer to model the use of stops using actual market data.

Any such models must religiously include reasonable estimates for slippage as a minimum. The entire path must be considered as well, including highs and lows reached during the period. Additionally, in the event of a gap opening, the actual open price must override the presumed stop price. Failure to take into account all of these details has led many an analyst to overestimate the benefits of stop-loss orders.

It is only after completing such an exercise that one can realistically evaluate the impact of stop-loss orders on the trading results. However, it is quite likely that empirical studies will follow the results of this chapter—on a qualitative basis, at least.

IDENTIFYING WHEN TO USE STOPS AND WHEN *NOT* TO

Clearly, we have shown that the use of stop-loss techniques is far from the panacea many on Wall Street make it out to be. However, it does have its place.

Clearly, we have seen that using the standard normal distribution model, the benefits of stops are lukewarm at best. In order to identify the situations when one might profitably employ stops, it is necessary to explicitly test that question using the empirical distribution. Any such test must include explicit recognition and testing of intraday (or intra period) highs and lows. If one fails to include these extreme values in price, any study is fatally flawed.

One very useful concept in studying stop-losses is the idea of the *maximum adverse excursion*. Essentially, the idea is that when we evaluate an historical data set of individual trades, we not only look at the outcome of each to its conclusion, but we look at how each trade did at all intermediate time frames as well.

Suppose we bought a stock at 50 and eventually sold it at 45 for a 10 percent loss. However, if at one point during the time we owned the stock, it went down to 40 at its nadir, the maximum adverse excursion was −10 points, or −20 percent. This concept can be useful when studying the effect of stops on a trading strategy.

In order to model stop-losses empirically, we must first set the stop rule. Usually this is a fixed percent loss. Some technical analysts like to use a fixed multiplier times the Average True Range (ATR). Others use trailing stops that move up if the price increases. Whatever method is chosen, it must be rigorously defined and tested.

After the method is defined, we (or our computer) examine each individual trade following its path during each time period to see if the stop would have been executed because the lowest price for the period slipped below the stop-loss point.

At this point, we must calculate a price at which the stop would have been executed. This is trickier than it might seem at first glance. As a minimum, the price should include something called slippage. This is the amount by which the actual execution price will slip below the stop price. As a minimum, the slippage should include the typical bid–ask spread.

However, often this is not enough. Many times, a stock will open for trading at a price much lower than the previous day. This is known as a gap opening because of the telltale gap that shows up on a chart of the stock. Often, such a discontinuous price jump will occur as the result of news. At other times, it is simply because a large seller wants to unload his stock on no obvious news. In any event, in order to model gap openings, the trader must recognize that the gap occurred and that the open price is the price to use, not the stop-loss price less slippage.

The problem of gaps is even more insidious when we consider that trading gaps can occur during the trading day. Often, they are the result of fast markets. Sometimes they result from news. Other times, the cause is the penetration of some important technical level. Traders who place their stops based on obvious technical levels such as previous highs or lows may be more susceptible to having their stops run by floor traders, much to their chagrin.

In any event, modeling stops should include the consideration of intraday gaps, as well as opening gaps. The only effective way to do this is to use tick data that considers every trade as it occurs. Such data is more expensive and more voluminous.

Although there are numerous problems and pitfalls associated with modeling stops, it can be done. However, we need to consider the fact that the model essentially helps us to analyze only one value for the stop-loss. The obvious question is whether the value we chose is the best. Naturally, to do this, we must define what is meant by *best*. Is it maximizing the mean return, minimizing the standard deviation, or improving the probability of success?

Another issue is that when we optimize the stop-loss value, we are creating several other problems for ourselves that are undesirable. First, we are trying many different models with the stop-loss value s allowed to vary. Statistically speaking, this can be viewed as either reducing the degrees of freedom or adding additional hypotheses. The point is that when we do this, we are increasing the chances that the result we ultimately obtain will be spurious. We make it more likely that the result is due to chance because we tried more ways until one finally worked.

Any statistical tests that we perform on the data will be reduced in power because of the need to adjust for the added number of tests tried. Potentially, even more dangerous is the possibility that the needed adjustments will not be made by the novice trader and that a result will be accepted for live trading that was wholly the result of chance.

As an example, suppose we had a data set and we found that the optimal stop value was −17.3 percent. The tests showed a profit at that level. But when we look at the other values tried, the trading method showed a loss at the −17 percent and at the −18 percent levels for the stop-loss. It simply is not credible that the testing actually found a sweet spot at −17.3 percent. Rather, it is more likely that the so-called sweet spot is due to inclusion or exclusion of one or a few observations that skewed the result. It is roughly akin to a trading system that includes the rule "Buy Google at 100." Well, the rule looks good on paper when we backtest it, but going forward it is likely to offer us no useful trades.

This issue is an example of a broad class of issues that some have dubbed *overfitting*, and others call data mining. Whenever we add more rules but each added rule only serves to eliminate a few observations, then it is time for the red flag to go up. The best policy is to keep the number of rules and fitted parameters to as few as possible, and the number of observations in our data as large as possible.

STOP-PROFITS

There is another order strategy that is quite different from the stop-loss order. That is the stop profit or profit target. It can be implemented as a stop order to sell at market or as a limit order at a given price target.

Either way, we can analyze the resulting distribution in just the same way that we did with the previous study of stop-loss orders. Each of the previous proofs also has an analogous proof based on the reflection principle applied to the profit target scenario. Because the proofs are essentially mirror images of those presented previously, we shall omit them here and leave them as an exercise for the reader.

However, the implications of the profit target are worth discussing and are presented as follows:

- Profit targets will not alter the expected return from a trade. They will neither add to nor subtract from the average return.
- Profit targets will reduce the variance and hence the standard deviation per trade. This can be a real risk reduction.
- The skew of the distribution will be altered in a similar, but inverse, way to that for stop-losses.

- The kurtosis will also be changed in an analogous way.
- The probability of a profitable trade will *increase* because the downside reflected paths from stop point *s* will have been eliminated. Some of those may have resulted in losses.

It is worth noting that investors who are so inclined may wish to utilize both stop-losses and profit target strategies in their trading. The combination of the two can be expected to have no impact on the mean return, but will result in a greater reduction in standard deviation than either alone.

PUTS AND CALLS

There are many similarities between put and call options and stop-loss or profit target strategies. In this section, we shall discuss the similarities, and some differences as well.

A call option gives the owner the right to buy 100 shares of stock at a fixed price for a fixed period of time. The fixed price is known as the *strike price* and the time is standardized by expiration months. Generally speaking, most stock options expire on the third Friday of the expiration month. A call buyer pays a price known as a premium to purchase the call option.

A put option is the right to sell 10 shares of stock at the strike price at any time up until the expiration period. The holder of a call option is not required to exercise this option. He or she will only do so if it is favorable.

If we compare a call option to a stop-loss strategy, we see that both offer a fixed downside loss limit. For this to be precisely true, we temporarily assume that the stop-loss is actually executed at the stop-loss price. In effect, the premium paid for the option acts as a limit on the loss. The buyer of a call can lose no more than his premium investment if held to maturity. Unlike the case for the stop-loss order, the loss to a call buyer is precisely and strictly limited. As discussed earlier, a stop-loss is not guaranteed to be executed at the stop price.

In a similar way, the probability distribution for the returns from a call option have a similar shape to the returns for a stop-loss analysis with a similar loss characteristic. Realization of these facts prompts one to wonder why more traders do not use call options instead of stop strategies.

For traders who employ profit target strategies, we find that the distribution of returns is quite similar to selling a put option. For example, suppose we sell a three-month put with a strike price of 50 for a premium of 5 when the current market price is 50. Our maximum profit is 5 if the stock goes to 55 because we get to keep the premium received for the put. In contrast, the profit potential is strictly limited to 5. It can never be any more.

However, this is the same profit profile that a trader who employs a profit target strategy would have. This trader has a profit outlook of a maximum of 5 if his 55 target is reached. In addition, he has a risk profile all the way down to a loss of 50 if the stock improbably drops to zero. This is the same risk that a put seller has. Hopefully, the reader can see that both stop-loss and stop-profit or profit target strategies are analogous to option strategies and can be modeled in the same way.

Conversely, we note that one can model puts and calls in much the same fashion if the positions are held to maturity. Thus, the probability models and arguments discussed in this section extend to options in a natural way.

One should hasten to add, however, that the resulting distribution for the returns on puts and calls themselves is fundamentally nonnormal. Again this is similar to the fact that using a stop-loss or profit target strategy results in a decidedly non-normal distribution as well. Thus, anyone developing such a model should be aware of that fact.

In the same way, the distribution for the stop-loss strategies and for the profit target strategies also results in a nonnormal probability distribution. Again, the trader is cautioned to avoid methods that assume the normal distribution for analyzing these situations.

Readers are urged to review the example program CD-ROM and the sample programs used to generate some of the charts in this book. In particular, the graphs relating to the normal distribution and the reflection principle can be very helpful in understanding this subject.

CHAPTER 5

Maximal Compounded Return Model

"Money begets money."

—Giovanni Torriano

*Foul cankering rust the hidden treasure frets, But
gold that's put to use, more gold begets.*

—William Shakespeare,
Venus and Adonis, 1593

Everyone wishes to make money on his or her investments. So maximizing investment return is an important subject in its own right. Some would argue that maximizing return is the only proper investment goal. This chapter should be very interesting for those folks.

For the rest of us who prefer to consider both return and risk in our investment decision making, this chapter is a start. It deals with how to maximize the compounded return on your portfolio. In a sense, this enables us to identify an upper bound on our risk taking. We shall see that there is a limit to risk taking. If we go beyond that limit, we will reduce return *and* increase risk. It is the worst of both worlds.

The basic concept of relative return is discussed as a foundation for this chapter. The essential difference between a simple average return for the stocks in a portfolio and the compounded returns on your portfolio are considered. Both types of averaging are needed, and the reader will see where each is appropriate.

Previously, we debunked some of the myths surrounding stop-loss orders. But that leaves us with a vacuum as far as good money management practices are concerned. One emphasis in this chapter is on the concept of proper position sizing as the best form of risk control. In addition, we shall see how and why position sizing is critical in order to achieve optimal compounded returns.

The chapter features a model that will maximize the long-term compounded return on a portfolio. The models have limitations that are thoroughly explained in the text.

From the idea of a model based on the theoretical distributions, the presentation moves on to consider the real-world model of the empirical distributions with its attendant warts and flaws. Modeling the empirical distribution is extremely important in order to be able to capture the real-world fat tails phenomenon. The techniques discussed also consider the all important issue of correlations between the variables.

Out of this frame work, the enhanced maximal investment formula is derived. The finale of the chapter discusses the reality that the maximal investment formula idea is cursed with large drawdowns and swings of capital that many investors will find unacceptable. Some ad hoc techniques to control the drawdowns are discussed.

Readers are encouraged to play along at home with the companion CD-ROM included with this book.

OPTIMAL COMPOUND RETURN MODELS

This chapter discusses the steps required to build and optimize a portfolio model that achieves the maximum possible return. In general, it is possible to optimize only one variable at a time. Thus, any model that seeks to optimize must somehow combine all of its objectives into a single function or formula. This function is called the *objective function*. It is essential in all optimization problems.

For the purpose of maximizing compounded returns, our objective function will most easily be expressed as a natural log function. The inputs to the log function will be in the form of a relative portfolio return for a discrete set of returns from backtesting. Each return will be weighted by its fraction of the entire portfolio. For an all-cash portfolio with no leverage, all of the weights should sum to 1, if the cash position is taken as one of the weights.

For portfolios that employ leverage, the sum of the weights may be greater than 1. For example, a portfolio that is leveraged 2:1 would normally have weights that sum to 2. Some hedge funds use short-selling techniques to reduce risk. In this case, the weight for the short positions will be negative. The sum of the weights for the entire portfolio could be anything. In particular, it could be negative.

RELATIVE RETURNS

We shall define a raw relative return as follows:

$$P_t/P_{t-1}$$

where

P_t = Price at time t

Thus, the raw relative return is simply the ratio of today's price to the price one time period before. Note that this definition is of a raw relative return. There is no consideration for dividends, stock splits, rights, or any of the other myriad distributions to share holders.

Accordingly, we must modify the previous definition to take into account such real-world oddities as dividends, stock splits, and many other types of corporate distributions. According to one study, there have been over 300 different types of corporate distributions throughout history. This number will only continue to grow as corporations invent new and exotic ways to distribute wealth to their shareholders. We shall combine all such distributions into an adjustment factor called D. This represents the value of the dividend or distribution during period t. The formula becomes:

$$\text{Relative return} = (P_t + D)/P_{t-1} \tag{5.1}$$

All of the inputs to the natural log function shall be in the form of relative returns. Relative returns give us numeric values that are centered on 1. When the price is unchanged, the relative return will be 1 and ln(1) is zero. Relative returns below 1 correspond to when the price declines, and relative returns above 1 will occur when the price rises. We also note that the relative return concept generalizes quite naturally to different time scales than 1 day, simply by changing the time scale. So time frames of a week, month, quarter, or even a year are all subsumed under this framework.

Normally, the price data would come from actual empirical price history. It could be all such prices for general portfolio work, or it could be selected trades from a mechanical system of some kind. It is theoretically possible to assume a random known distribution of some kind as well. In that case the data would be random realizations from the putative distribution. However, the data points are obtained, the formulas in this chapter are designed for discrete data, but that should not limit their general application.

Traditional portfolio modeling has assumed a theoretical distribution, but the orientation of this book is more toward an empirical approach. There are several reasons for this approach:

1. *The empirical distribution is a more general, assumption-free framework.* It is less prone to be dramatically incorrect.

2. *Considerable evidence has accumulated to the effect that the variance of the market exhibits bursts of serially correlated volatility.* The assumption of a stationary

variance seems to be incorrect. Thus, resorting to the empirical reduces the dependence of the model on the assumption of a stationary variance

3. *Formerly, the problem of running large simulations on empirical data was a nearly intractable problem for all but the most powerful computers.* In the present era of fast PCs with built-in hardware, floating-point coprocessors, and large memory, this capability is well within the reach of every desktop computer. What was once insurmountable is now commonplace.

4. *A certain amount of serial nonlinear relationships exists in the markets.* If and to the extent that this is true, then static models based on mean, variance, and covariance do not provide a complete basis upon which to model a portfolio. In contrast, using the empirical distribution appropriately can capture this nonlinearity. Conceivably, this can even be extended to intermarket relationships as well. To the extent that markets are interrelated or even cointegrated, then we need to resort to the empirical distribution for our analysis.

AVERAGE STOCK RETURNS, BUT COMPOUND PORTFOLIO RETURNS

Suppose we had a three-stock portfolio. Our stocks are called A, B, and C, and their returns for the period are given by a, b and c. If we then invest in each in the ratios 25:25:50, the formula to calculate our return at the end of the time period will be:

$$\text{One period portfolio return} = .25a + .25b + .50c$$

It is a simple weighted sum of the returns for each stock. If the weightings had been equal, then the formula would be equivalent to a simple average of the returns for each stock. The key point here is that returns within a period should be calculated as a weighted average of the individual returns. There is no compounding occurring within the period because money used to invest in one position is not available for another. Thus, there are no logs or other sophisticated formulas.

If we have n stocks in our portfolio and the returns are given by $x_1, x_2, \ldots, x_n$, then the formula for the total portfolio return for the period is

$$\text{Portfolio return} = \sum_{i=1}^{n} w_i x_i \qquad (5.2)$$

The weight of each stock position i is represented by the term w_i. This formula is the general formula for the weighted average of simultaneous positions held during a single time period. We note that the idea of a time period could be a year, month, week, day, or even higher intraday frequencies. For our purposes, the time frame is simply an arbitrary planning horizon. It can be taken as long or short as is reasonable for the given portfolio and trading style of the portfolio manager.

LOGARITHMS AND THE OPTIMAL EXPONENTIAL GROWTH MODEL

If single-period portfolio returns are found as a weighted average of individual returns, we may reasonably ask how to define the long-term compounded growth potential of a portfolio. As discussed in the previous section, the single period return is a simple weighted average. However, we know that the long-term compounded return is essentially an exponential growth function. Naturally, the usual method to compute this will involve logarithms. The resolution to this seeming conflict is to combine *both* ideas into one formula.

Specifically, we combine the simple weighted average into a single variable for period t as follows:

$$\text{Portfolio return for period } t = r_t = \sum_{i=1}^{n} w_i x_i \tag{5.3}$$

Then the contribution to overall long-term compounded return will be a function of

$$\text{Contribution to compounded return} = \ln(1 + r_t)$$

$$\text{The actual return is}: e^{\ln(1+r_t)} \tag{5.4}$$

Therefore, to maximize the compounded return we only need to maximize the ln term. Switching to exp( ) notation, for m periods we get

$$\text{Multiperiod compounded return} = \exp\left(\sum_{t=1}^{m} \ln(1 + r_t)\right) \tag{5.5}$$

POSITION SIZING AS THE ONLY GUARANTEED RISK CONTROL

In the preceding discussion, we dealt with how to calculate compounded return. The method combines both the arithmetic average of the individual positions within period and the compounded or geometric average for a sequence of portfolio returns over several periods.

However, it begs the question as to how to control risk. The method only addresses how to calculate return. The only inputs to the return function are the weights chosen by the portfolio manager. In effect, we are left with the rather obvious answer that the primary way a portfolio manager can control risk is via the selected weights.

CONTROLLING RISK THROUGH OPTIMAL POSITION SIZING

The contribution to overall compounded return for a portfolio of only one position with weight w is given by

$$\sum_{t=1}^{n} \ln(1 + wr_t) \tag{5.6}$$

where w is the respective weighting for the position. And each r_t is the return from an historical simulation or study of previous returns. To convert this contribution to absolute dollars it only requires taking the exp( ) function of equation 5.6. To find the optimal position size, one needs only to optimize w with respect to the given historical data.

A few caveats are in order, however. First, equation 5.6 deals only with a single position. Effectively the one position comprises the entire portfolio. As such, it is appropriate only for that case. In the event of more than one position, the formula only helps one identify an *upper bound* for the position size. In other words optimizing for w in equation 5.6 only identifies the *largest* amount one should invest in the given position. The true optimal position size in a multi-investment portfolio is likely to be considerably less.

Under no circumstances should an individual position ever exceed the upper bound given by this formula. Traders often term this situation *overtrading*. In essence, what an investor is doing when the position size exceeds this limit is to actually *reduce* return and increase risk. Literally, it is the worst of both worlds.

It is simply not rational to exceed this value in a single position. To do so exposes the portfolio to added risk without compensating return. It is nothing more or less than gambling. However, it is one of the most perfidious forms of gambling in the sense that exceeding the upper bound on position also exposes the portfolio and the manger to total risk of ruin. Clearly this is not a desirable situation.

MAXIMIZE COMPOUNDED PORTFOLIO RETURN

The more general case for portfolio returns is the case in which multiple investments are held at the same time. In order to deal with this case, we shall need to consider both the average return within a period and the effect on sequential compounding that results.

But the overall goal shall be to optimize the portfolio allocation so that the maximum compounded return is achieved.

Assuming weights $w_1, w_2, \ldots, w_n$ where n is the number of positions, and expected return vector r where each r_i is a return for the given security in that period. The word *vector* here simply means a list of returns. Note that r is a vector containing observations for the same period.

Nominally, it would come from a historical study of past prices. However, for our purposes it could also come from a lognormal simulation that takes appropriate measures to account for correlation between assets. Because the correlations between financial assets tend to be high, it is important to view this return vector as returns from the same period. This treatment effectively captures the dependency caused by correlation.

We only need to set up and solve the optimization problem. In keeping with the philosophy of this book, we shall let the computer do the actual optimization. The objective function is taken first from equation 5.3, repeated as equation 5.7, which gives us the simple arithmetic average return for the period.

$$\text{Portfolio return for period t} = r_t = \sum_{i=1}^{n} w_i x_i \tag{5.7}$$

$$\text{Multiperiod compounded return} = \exp\left(\sum_{t=1}^{m} \ln(1 + r_t)\right) \tag{5.8}$$

where m is the number of time periods.

MAXIMAL COMPOUNDED RETURN MODELS

In order to maximize the long-term multiperiod return of a portfolio, we must maximize the return expressed in equation 5.7. For now, we shall not consider *how* to maximize. Rather, the important first goal is to further consider *what* to maximize. Equation 5.7 gives us the long-term formula, but it is important to realize that the overall objective is reached by a series of steps. Each period represents a step in the long-term process.

Compound interest is a multiplicative process. It is not an additive process. In contrast, the average return within period of a portfolio is an additive process. We add up the weighted returns and compute the average. To reflect the fact that the long-term process is multiplicative, at each step we should seek to maximize the log of the portfolio's contribution. Thus, the appropriate formula to optimize is

$$\text{Max } \ln(1 + r_t) \tag{5.9}$$

This simply represents the inner part of equation 5.8. This is the part that represents the within-period returns. So when we maximize this formula, we maximize the ongoing multiperiod returns.

The best way to view such formulas is as a maximal investment size formula. It is the amount to invest if one had no aversion to risk at all. The person or portfolio manager who is risk indifferent would seek to maximize this formula. Essentially, this is a mathematical statement of how to maximize one's long-term compounded wealth if one is risk neutral.

WHAT THE MODEL IS AND IS NOT

The important thing to understand about equation 5.9 is that it maximizes the long-term compounded return of the portfolio. In one sense, that is what we want. Clearly, maximizing return is a very important part of investing. The drawback is that maximizing return is merely that. It does not fully address the issue of risk. Many investors and portfolio managers dwell exclusively on return to the exclusion of all else. A problem lies therein.

When one exclusively focuses on return to the exclusion of all considerations of risk, it creates a situation in which volatility is ignored. In particular, for the case of one investment per period, using equation 5.9 to optimize return results in an ultimate volatility of returns that is unacceptable to most investors.

An examination of the optimization function shows that it gradually rises up to the maximum point but then suddenly plummets after the maximum value is reached. The lesson to take away is that missing the maximum point on the low side has little cost. But an error in finding the optimum value beyond the actual maximum has dire consequences. It is an example of an asymmetric risk–reward function (see Figure 5.1).

In Figure 5.1 we have a typical example of a Maximal Return function. The sample returns used to construct this were simply made up from typical return numbers. In normal modeling, these returns would come from historical backtesting or from actual trading results in the past.

We see in Figure 5.1 that the return starts out positive for small values of the weighting function. In this fictitious example, it reaches its maximum value at 59 percent of the portfolio invested in the market.

One salient feature of this graph is that so much of the right side of the function actually leads to large losses. The given set of returns has a positive expectation in the usual misguided statistical sense so that is not the problem. The real issue is that as more money is invested, the compounded returns increase at a slower and slower rate. Ultimately, at about 59 percent invested, the returns actually start to diminish at an ever faster pace.

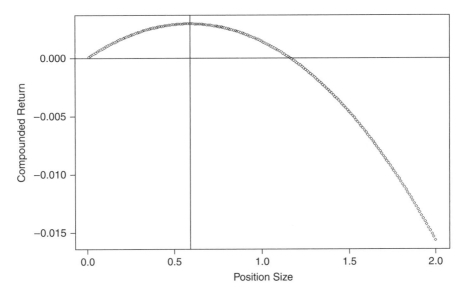

Figure 5.1   Asymmetric Risk–Reward Function

The weightings on the right side greater than 1.0, represent the use of leverage. At 1.0, the investor is fully invested. Whereas at 2.0, the investor is leveraged 2:1, which corresponds to using 50 percent margin. Clearly, the excessive use of leverage in this situation can be catastrophic.

MODELING THE EMPIRICAL DISTRIBUTION

In order to model the empirical distribution, as opposed to the theoretical, we must create a random reordering of the historical record. The key consideration is to preserve any sequential correlations in the data. The good news is that there generally are few linear correlations in the data. That fact is generally promised by the efficient market hypothesis. However, there may be relationships in the data that are nonlinear. Preserving these is the essence and the art of good portfolio modeling.

To model empirical data, yet preserve nonlinear relationships at various lags, we must preserve both the data and most of the lag relationships. By simply randomizing the start time and adopting a relatively long window until the end time, we can effectively preserve any nonlinear relationships in the data.

The primary considerations when modeling with a randomized time model are to decide on the size of the data window and the number of randomizations to be performed. With respect to the window, it should fit the desired holding period or it should be compatible with the desired reevaluation period. For example, if we want to evaluate our portfolio on a monthly basis, then a look-back window on the order of a month would be appropriate.

Another consideration is if some past data is needed. For some trading systems, a certain amount of data from a prior period is needed. For example, if we need to calculate a moving average of 20 days, then we will need to allow for at least 20 extra days in our data prior to the random time chosen. Thus, if we randomly chose time t, then the data window must include day $t - 20$ through day $t - 1$ in order to allow for the moving average.

In addition, we must allow for the actual window of data we wish to analyze. Thus, our total required data for this case would be the window plus 20. Although it is certainly possible to ignore this issue initially, in the opinion of the author it is better to address this in the planning stages of any model. The alternative—to allow the computer model to blow up with an error message—generally occurs at the most inopportune times. Ignoring this issue can lead to unknown errors that the computer does not detect. For example, it could result in data values of zero inadvertently being used in place of real data, or any of a myriad number of other problems.

CORRELATIONS

Correlations are handled as an explicit part of traditional portfolio theory. In that field, they are crucial to the calculations and need to be handled directly. However, if we use the empirical distribution, relationships may be embedded in the data possibly in a non linear way. It is important to sample all of the data points from the same time period for all of the investments in that period. Only in that way can we capture the actual underlying relationships.

One example of this might be if we were analyzing a macroportfolio consisting of stocks, bonds, gold, and the dollar. We might well find that stocks and bonds are positively correlated at times and at other times they are negatively correlated. So, too, we might find that the correlation between the bonds and the dollar waxes and wanes at certain times in the business cycle.

The only effective way to capture these relationships is to pick our sample from a randomly selected window in time that includes all of the relevant data points varying together as they varied then. We need to resample the entire multivariate distribution, not just one isolated variable at a time. In other words, each sample window in the preceding example would have to include data for stocks, bonds, gold, and the dollar for the entire window.

As an example, we would sample a window beginning at randomly selected time t. To capture all of the hidden relationships, we need to consider all of the data for stocks, bonds, gold, and the dollar at time t as they occurred at that time. We then walk forward through the entire sample window taking all the observations for that time period. This technique captures both the contemporaneous correlations that occur within a single period as well as any sequential relationships that may exist.

We also note that this sampling technique preserves not only linear correlations but also other nonlinear relationships. Looking at correlation coefficients is usually sufficient to detect linear correlations, but it is no assurance that there are not nonlinear effects present.

It has often been noted that during financial crises all markets tend to be correlated. This includes markets that were not previously related, at least not linearly. Using the window sampling technique helps to preserve this structure in the empirical data.

THE ENHANCED MAXIMUM INVESTMENT FORMULAS

Earlier in this chapter, we discussed optimization of the single-period portfolio returns, and specifically for a single investment. Although this may seem risky or foolhardy at first blush, in fact sometimes it is quite reasonable. For example, suppose an investor is invested only in the Standard & Poor's 500 index fund. These go by the moniker the *Spyders* with ticker symbol SPY. Effectively, this fund is a diversified portfolio of some 500 large-cap stocks weighted by capitalization. No one could argue that the portfolio is not sufficiently diversified. Naturally, this generalizes to any index fund or future product with similar properties.

Therefore, it is actually reasonable to consider investing in what amounts to a single entity. Thus, the discussion of the previous section is quite reasonable under certain circumstances.

However, we can also consider the case of multiple positions. In this case, the same basic formula applies, but we note that the formula to calculate r_t now must include all of the portfolio positions. We then have:

$$r_t = \sum_{i=1}^{n} w_i x_i \tag{5.10}$$

Where the w_i is the weight given to investment i *and* x_i is the return from that investment during period t. Now r_t is the weighted portfolio level return for period t given the selected weights for each position.

At this point it only remains for us to optimize the overall return by proper selection of the weights, all the w_i choices. So we let the computer optimize by maximizing the following objective function over all the weights.

$$\text{Max } \ln(1 + r_t) \tag{5.11}$$

EXPECTED DRAWDOWNS MAY BE LARGE

The major drawback to using the return optimizing formulas is that the variability is likely to be too great. The formulas do maximize long-term compounded return, just as advertised. However, because risk is not included explicitly, they are subject to wild swings and potentially catastrophic drawdowns.

Earlier, we cautioned against the folly of investing beyond the recommended optimum. In fact, returns fall off dramatically. Overinvesting can actually cause a negative expected return in a logarithmic sense. At the same time, risk as measured by the variance increases. It is the worst of both worlds—lower return and increased risk. Some writers who have experimented with similar formulas have suggested that the maximal investment be reduced from its existing level to a level one fourth of the calculated size.

One advocate of the one-fourth heuristic is Ed Thorpe, former M.I.T. professor of statistics. He is, perhaps, better known as the author of the best-selling book *Beat the Dealer*. The book chronicles his successful attempt to beat the casinos at the game of blackjack. Thorpe's one-fourth suggestion is merely a heuristic designed to produce a more palatable money-management formula. However, it leans in the right direction. More importantly, it demonstrates how the blind use of the maximal optimization formula leads to results that many find unacceptable.

CHAPTER 6

Utility Models— Preferences Toward Risk and Return

"Be careful what you wish for, you might get it."

—Anonymous

T he purpose of this chapter is to discuss the all-important subject of utility models. The word *utility* essentially means "usefulness." If the goal of investing is to create and enhance wealth, then we need to answer the perplexing question of how to value wealth. Here we address the broad subject of how useful is a dollar.

First, we introduce the idea of a utility model on the simple grounds that we must define what it is that we want before we can devise a plan to go after it. The utility model becomes our goal. We must come to grips with our desired rate of return and our feelings toward risk.

The chapter covers the history of logarithms and relates some of the theories that have used logs to model investments. An overview is given of some of the great thinkers and theories of the utility of money. The discussion ranges from the St. Petersburg Paradox to the relatively modern work in game theory and utility models such as Arrow's work.

The focus is kept on the salient properties of a good utility model. This concept is developed into a utility model that will define and is consistent with optimal long term growth of capital at the portfolio level.

The text also discusses the Sharpe Ratio, an investment metric that seems to be ubiquitous in the industry. A model is developed that will optimize the Sharpe Ratio for a given portfolio.

There is a general discussion of the many optimization routines available in the R library. Typically, each routine can be invoked simply by a single line command. The section provides an overview of the most useful commands and a brief description of the situations in which each one applies. The reader will find information on how to obtain full detailed online help in that section as well.

The Excel add-in package Solver is used as an example of how to set up a spreadsheet to optimize the Sharpe Ratio. The discussion in the text relates to the example provided on the CD-ROM that accompanies this book. As always, emphasis is on the concepts and understanding how to interpret the results. The Solver package already knows how to do the optimization so that you do not have to.

Optimization examples are provided on the CD-ROM in both Excel and R. Readers are encouraged to review these after or during their reading of the chapter.

BASIS FOR A UTILITY MODEL

The anonymous aphorism quoted at the beginning of this chapter illustrates the dilemma that investors face. In order to make an intelligent investment choice, they must first define what it is that they actually want. Defining the investment goal is the first step in achieving investment success. However, it is equally important to understand the consequences that are attendant on the investment goal being considered.

For example, most people know that they want to maximize return on investment. But with that usually comes added risk. So to solely focus on return is certainly faulty and likely will lead to undesirable consequences. Some consideration of risk must be included. Additionally, we can and should consider other investment measures, such as probability of gain, compounded portfolio return, skew of the resulting distribution, and perhaps even the kurtosis of our chosen investment goal.

For the remainder of this chapter, we shall use the term *utility function* for our investment goal and discuss how to derive a suitable utility function.

Clearly, any reasonable utility function should include the average portfolio return, as discussed in previous chapters. This then forms the basis for calculating the compounded portfolio return that should also certainly be included in any goal.

Because very few of us are risk averse, we should also include a reasonable measure of risk in our utility function. Risk has always been a rather ephemeral concept in finance. Some would say it is only the amount lost that should be considered in risk. Others argue that all of the volatility should be considered, with the largest outliers weighted the most.

Effectively, this is what the standard deviation function of statistics does. It weights the resulting deviations from the mean by their squares and has been shown to achieve a maximum likelihood with its weighting. Largely as a result of this, the field of finance has settled on the standard deviation as the most accepted measure of variability of return. It is effectively equated with risk. We shall adopt this standard as well.

It is customary in the U.S. investment world to measure everything in dollars. Even if one's currency is euros or yen, there is a simple conversion at any given time that will convert to the desired numeraire. But is a dollar really worth a dollar? Earlier, we discussed the fact that most people would not play the St. Petersburg Paradox game at its stated mathematical expected value nor even anything close to that value. As Daniel Bernoulli argued, the reason was that people actually had a logarithmic sense of the value of money. Thus, it may be reasonable to impute a utility function based on the natural log of the dollars in question.

It should be emphasized that this is different from, and in addition to, the use of logarithms that we employed previously in maximizing the compounded return of the portfolio. That return is still expressed in dollars. However, those dollars require an additional log function to be converted to utility units. Thus, one of the fundamental assertions of this book is that the utility function of choice should include an explicit ln ln function or iterated log function.

Undoubtedly, many of the readers of this book are professionals employed in the investment field. For those people, there is another special kind of utility function that must be acknowledged. Specifically, it is the metric by which they are measured as managers. In modern portfolio management, the metrics have grown ever more sophisticated and typically do include some sort of explicit recognition of both risk and return, as well as other measures. In particular, the Sharpe Ratio has become nearly ubiquitous. The popular Morningstar mutual fund tracking service routinely calculates a Sharpe Ratio for each of the funds tracked. In addition, other measures of performance are widespread.

The famous beta calculation that measures the sensitivity of a portfolio to market moves in the designated index is widely available. Many clients wish to reduce their exposure to equities to a particular level and thus, wish to minimize the overall systematic correlation with equities.

For each security or individual investment, there is a beta that measures its intrinsic systematic relationship with the overall market. The amount of variance explained by that beta regression is the R^2 of that regression. This is separate and distinct from the total variance that measures the total variability of the investment. Thus, in defining one's utility function, the beta represents the market correlation that cannot be eliminated through simple diversification. In a similar fashion, the R^2 measures the amount of variance that cannot be eliminated through diversification.

HISTORY OF LOGARITHMS

No discussion of the history of logarithms would be complete without a reference to John Napier. In many ways, he can be considered the father of the logarithm. In 1614, Napier published a book titled *Mirifici Logarithmorum Canonis Descriptio*. It represents the first publication of the logarithm concept.

Clearly, the concept of logarithms or the logical prerequisites for its conceptual genesis were extant at the time. In particular, the Swiss mathematician Joost Burgi published his technique for logarithms in 1620 just six years after Napier. For perspective, this is the same year that the Pilgrims landed at Plymouth Rock. Burgi may have privately developed his technique as early as 1588 but was moved to publish only after prompting from Johannes Kepler. Although Napier's publication was already well known at the time throughout Europe, the method used by Burgi was quite distinct from Napier's, and thus, clearly had been developed independently. For his contribution, the lunar crater Burgius has been named in his honor.

Given today's electronic technology, few realize that two rulers can be used as a simple adding machine. The idea is very simple. If you want to add $2 + 3$, all that is required is to line up the rulers and then slide one of them to the right so that its zero point lines up with the numeral 2 on the other one. Then look to the right on the one that was slid to find the 3. The numeral 3 should now line up with the numeral 5 (the answer) on the other ruler. Essentially, the idea is to add the length 2 to the length 3 and we find that the total length is 5.

Napier used the same basic idea to construct a simple device that acquired the moniker *Napier's bones*. The key idea was to construct the two rulers on a logarithmic scale rather than an arithmetic scale as on a standard ruler. Thus, when the top ruler was slid to the right, the device was now adding the logarithms, which is the equivalent of multiplying. The answer could be read directly from the opposite ruler because the scale was in logarithms as well. Thus, Napier invented the slide rule, which greatly simplified multiplication and division right up until the time that modern calculators were invented.

In 1728, the Swiss mathematician Gabriel Cramer wrote a letter to his friend Daniel Bernoulli. In the letter, Cramer outlined his thoughts on the St. Petersburg Paradox and how to resolve its paradoxical nature. Cramer's contribution was to explicitly include a utility function as part of his analysis. His proposed utility function was based on the square root of the amount in question. Cramer reasoned as follows:

> *Mathematicians estimate money in proportion to its quantity, and men of good sense in proportion to the usage that they may make of it.*

Thus, he conjectured that the value of money did not rise in linear proportion to the arithmetic amount, but rather, rose monotonically but at a decreasing rate as the amount of wealth increased. He posited an absolute upper bound of 2^{24} coins as the upper limit of utility. He was also the first to propose the St. Petersburg Paradox in its modern form with coin flipping instead of a six-sided die.

Although Cramer's choice of the square root was not quite correct, it was his thinking that led Bernoulli to propose the natural log function as the basis for the utility of money. Bernoulli added the concept that one's wealth must be a factor in the concept of utility. Cramer had missed this latter point completely, presumably seeking a pure, more universal definition of utility.

Unfortunately, Bernoulli's utility function and the St. Petersburg puzzle were effectively lost to modern thinkers. It was only in the 1950s that the paper was rediscovered and translated for modern scholars.

In late 1944, Jon Von Neumann and Oscar Morgenstern published their groundbreaking work, *Theory of Games and Economic Behavior*. Their contribution was to axiomatize the idea of a utility function as a *monotonically increasing* concave function of wealth. *Monotonically increasing* can be interpreted as "more is better." The concavity property means that investors are increasingly sated with greater wealth. In other words, a dollar more to a millionaire is not worth as much as a dollar to a pauper. The value of a dollar increases, but at a marginally declining rate.

K. Arrow, G. Debreu, and J. Pratt all made important enhancements to the development and further rigorous development of utility theory. The important take away from these ideas is that a proper investment utility function is monotonically increasing (everywhere of interest) and concave. The concavity can also be stated as saying that the second derivative is everywhere negative. Importantly, the log function family satisfies these requirements (see Figure 6.1).

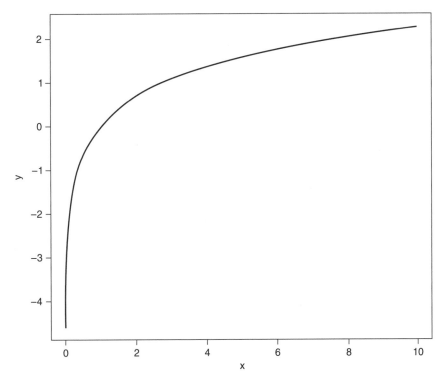

Figure 6.1 Log Function

More recently, Professor Mark Rubinstein of the University of California, Berkeley, has published a paper discussing the implications of an investment policy that solely maximizes growth. The paper offers a straightforward proof of the proposition that optimizing the expected compound growth is the long-run optimal strategy. In addition, he addressed the question as to how long it would take for an investor to be 95 percent confident that his or her optimal growth maximizing policy in stocks would be superior to other more mundane strategies, such as investing in fixed short-term money market rates.

The resulting time frames were surprisingly long using reasonable assumptions from the market's own historic rates of return and variability. For example, to achieve a 95 percent confidence that the optimal strategy would be superior, the investor would have to wait more than 200 years. For 99 percent assurance, the wait time is about 4,000 years! Reassuringly, the probability that the strategy will be superior eventually approaches 1. However, it takes much longer than 4,000 years. This raises the obvious rhetorical question—can an investor wait so long?

Clearly the log-maximizing strategy is optimal in an expected log sense. However, it may not necessarily be the most desirable. Rubinstein also adds the point that it does not necessarily maximize the probability of being the best strategy at all intermediate time frames. So if maximizing probability of meeting a certain benchmark return is the goal, another utility function may be in order. Specifically framing the utility in terms of the probability of success at a given point in time might be one reasonable objective function.

OPTIMAL COMPOUNDED UTILITY MODEL

We are now ready to proceed with the development of a formal model based on logarithmic utility. The key is to define our utility function that will explain what a dollar is worth to us. Clearly, by historical precedent and sound logic, the natural log is a clear choice as our utility of wealth number.

We also wish to maximize the overall compounded portfolio return *as measured in utils*. Instead of maximizing wealth directly, we now seek to maximize utility as measured by *utils*. We shall use the term *utils* as an arbitrary unit of measure to emphasize that we are not speaking of dollars but rather in utility units. From our earlier discussion, the ln function is the natural choice. So our utility function for wealth at time t becomes

$$U_t(w_{it}) = \ln(r_t/W_{t-1}) \tag{6.1}$$

where W_{t-1} is the wealth or portfolio value from the previous period $t-1$ and r_t is the portfolio return for the period from Eq. 5.3.

Then the objective function is to maximize the compounded utility. That is, we wish to maximize compounded $U(t)$ at time t. But the contribution to compounding for each $U(t)$ is $\ln(1 + U_t)$. Substituting from equation 6.1, our objective function becomes

$$\text{Objective} = \max \sum (\ln(1 + U_t)) \tag{6.2}$$

We note in passing the use of the iterated logarithm notation. Intuitively, this is motivated by the fact that the utility is a log function and the contribution to compounding of the utility is also a log function. Hence, the ultimate objective function is in the form of the log of a log.

THE SHARPE RATIO

The performance of many professional money managers is measured by the Sharpe Ratio possibly along with other metrics:

$$\text{Sharpe Ratio} = (r_p - r_f)/s_p \tag{6.3}$$

where

r_p is return for the portfolio
r_f is the risk-free rate of return (usually three-month T-bills)
s_p is the standard deviation of the portfolio returns

Essentially, the numerator measures the excess return the portfolio received over and above the riskless rate. The excess return is then divided by the number of units of risk as measured by the standard deviation. This gives us the excess return received per unit of additional risk taken. This seems to be a reasonable measure of portfolio performance.

In any event, this is the measure of a portfolio manager's performance that is most prevalent in the industry. Everyone who manages money should be aware of what it is, how to calculate it, and what it measures. Any manager who is routinely measured by this yardstick may wish to consider adopting the Sharpe Ratio as the portfolio objective. In so doing, the money manager will be adopting a reasonable objective function as the portfolio goal and will be simultaneously optimizing personal performance as measured by the Sharpe Ratio metric.

OPTIMAL MODEL FOR THE SHARPE RATIO

In the preceding section, we discussed what the Sharpe Ratio is and what it purports to measure. It is an important measure of portfolio performance and is widely used in the industry. Many managers are judged by it. It is probably fair to say that most are at least partly measured by the Sharpe Ratio.

Thus, it is important to know how to optimize this ratio and how to target one's portfolio to achieving the best possible Sharpe Ratio. That is the goal of this section. More generally, this section can serve as a case study of how to perform portfolio optimization for any desired objective function.

One of the goals of this book is to elucidate the concepts of portfolio modeling in an intuitive and easily accessible manner with a minimum of math. In keeping with this objective, we shall focus on how to calculate the answer for any given optimization problem. We will eschew all attempts to derive theoretically elegant optimal solutions and support those formulas with proofs. Instead, the focus shall be on obtaining the right answer with a minimum of effort. To a practitioner, this simply means we need to find out how large each position should be in order to optimize our objective function. Implicit in this is the transcending question of the optimal amount of leverage or cash that one should employ.

Fortunately, there are at least two readily available solutions:

1. *Microsoft Excel has an excellent add-in package called Solver that will perform the necessary optimization.* To use Solver, first define the objective function as a single cell in the spreadsheet. For the Sharpe Ratio, the formula would be based on the following (patterned after equation 6.3):

$$\text{Sharpe Ratio} = (r_p - r_f)/s_p$$

Thus, one only need define the portfolio return r_p, risk-free return r_f and portfolio standard deviation s_p based on the weightings and some past data for the positions being considered. The Solver program will need to know where the weightings are to be placed. Often, it is helpful to start with some reasonable initial values. Good choices would be equal weighting or capitalization weighting. If we select a reasonable choice such as these, Solver is able to run a little more quickly. Essentially, Solver will find the weightings that represent the "answer" as far as a practitioner is concerned. The weightings are the amounts one should invest in order to optimize the Sharpe Ratio.

2. *The other way to optimize the objective function is to use the statistical language R (or its close cousin S) as the optimization tool.* R will generally be faster than Excel, and it will often be easier to implement than the spreadsheet approach. This latter point is especially relevant as the number of desired portfolio positions increase.

The *optim* routine in the R stats library will generally suffice for most purposes. The calling sequence for this function is as follows:

optim(par,fn,gr=NULL,
method=c("Nelder-Mead",
"BFGS", "CG", "L-BFGS-B",
"SANN"),
lower=-Inf,upper=Inf,
control=list( ), hessian=
FALSE, ...)

For our purposes, the parameters are as follows:

par   Initial values for the various parameters (weights) to be optimized.

fn   The objective or goal function to be minimized (or maximized). The first argument is the vector of parameters over which minimization is to take place. It should return a single valued scalar result.

gr   A function to return the gradient for the "BFGS", "CG" and "L-BFGS-B" methods. For our purposes, set this value to NULL, and a finite-difference approximation will be used.

method   The method to be used. For our purposes the default method is fine. Type help(optim) and see *Details*.

lower, upper   Bounds on the variables for the "L-BFGS-B" method.

control   A list of control parameters. See *Details*.

hessian   Logical. Should a numerically differentiated Hessian matrix be returned? Most users will set this to false or omit this variable.

One tip that is well worth knowing is that any maximization problem can easily be changed into a minimization problem, and vice versa. To accomplish this feat, one need only place an artificial minus sign in front of the function to be minimized. It will then become a function to be maximized. If the function is one we wish to maximize, such as the Sharpe Ratio, placing the minus sign in front will allow us to use a software routine that minimizes the function to find the desired answer.

For our purposes, it is best to present the problem as a minimization problem in contrast to the fact that we usually wish to maximize the Sharpe Ratio. The par vector should be a simple list of starting values for the weightings of each investment in the portfolio model and one for cash. Setting the gr or gradient parameter to NULL allows the routine to calculate its own finite difference derivatives rather than requiring you as the user to derive and provide a matrix of derivative functions. Again, the emphasis is on simplicity. The optim routine will work fine without the added help from the user.

For more details on this routine, type help(optim) in the R environment to view the complete documentation.

For those users who are more venturesome, another optimization routine worth exploring is nlminb. Again, more information can be obtained by typing help(nlminb).

Some other routines that can be of interest in R and its sister language S are the following:

- Optimize
- Uniroot
- Univariate
- Glm
- Ms
- Nlm
- Quadprog—for traditional Sharpe Markowitz quadratic programming

Each of these routines differs somewhat in their purpose and input parameters. The first two routines only deal with univariate optimization. In other words, they are designed for optimizing a function of only one variable. For the general case, we are dealing with functions of as many variables as we have candidate portfolio positions. The weighting of each position is the variable that we seek. Thus, these first two routines are designed for the special case in which only a single trading vehicle is being considered, such as the SPY exchange traded fund or the S&P futures contracts. In this case, the variable that is optimized is the amount of cash or leverage that should be employed.

The R environment provides excellent help support that includes all the details on the calling parameters and details on the options available in each routine. The complete help description and parameters can be called up simply by typing help (functionName).

OPTIMIZATION WITH EXCEL SOLVER

Suppose we wish to optimize a simple portfolio consisting of stocks in the form of the SPY ETF, bonds in the form of the TLT bond ETF and risk-free cash via short-term Treasury bills. A spreadsheet to optimize the Sharpe Ratio for such a portfolio is shown as Figure 6.2. The actual spreadsheet program is included on the CD that accompanies this book. Interested readers are invited to review the simple formulas that are in that spreadsheet.

	A	B	C	D	E	F
1	**Sharpe Ratio Optimizer**					
2	Sharpe Ratio	0.40				
3	Avg Return	0.84%				
4	Std Dev	1.60%				
5	SPY weight	70.00%				
6	TLT weight	20.00%				
7	Cash weight	10.00%				
8	Total Invested	100.00%				
9	Riskless rate / mo	0.20%				
10				Portfolio		
11		SPY	TLT	In Return		
12		2%	1%	0.0161		
13		-3%	2%	-0.0169		
14		2%	-1%	0.0121		
15		-1%	1%	-0.0048		
16		3%	-1%	0.0190		
17		3%	2%	0.0249		
18	Average	1.00%	0.67%	0.84%		
19	Std Dev	2.45%	1.37%	1.60%		
20						
21						

Figure 6.2 Sharp Ratio Optimizer

A few key values in the spread sheet are worthy of note.

- Cell B2 contains the formula for the Sharpe Ratio. This is our objective function. In this case the formula is simply the spreadsheet version of equation 6.3.
- Cells B11 through B17 contain imaginary monthly return data for SPY.
- Cells C11 though C17 contain imaginary monthly return data for TLT.
- Cells B5 through B7 are assigned arbitrary guesses as to portfolio weightings for the three investments: SPY,TLT and cash.
- Cell B8 is the sum of the three weightings and thus adds up to 100 percent.

The problem assumes that the portfolio is 100 percent invested in one of the three assets at all times. Also assumed is that the portfolio is not allowed to use leverage. In other words, the total investment can never exceed 100 percent. The final restriction on the portfolio is that it is not allowed to sell short. In other words, position weightings for each position have to be zero percent or more. Negative values are not allowed under our assumptions.

Figure 6.3 Solver Parameters

To solve this problem. we seek to maximize the Sharpe Ratio subject to the constraints given above. The answer we are seeking is the amount of the portfolio weightings that will maximize the Sharpe Ratio given the data presented. In order to do this, it will be necessary to use the Excel Add-In routine called Solver. It should have come standard with your software, but may need to be installed if it has not been installed already.

The Excel Add-In Solver can be installed by simply typing Tools/Add-Ins and selecting the Solver Add-In package. You may have already installed the package; if so, then that step can be skipped.

Once installed, Solver can be invoked by clicking Tools/Solver. If Solver has been newly installed, it may be necessary to click the down arrow at the bottom of the drop-down menu to make it appear for the first time. Once Solver is selected, a pop-up window will appear in the form of Figure 6.3.

Note that the Solver pop-up window has been filled in with some cell values. These refer to the cells in the main body of the spreadsheet. In particular, the box labeled *Set Target Cell* has been filled in with B2, our Sharpe Ratio target function. The box titled *By Changing Cells* has the cell range B5:B7 that are our three weightings for the three portfolio positions.

The pop-up window also has another larger box titled *Subject to the Constraints*. The four lines in there are the portfolio constraints already discussed. The first three are that B5, B6, and B7 cannot be negative. This is the prohibition against short selling. The final line is B8<=1. Cell B8 is the sum of the weightings of all three positions. Because leverage or borrowing is not allowed for this example, the sum of the three positions cannot exceed 100 percent that is represented by the number one in this case. So the sum of the three weightings must be less than or equal to 1.

We also note that the *Equal To* section is checked as Max, indicating we would like to maximize the target function Sharpe Ratio. Solver is perfectly capable of solving minimization problems as well. If this had been a problem in which we seek to minimize risk, that might be the appropriate choice.

Normally, the user would fill in these parameters and constraints in order to set up the problem. Then, when the pop-up window is filled in, we only need click the Solve button to find our solution. Almost instantly (for this problem), a solution will be found and another window will ask if we wish to use the Solver solution and to update the spreadsheet. Click OK to see the answer. The solution is the new weightings that have replaced our original guesses in cells B5 through B7. The new optimized Sharpe Ratio

	A	B	C	D	E	F
1	**Sharpe Ratio Optimizer**					
2	Sharpe Ratio	0.65				
3	Avg Return	0.78%				
4	Std Dev	0.88%				
5	SPY weight	35.44%				
6	TLT weight	64.56%				
7	Cash weight	0.00%				
8	Total Invested	100.00%				
9	Riskless rate / mo	0.20%				
10				Portfolio		
11		SPY	TLT	In Return		
12		2%	1%	0.0135		
13		-3%	2%	0.0023		
14		2%	-1%	0.0006		
15		-1%	1%	0.0029		
16		3%	-1%	0.0042		
17		3%	2%	0.0233		
18	Average	1.00%	0.67%	0.78%		
19	Std Dev	2.45%	1.37%	0.88%		
20						
21						
22						
23						

Figure 6.4 Sharpe Ratio Optimizer

value is also shown, along with the recalculated average return and standard deviation. The recalculated spreadsheet solution is shown in Figure 6.4.

The reader should now be able to generalize these concepts from this example to other portfolio modeling problems simply by using the relevant formulas and concepts of this book to set the Solver model. Each problem only needs a target function, the constraints, and usually some data. For most of the application covered in this book, the weighting values are the desired solution to the problem.

CHAPTER 7

Money Management Formulas Using the Joint Multiasset Distribution

The safe way to double your money is to fold it over once and put it in your pocket.

—Frank Hubbard

There is a very easy way to return from a casino with a small fortune: go there with a large one.

—Jack Yelton

Correlation is an inescapable fact of financial life. Virtually all stocks are correlated, and in fact, they are highly correlated. During the same day, stocks will often show positive correlations on the order of 80 to 100 percent. In a highly correlated environment, the usual statistical assumptions of independent identically distributed variables go all awry. Nothing is independent, because everything is highly correlated.

This chapter deals with the issues of many variables that may or may not be correlated. Initially, the discussion starts with the continuous theoretical distributions and how correlation plays a part. The role that correlation plays in the maximal log log model is further discussed.

The next section develops the concept of how correlation impacts the Sharpe Ratio. From there, the discussion turns to the empirical distribution. The end of the chapter addresses the question of using the empirical distribution in the presence of correlation in order to develop the maximal log log model for publication, as well as how to analyze the empirical definition.

THE CONTINUOUS THEORETICAL DISTRIBUTIONS

Previously, we have only slightly considered correlation in the discussion of portfolio modeling. In this chapter we consider the very important real-world consideration of correlation between investments. This discussion naturally breaks down into two basic discussions.

First, if one wishes to assume one of the continuous theoretical distributions, we can use the technique of random sampling from known distributions such as the lognormal. Second, if one wishes to avoid any unnecessary assumptions regarding the underlying distribution, it is best to use the empirical distribution and perform resampling from that to model the portfolios. In either event, the correlation between assets and any other known and possibly nonlinear relationships should be modeled explicitly.

Typically, the correlation between stocks is somewhere between 50 percent and 90 percent. The correlation between broad-based indices is almost always greater than 90 percent. Correlations between exchange traded funds (ETFs) can be anywhere from 50 percent to 90 percent, depending on how broad-based they are. The reality is that financial markets are inescapably correlated and interrelated in many ways. Any practical model of portfolio behavior must inevitably take this into account.

For the theoretical distributions, one way to take into account the correlation between assets is to calculate the correlation based on the past correlation relationship. For this purpose, the formula for the variance of two correlated assets illustrates the importance of explicitly incorporating the correlation into our model. In equation 7.1, we note that the variance of the joint probability distribution of X and Y increases by twice the covariance between the two variables:

$$\text{VAR}(XY) = \text{VAR}(X) + \text{VAR}(Y) + 2\text{COV}(XY) \qquad (7.1)$$

We emphasize that the formula doubles the impact of the covariance between the two variables. Thus, a portfolio of positively correlated assets will always have more variance than the simple sum of the individual variances of the positions.

Alternatively, we can randomly resample from the putative theoretical distribution. In so doing, we must explicitly include recognition of the correlation between the assets. Equation 7.1 can be quite helpful to model random samples from the joint probability distribution of a pair of correlated assets.

MAXIMAL LOG LOG MODEL IN THE PRESENCE OF CORRELATION

In the previous chapter we discussed the innovative *log log model* proposed in this book. However, the discussion assumed no correlation between assets for simplicity and intuitive appeal. It is now time to discuss the real-world framework in which correlation is an ever-present fact of life.

We now take our log log utility model from the previous chapter and incorporate variance and covariance into it. Thus, our discrete portfolio return model at time t becomes

$$r_t = \sum_{i=0}^{n} w_i\, r_{it} \tag{7.2}$$

where r_{it} are the individual security returns at time t for security i.

$$U_t = \sum (\ln(1 + \ln(1 + r_t))) \tag{7.3}$$

Equations 7.2 and 7.3 appear to have no explicit term for correlation. The reason such a term is not needed is that the returns are treated as a contemporaneous vector of returns. We recall that a vector is simply a list. In this case the list is a list of returns from the same period in time.

Thus, any correlation between the different returns is already taken into account by treating all of the returns from a single period together as a group. The correlation is built into the calculation of the individual returns themselves. So we need add no special term to treat the correlation separately for the discrete case.

It is important to note that the returns for each period must be taken together as a group for this type of analysis to work correctly. The returns for period t already include the effects of correlations between them and so must be taken together. Conversely, taking returns for security i through all periods separately would not take into account the effects of correlation between the different positions within a given period. That must be explicitly considered for each return calculated.

OPTIMAL SHARPE MODEL WITH CORRELATION

The standard Sharpe Ratio developed by William F. Sharpe and now included as part of the CAPM model is given by

$$\text{Sharpe Ratio} = (r_p - r_f)/\sigma_p \tag{7.4}$$

where the subscript r_p stands for portfolio return and r_f is the risk-free rate on short-term Treasury bills. Effectively the Sharpe ratio measures the amount of excess return of the portfolio per unit of risk taken. It is the measure of portfolio performance that is most widely used in the financial industry. Thus, by any reasonable standard it represents an important metric by which portfolio managers are judged.

A potentially more useful variation of the Sharpe Ratio would be to calculate within-period returns as usual, but treat overall returns as continuously compounded via the use of the logs of the returns. Effectively, we would be calculating an average of the logs of the returns and the standard deviation about that average.

As further enhancement of this idea, the concept can be combined with the use of the log log utility function to obtain an objective function that incorporates the concept of maximizing the log log return per unit of log log risk undertaken.

Thus, our modified log log Sharpe ratio would be based on the expected log log return less the riskless rate per unit of risk taken in a log log sense. We can define r_{LL} to be the expected log log return as follows:

$$r_{LL} = \ln(1 + \ln(1 + r_p)) \tag{7.5}$$

In a similar fashion, we have for the log log standard deviation the formula as follows:

$$\sigma_{LL} = \sqrt{VAR(\ln(1 + \ln(1 + r_p)))} \tag{7.6}$$

THE EMPIRICAL DISTRIBUTION

The disadvantages of using theoretical distributions such as the normal and lognormal have been previously discussed. Although such distributions offer some advantages in intuition on occasion, and can provide us with closed-form solutions, generally they are to be avoided. A much better practice is to use robust resampling from the empirical distribution to model one's portfolio. This avoids all of the issues of nonnormality and fat tails.

Essentially, the idea is to randomly select past periods and then use all of the stocks or trades from that period together as a group. This effectively captures the correlation between them in a simple, straightforward manner. It also obviates the need to deal with the correlations via the variance–covariance matrix with its associated Cholesky decomposition.

The procedure is to randomly select each time period and then calculate the portfolio returns for the given weightings. Then take the desired utility function or goal function of the computed portfolio return. The final step is to maximize the goal function by varying the weights during successive resampling iterations. This step can be handled either by Solver or by the various multivariate optimization routines available in R.

Using the formulas given earlier for the log log case we have:

$$r_t = \sum_{i=0}^{n} w_i \, r_{it} \tag{7.7}$$

where r_{it} are the individual security returns at time t for security i.

$$U(t) = \sum_t (\ln(1 + \ln(1 + r(t))))$$ (7.8)

Intuitively the $U(t)$ function is to be interpreted as the utility of the log log function.

We substitute the actual returns from randomly selected time t into equation 7.7 and the resulting portfolio return r_t is used as input to the $U(t)$ function per equation 7.8. The standard optimization routines from Excel, S, and R can be used to find the optimal portfolio weighting vector w.

MAXIMAL LOG LOG MODEL IN THE PRESENCE OF CORRELATION

It is important to understand what the maximal log log function is and what it is not. The maximal log log model is that weighting of portfolio investment sizes that will maximize the long-run log log return of the portfolio. It is optimal in that sense only. We recall that, in general, it is possible to optimize only one thing at a time.

By definition, the log log utility function includes a log term. One of these log functions maximizes the compounded return of the log of the wealth ratio. The other log function of the two provides us with a measure of the utility of the wealth that we are compounding.

It is useful to note that the log function is concave. The slope of the line is everywhere decreasing. Thus, the log function contains a kind of built in risk aversion when considered from an arithmetic viewpoint. This can be seen more clearly in Figure 7.1.

The iterated log function has a double risk aversion built in. Each of the log functions adds additional concavity to the function. In that sense, it is clearly more risk averse than the simple maximal return formulas presented earlier. Figure 7.2 illustrates the additional concavity of the iterated log function.

The reader will recall that one of the well-known problems with the maximal returns type of formulas is that they result in unacceptably large volatility. The conservative double-risk reduction of the iterated log function directly addresses this in a way that also optimizes a reasonable utility function. The reader is strongly encouraged to consider this function as the basis for one's portfolio modeling efforts.

MAXIMIZING THE SHARPE RATIO IN THE PRESENCE OF CORRELATION

The presence of correlation between variables can also impact the calculation of the Sharpe Ratio when one assumes the empirical distribution as the governing premise. There are really two issues in this discussion.

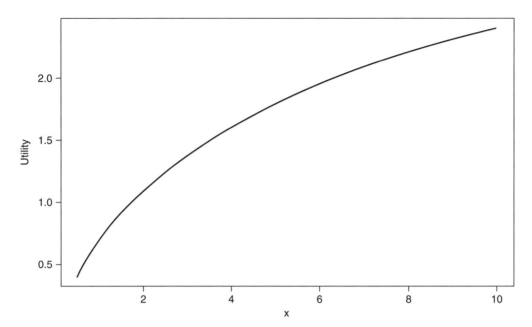

Figure 7.1   Log Utility Function

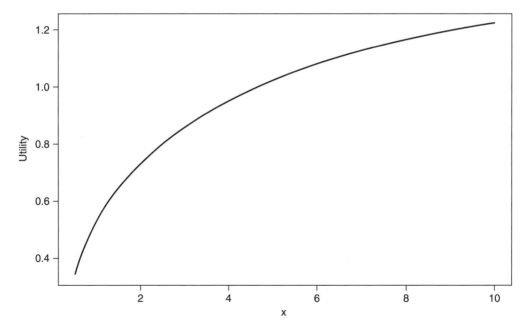

Figure 7.2   Log Log Utility Function

First, the variables can be simultaneously correlated. When IBM goes up, then GM is likely to go up during the same period. This type of correlation goes by many different names. One would be simultaneous correlation, while another would be coincident correlation. When speaking in a time series context, the term might be *correlation with lag zero*.

The second type of correlation involves a serial dependence between one day and the next day's trading. The efficiency of the markets guarantees us that this correlation is likely to be rather small. However, it should be considered anyway. The name for this is *autocorrelation*, implying that the data is correlated within at some earlier period. Another name for this type of correlation is *serial correlation*. For this type of correlation, the number of time periods between two correlated observations is known as the *lag*.

There is another type of serial relationship that may not be a true correlation at all. In ordinary correlation, there is a presumed linear relationship between the variables, even if the variables are returns from the same stock separated by a certain number of days called lag. If the correlation is zero or nearly so, then we can say that there is little or no linear correlation between the variables under consideration.

However, this does not preclude a nonlinear relationship between variables. There are very many possible nonlinear relationships that we could imagine. For example, it is well known that the volatility of the market is autocorrelated. If the market has been recently volatile, it is likely to continue to be volatile. One way to measure this is to look at the correlation coefficient for consecutive values of the returns, squared terms for the market. There is a consistent positive correlation for this variable despite the fact that the linear values of the returns generally show little or no correlation.

MODELING COINCIDENT CORRELATION

In order to deal with coincident or coterminal correlation from an empirical multivariate distribution we need to obtain our random sample from all of the variables in question for that time period. It is not sufficient to only sample one variable from a given time period and another variable from a different time period. It would not effectively capture the correlation that may be present.

Because we know that correlations between return variables during the same time period will be highly correlated, it is imperative that all of the variables come from the same period. This will effectively capture the correlation, as well as enable us to consider the effects of the correlation on the variance.

Alternatively, if we were only to capture variables from different periods, we are assured that they would not have the necessary correlations. The efficient markets hypothesis assures us of this fact. Thus, the only way to perform an analysis using the empirical distribution is to collect our randomly sampled data as a set of points or as a vector of the given variables in question.

Modeling Nonlinearity and Autocorrelation

In order to randomly sample from the empirical distribution and compensate for nonlinear relationships, we must take certain precautions. Ideally, we wish to include all of the variables from a time period according to the previous discussion. However, often that is not enough. It will only eliminate correlations and relationships that exist within that time period.

If we suspect nonlinear relationships exist, then we need to take a more general approach. We need to remember that these relationships may not even show up as simple linear correlations. Thus, they may exist, but we cannot even guess at their correct mathematical form.

There may also exist autocorrelations and cross-correlations between variables at different time lags and for different periods of time. In order to capture these, it is not sufficient to merely include all of the variables from one period in time. We must include variables from a recent window in time in order to model these sequential relationships in time.

Therefore, the correct way to randomly sample our data would be to randomly select a time period t. Then, each time t represents a window of multivariate data, the data variables for each time period must be captured. But more than that, the same set of variables for previous periods prior to time t must be captured and used as our sample.

Ordinarily, for statistical testing and modeling, we would prefer to consider nonoverlapping periods. We would also consider each one only once. The idea is to avoid double counting and keep the observations statistically independent from one another.

However, for our empirical sampling models, we can and should allow overlapping time periods. Effectively, we are letting the sampling technique perform our analysis for us, even if the data we feed it have dependencies, as they must. We are resampling at random times and not just random data.

Those who feel uncomfortable with this technique can adopt fixed periods and simply resample from those. However, this technique has the drawback of reducing the number of permissible data samples by a factor of the window size. Suppose we had a sample of 500 days and chose to model a 20-day look-back window. This will give us about 24 nonoverlapping time periods. But if we allow any day to be randomly selected, the number of possible starting points is now about 480. Note that we need to allow for an initial look-back window of 20 days at the beginning of our data.

To summarize, either method will produce good results. However, the method of randomly sampling any time period is generally to be preferred, provided a sufficiently large number of samples is used.

CHAPTER 8

Proper Backtesting
for Portfolio Models

M ost work with models is based on backtesting a given concept with historical data. Invariably, the issue of good-quality data arises in every study based on historical data. This chapter deals with the issues of ensuring good data and how to deal with empirical data in general.

In particular, the discussion inevitably leads to how to synchronize data between different markets in different time zones, with consideration to the varying days and holiday schedules in different countries. In order to conduct a proper study, most analyses require the use of net change data in lieu of price level data. In addition, the chapter discusses the need to use intraday highs and lows in one's work.

As always, the focus is on predictive studies versus retrospective nonpredictive studies. Numerous data pitfalls are discussed, including the fact that adjusted data may be erroneous, for many possible reasons. The user is urged to maintain his own adjusted database for the sake of data integrity.

Finally, this chapter deals with the important topic of robust resampling methods to analyze the data. The reader is shown how robust methods can be used to develop confidence limits for everyday statistics in a way that does not depend on the quirks of the underlying distribution.

In this way, the serious portfolio modeler can be freed from the curse of the fat-tailed underlying distribution.

ASSURING GOOD DATA

Any historical study of investment vehicles is only as good as its data source. For that reason, it is important to discuss the data sources and the myriad of pitfalls that can befall someone who uses historical data sources. First, we shall deal with the seemingly simple matter of assuring data quality.

Perhaps the simplest and best method to assure quality is to find two reputable and independent sources of data and to simply compare them against each other. Such a test should include a simple comparison of same price on the same date. It would also include a count of missing days for each vendor. An additional test should be made to find extra days that may have been added or omitted.

For daily or weekly data, the data fields should include Open, High, Low, Close, and Volume. An often-overlooked factor is that stock data needs to be adjusted. Such adjustments include stock splits, as well as dividends and other corporate distributions. Thus, accompanying each stock should be a file of adjustment data or something similar embedded in the data itself. For each date, the date should be explicitly included as a separate field. For Futures or Options, the Open Interest field should be available as well.

SYNCHRONIZE DATA

There are many reasons data must be synchronized. One reason is that some markets do not trade when other markets do. For example, the bond markets observe more holidays than the equity markets. Different countries observe different holiday schedules. Thus, one market may be open and a similar market in a different country is closed for the local holiday.

Synchronization is important for several reasons. First, most studies of price movements should be performed using net change data. Thus, for comparability the net changes should be for the same period of time. Irrespective of whether the time frame is daily, weekly, or even hourly, it should reflect the same period of time.

For example, when we are trying to measure the correlation between two stocks, there will be subtle bias issues if sometimes the net change figure is for two days compared to one day. By its very nature the two-day net change will typically be about 1.41 times larger than the one-day change. This will impact the correlation calculation that relies on the cross-product between the two data series.

There are several ways to synchronize data. One way is to simply defenestrate any days that show missing data for whatever reason. We simply remove those days from our sample in *all* of our data series. If even one day is missing from, say, a German stock, that day is removed from all of the other series as well. Thus, each net change in the data we keep is still comparable to the other data series.

Another way to synchronize the data is to keep only the latest data for which all of the dates that are equal. Yet another technique is to combine added dates so as to artificially create matching pairs of dates.

USE NET CHANGES *NOT* LEVELS

It is important to use the net changes rather than price levels for several reasons. One of the more important of these reasons is that the levels are always autocorrelated in a random walk time series. It is easy to understand why this is so. For an additive random walk model, today's price is the sum of yesterday's price plus a small random innovation. Each successive price level is the sum of all of the recent innovations. Thus, it is correlated with each, at least to some extent. For example, the sum of the last 20 days' innovations will not change much when one more daily observation is added. The previous 20 days still represent about 95 percent of the total variation. It follows that the correlation will be comparably large.

In fact, empirical studies done by the author show that artificially constructed random walks are generally positively serially correlated in the neighborhood of 65 percent to 95 percent. These correlations are quite large and will doom any statistical study to many false positives. It is to be emphasized that these were *randomly* generated data studies, and thus, there should be no correlation except what was artificially induced by the process. The inescapable conclusion is that using levels of prices is a faulty process and will cause spurious correlations where no real correlation actually exists.

Strictly speaking, this applies only to an additive random walk. As previously discussed, stock markets are probably best modeled as multiplicative random walks. This type of model best accounts for the positive compound returns of stocks over very long periods of time. However, the same arguments are valid here as well, because a multiplicative model can also be expressed as an additive model in the logs of prices. Thus, large spurious correlations will be induced in the logs by using price levels. Simply put, the research based on correlations involving price levels will find correlations that are not real.

There are several ways to calculate the net change for a given time period. The simplest is to take the net difference in points. This is literally the net change as measured in points.

Over time, stock prices tend to drift higher. The longer the time, the greater the upward drift. If we are studying a period of time during which the drift has been large, it is quite likely that the net point changes later in the time series will be larger than those earlier. The variance of the time series will increase with time. Statisticians call this *heteroskedasticity*. It simply means *different variances*.

Statistically speaking, it is a situation that we wish to avoid. The variance in the second half of the series will be larger than the variance in the first half. Thus, the standard deviation of the second half will be larger than the first half. Equally important, the data will appear to be dominated by the latter part of the price series.

To address the problem of heteroskedasticity, we need only recast the net change as a percent change. Generally speaking, this will render the changes of the first half comparable to those of the second half. For any longer-term studies of more than a year, using percent changes should be the norm and is highly recommended as a best practice. For time periods shorter than a year, the net point change is probably good enough.

We have discussed the fact that the equity markets exhibit long-term compounded growth. This is in contrast to other markets, such as commodities and bonds, that generally show no long-term growth. The ideal way to measure price change in compound growth situations is to use the logs of price changes. We take the relative price change and then take its natural log.

$$\text{Relative price change} = \ln((P_{t+1} + D)/P_t) \tag{8.1}$$

Where P_t is the price at time t and D is the shareholder distribution (usually a dividend or split).

ONLY USE INFORMATION FROM THE PAST

Anyone who has watched a science-fiction movie about time travel knows the dangers of knowledge of the future. It seems that every work in the field invariably raises the question of the great time travel paradox. If you go back into the past and kill one of your ancestors before he passed on his genes, you will never exist. If you never existed, then how did you go back into the past to kill your ancestor?

The theme of altering the future seems to be mandatory for this genre. The plot often revolves around the temptation to use one's knowledge of the future to improve it and the stern warning that any such attempt is evil and ultimately doomed to failure.

Such dire warnings apply equally well to one who performs studies based on historical data. *Only use information from the past.* One should never let knowledge of the future creep into the results.

This point may seem obvious and almost need not be stated. Yet countless studies suffer from the problem of knowledge of the future. In fact, the problem is so insidious that it tends to arise without the researcher being cognizant of the fact.

One way knowledge of the future can creep in is through simple software mistakes. In most programming languages such as R, there is a facility for specifying the date of a particular price. Often, this boils down to a simple subscript or integer index. If we were programming a simple moving average and the subscript were off by one, then the average might include data from one day in the future. In Excel, the analogous situation would be when a range specification is off by one or more. If the range includes information from the future, the results are likely to be too good to be true.

One good diagnostic is to be suspicious whenever the results of a study are too good to be true. It is natural to be happy when a study seems to work out well. Rather than becoming elated that a study has seemingly worked out very well, we should immediately *assume* that knowledge of the future has somehow crept in and figure out how and why.

Another insidious form of knowledge of the future occurs when using retroactively adjusted or edited data. If we were doing a study based on fundamental data and arbitrarily used a historical database provided by some supposedly reliable vendor, we may be subject to significant knowledge of the future biases. Many vendors retroactively adjust their data to reflect the latest reported changes. Sometimes these are accounting changes that are only announced months, or even years, later.

The classic example is the Enron fraudulent accounting scandal. Just prior to the revelations about Enron, the fundamental data seemed to scream that the stock was incredibly cheap by any reasonable accounting valuation metric. Yet, when viewed in the light of later released and retrospectively corrected accounting statements that reflected the true situation, it was clear that the stock was a scam. The problem was, the corrected accounting data were only made available years later. At the time of Enron's demise, one could not have known simply by looking at the current published information.

Enron is an extreme case, but many more subtle cases arise all the time. The key issue is knowledge of the future. Any study that includes such knowledge is suspect, and such trading strategies are to be avoided.

Historical price data can include such pitfalls as well. For example, it is fairly common for price reports and quotes to be erroneous. In particular, a single quote can be typed incorrectly, or data transmission problems can result in a single bit being dropped and a digit will be off by 1. Most such errors will show up as the reported high or low price for the day. The reason for this is simple. Errors tend to be large. A 5 that is changed to a 6 can result in a 20 percent error in the reported high for the day if the price is changed from a 51.14 to 61.14. A 51.14 price can be morphed into 52.14. It all depends on the decimal place in which the error occurs.

A good way to avoid such errors is to use a price continuity filter that screens out discontinuous jumps and large changes. At first blush, it may seem that the way to deal with these is to retroactively adjust the prices when the corrected data is known. The point of this section of the book should be clear by now. You cannot use knowledge of the future. If the corrected prices are not known *at the time*, the information should only be used when it is known. Obviously, this requires some additional bookkeeping or complexity in the way data is handled. At a minimum, new information should be time stamped and never altered once it is captured. Even if corrected information comes in, that, too, should be time stamped and only made available to a retroactive study after it is known. Databases that are permanently burned onto CDs or DVDs are excellent ways to ensure against retroactive data corruption. The data on a write-once medium cannot be altered. Even so, time-stamping individual transactions is still essential.

Sample selection can also introduce knowledge of the future biases into a study. For example, it is well known that mid-cap stocks that have grown large enough to be included in the S&P 500 index provide a profitable universe of stocks to buy. Several hedge funds and astute traders have developed strategies that seek to identify which stocks will be dropped and which added to the index. The strategy usually involves buying those that are to be added and short selling those that are to be dropped. Implicit in this theory is the idea that fixed-strategy index funds will be required to buy the newly added stocks and sell the dropped issues. The hedge fund hopes to profit on the differential regardless of market direction.

Suppose we start with a list of the current members of the S&P 500 index. We then propose to perform a historical study of these issues. Where is the harm in that?

There is a subtle bias, contained in such a study. By selecting *current members of the index*, we are incorporating knowledge of the future. We could not know with certainty which stocks would be in the index five years later. Nor could we know which would be dropped. By avoiding all issues that were subsequently dropped, we may well have a sample that avoids all negative growth and companies that fell by the wayside. Similarly, our sample includes all those companies that were not members of the list years ago but joined the select group presumably through superior growth. This illustrates that knowledge of the future need not be quantitative, but can be transmitted merely by qualitative membership in a class or group.

PREDICTIVE STUDIES VERSUS NONPREDICTIVE STUDIES

Recently, it has become a fad on Wall Street to look at coincident correlations of price *levels* as though they are some how predictive. An analyst will present a chart of two price levels that are both rising and nod sagely that there is a correlation between the two. The entire analysis is predicated upon the fact that both are rising at the same time. Alternatively, the chart might show that both are falling at the same time.

In his book *Statistics on the Table* (Harvard University Press, 1999), Professor Stephen M. Stigler uses the example of a tree and a boy. Both are growing taller every year. But the two are not correlated. The growth spurts of a tree will have much to do with its own life cycle, sunlight, and annual rainfall. The boy's growth rate will correspond to his feeding, family history, and life cycle—notably, puberty. The annual differences will show little correlation, even though both are growing. A correlation analysis of two time series that are both growing will often show spurious correlations simply because the analysis is based on levels of a price series.

Knowing how much the tree grew last year will not allow any reasonable prediction of what the boy's growth will be in the next year. To be predictive, we must have two properties. First, there must be a correlation. Second, the correlation must extend from the past values of the predictor variable to the future values of the variable that we wish to predict. In other words, the predictor must lead to the variable to be predicted. A relationship that is only correlated in the present is at best a descriptive relationship. It shows only comovement, but is not predictive.

It should be emphasized that this discussion is directed to the question of what is a predictive relationship. This is to be distinguished from the coincident correlation that most stocks have with each other and the market overall. As we saw earlier, the coincident correlation relationship can be very important in analyzing a portfolio model and how best to optimize it. Two stocks that move together do not serve to reduce risk as well as two stocks with little correlation. The best of all is two stocks that are negatively correlated. However, knowing this does not allow us to predict the direction in which the two stocks will move. We only know they will move together.

USE INTRADAY HIGHS AND LOWS FOR MODEL ACCURACY

Often traders will seek to use limit orders or stop-loss orders for entry and exit of market positions. Modeling these can be tricky. For example, a limit order at a price of 50 may appear to be a simple thing to model. But if one only uses closing data, and yesterday closed at 50.20 and today at 50.30, the order may or may not have been executed. Based solely on closing data, we cannot tell what the true story is.

Obviously, what is needed is the ability to include intraday highs and lows in our analysis. But even that remedy is not without pitfalls. Suppose the low for the day was exactly 50 and our order was at 50. Again, there is no way to tell if the order would have been executed or not executed with a report of "Stock ahead" in line. Although this is a relatively rare case, it still must be addressed by the serious researcher. One way to handle this is to assume that the limit order is only executed a percentage of the time if it coincides with the high or low. This percentage can vary from zero to 100 percent.

Another way to handle it is to analyze it both ways. Once with the assumption that the order is always executed and once assuming it is never filled. If the two are significantly different, then the matter should be investigated further. If not, then it may be a nonissue. In any event, it is likely that limit orders at the extrema for the time period will be *adversely selected.* Simply put, you will get orders filled when you do not want them filled and never get them when you do want them filled.

A similar situation arises with stop orders. One would think that when a stop price is hit the trade will occur at that price. In fact, this rarely happens. Once the stop price is hit or exceeded, the order then becomes actionable—usually as a market order unless a limit was specified. In that eventuality, the trader must expect to pay the then-current bid–ask spread. So too, for any market order that is given. One must expect to pay the spread. This is a phenomenon often called *slippage* in the vernacular of Wall Street. Any historical study must explicitly take into account slippage by some means. Naturally, we must add commissions to the slippage.

One final caveat is in order. The highs and lows for the time period are notoriously susceptible to error. Although the use of highs and lows is highly recommended for trading studies, it must be accompanied by thorough scrutiny of the quality of such data.

ADJUSTED DATA MAY BE ERRONEOUS

Yahoo finance has an excellent source of historical price data for stocks. In many cases, the daily price histories go back 40 or 50 years. The short Internet URL for Yahoo is:

`finance.yahoo.com`

Google finance has recently entered the arena with its own price history data as well. Undoubtedly, the competition between the two companies will stimulate even better data sources and improved quality in the future. The short form of the Google address is:

`www.google.com/finance`

Yahoo has a data column that displays the adjusted closing prices. The open, high, low, and close data are unadjusted. This means that the user must adjust the other fields individually. This is easily accomplished by either taking the difference between the adjusted close and the original close, or by taking the ratio of the two prices as an adjustment factor.

However, there is a hidden catch with this procedure that can lead to serious problems in the data. This problem is round-off error. Yahoo! and most other data vendors round their data to two decimal places. A classic example of this would be Microsoft stock. From the 1980s to the present, MSFT has enjoyed dramatic compounded growth. The stock followed the good fortunes of the company and maintained an ever-increasing upward trajectory, at least until the year 2000.

The upward trajectory of prices is one piece of the problem. The other is the fact that prices are reported and stored in fixed decimal format. Typical, is a two-decimal-place format, but a few data sources preserve four-decimal-place accuracy. In the case of Microsoft, the Yahoo! finance site shows the adjusted prices for the stock from April 18, 1986, through April 11, 1986, to be $.09—an adjusted price of 9 cents per share. For seven straight days, the price was supposedly unchanged.

Obviously, something is wrong with this picture. At the time, Microsoft was a darling of Wall Street, one of the high-flying glamour favorites. In fact, the problem is the double whammy of the extreme growth in Microsoft to date and the use of the fixed decimal format by the data vendors. Thus, the real adjusted price for MSFT may have been anywhere from 8.5 cents to 9.5 cents. We have no way to know. But when the price crossed the round-off threshold from above 8.5 cents to below 8.5 cents, the price appeared to drop precipitously from 9 to 8 cents per share. Thus, when we look at the net change on a percentage basis, it appears to be a rather largish 11 percent decline. In fact, the drop at the time may have been minimal, but just enough to push the stock below the 8.50 threshold on an adjusted basis. We cannot tell from the adjusted data as it is.

ADJUSTING YOUR OWN DATA

Clearly, the foregoing discussion indicates a serious problem with the adjusted historical price data provided by many, and perhaps most, vendors. Effectively, the original data for MSFT prices have been reduced to only a single digit. All numerical significance greater than a single significant digit has been lost. Fortunately, there is a remedy. The solution is for investors to do their own data adjustment.

Essentially, the key is to find a vendor who offers the necessary data to perform your own adjustments. Yahoo! is one such vendor. It offers stock-split data as well as distribution data such as dividends. Then you can perform the necessary adjustments to as many decimal places as your software can handle. Under current double-precision technology, that is usually about 16 decimal places. Using that level of precision, the calculations are more than adequate to fix the round-off error problem.

MISCELLANEOUS DATA PITFALLS

There are several other data issues that can arise. One is the issue with fundamental data whereby the data is retroactively adjusted by the data vendor. Literally, the vendor will go back and edit his historical database as revised information is reported. The trouble with this is that it renders any sort of historical study impossible and unreliable. The only way to do this is to either obtain dual data sets from the vendor or do it yourself.

A dual data set would include a complete time-stamped database of information that was available at the time. It must have a guarantee that there were and will be no retrospective alterations. The other part of the dual data set would be the retrospectively adjusted data. For the purposes of the investment manager, the latter data is nearly useless.

There are also numerous errors that are reported in simple pricing data. Most often, these occur in the highs and lows for the day. Simple filters to assure continuity of price histories can go a long way toward identifying and eliminating such errors. However, it is important to mention that if these cannot be identified and eliminated by simple filters, they should be captured, time stamped, and recorded as they were known at the time, just as was done for the fundamental data.

TABULATE AND SAVE THE DETAILED RESULTS WITH DATES

Any good study should, as a minimum, include a detailed tabulation of which days were included if a selection of some sort was made. This detailed tabulation can be used as the basis for portfolio modeling when the results of the study are subsequently utilized for trading. The saved results become the inputs for the robust analysis of optimal portfolio position sizes and correlation studies.

OVERLAPPING DATES ARE IMPORTANT FOR CORRELATIONS

It is important to synchronize and reconcile dates in one's data. Some people have always thought of the bond market as a gentleman's club. Although ladies are now permitted to enter, there is still some truth to this perception. One example of this is the fact that the bond market, in its wisdom, seems to have more holidays than the equity markets.

Suppose we were doing a study and using yesterday's change in bond prices to help predict the stock market for tomorrow. However, the bond market was closed for a holiday yesterday. Does that mean that the price change from two days ago is now predictive of today and tomorrow in the stock market? Alternatively, should we exclude this signal from one day or the other? These questions can be tested, although the samples will be small. Nevertheless, the issues are real and must be handled by data synchronization.

A similar issue arises when dealing with international markets. Different countries have completely different holiday schedules. Thus, data synchronization is important in these realms as well.

Another critical consideration in the international arena is to get the time zones right. For example, the FTSE is traded in London and opens before the New York markets start trading. However, that does not mean that it is safe to use the FTSE price change for today as a predictor of the New York market move for today. In fact, both markets share some trading hours in common. Currently, it is the first hour of New York trading that coincides with the last hour of London trading.

Thus, there is a built-in correlation, but it is a simultaneous relationship that cannot be used for prediction without considerable care. Generally, the use of conditional predictors based on intermarket relationships in which the markets overlap trading hours should be avoided.

CALCULATE MEAN, STANDARD DEVIATION, VARIANCE, AND PROBABILITY OF WIN

As a minimum, any good study should calculate at least a few key statistics. Certainly it is important to find the mean return. Then either the standard deviation or the variance should be computed. Either one of the latter is usually sufficient. Summary statistics should include a recitation of n, the number of observations included. Often overlooked, but always quite useful, is the probability of a win or winning percentage of trades.

Other helpful statistics would include a summary of the quantiles of the return distribution, the skew, and kurtosis. These latter figures can be readily found in R. Many traders prefer to use the drawdown statistic, which is a measure of the decline from the highest level of the equity curve to the nadir of its greatest drop. Although the statistic is somewhat flawed, nevertheless, it is in common use and generally well understood. The flaws are that it is a highly variable statistic and subject to runs of good and bad luck, more so than measures of risk such as standard deviation. The drawdown metric is not a relative measure. It is also subject to manipulation. For example, if the largest drawdown was seven years ago, then the unscrupulous operator need only present the last six years of history to exclude the offending item.

Another important measure to calculate is the Sharpe ratio and perhaps the Sortino ratio as well. These are generally accepted measures of risk and can be quite helpful in evaluating the results of a study. It is also useful to perform the beta regression analysis. From this we get the alpha as a measure of relative market performance. We also calculate the beta to look at the relative market multiplier and as a measure of correlated risk. The R^2 is helpful as a measure of market correlated risk.

ROBUST METHODS TO FIND STATISTICS

In earlier chapters of this book, we discussed the fact that the normal and lognormal are inadequate distributions to perfectly describe the distribution of market returns. In order to analyze returns without assumptions about the underlying distribution, it is best to use robust resampling methods. Essentially, these randomize the data and allow us to repeatedly resample from the distribution. This facilitates building confidence intervals and quantiles for the actual empirical distribution, whatever it may be.

Robust methods can also be used with multivariate distributions. However, in this case the usual best practice is to combine together observations for each variable at the same time. The import of this can be seen if one looks at the wild fluctuations around the time of the 1987 stock market crash. Not only did the stock market exhibit extraordinary volatility, but most other markets did as well. Markets such as bonds, currencies, gold, and oil all exhibited extraordinary volatility. Therefore, keeping those observations together serves to preserve the correlation structure of the intermarket relationships.

An even better practice is to resample the data at random times, such as random weeks or months, but to keep the sequence of data at the random time intact. This technique can help to preserve any suspected or unknown sequential relationship in the data set. If we approach the random resampling in this manner, then we can be less concerned about issues such as the fact that the GARCH models have shown us that the volatility as measured by variance is not stationary but seems to change regimes over time.

CONFIDENCE LIMITS FOR ROBUST STATISTICS

The importance of confidence limits cannot be overemphasized. For example, if we wish to know if a given mean is really greater than zero, we can simply look at the confidence limits at the 95 percent level. If the range bounded by the limits does not include zero, then we can be confident that the mean is truly above zero and not simply due to chance this time around.

To compute any robust statistic, we resample from the original data a subset of, say, 80 percent of the total observations in the data set. For each resampled subset, we calculate the desired statistics—mean, standard deviation, variance, correlation, and anything else. Each such statistic is saved in an array of, say, 1,000 items. To tabulate the frequency distribution for that particular statistic, we sort the array from smallest to largest. Assuming we chose 1,000 elements in our array, then the 5 percent level is given by the element in the sorted array at position 50. The element at position 950 represents the 95 percent percentile of the cumulative probability distribution for that statistic. Thus, the position can be read directly as a probability percentile that is usually abbreviated as p.

CHAPTER 9

The Combined Optimal Portfolio Model

In many ways, the goal of this chapter is to put it all together. To a large extent, the earlier chapters have laid a good foundation. Thus, to some extent the work of finalizing is made easier. For the most part, the reader should have now acquired the necessary skills to understand how to accomplish the goals of portfolio modeling.

This chapter discusses the broad subject of when to choose the theoretical and when to choose the empirical distribution for one's model. In general, the empirical is to be preferred, but there are important exceptions discussed in the text.

From there, the concepts naturally flow to the choice of the objective function or utility model. A thorough discourse follows on whether you should choose the ubiquitous Sharpe Ratio or the innovative Log Log utility model proposed in this book.

Beyond that, the chapter addresses the ideas involved in model simulation. Of special import are the concepts relating to the joint multivariate distribution, with the possibility of correlative relationships. The reader is shown how to deal with this particular circumstance.

Finally, the chapter and the book closes with a discussion on the differences between professional money managers and simple private investors. The reader is shown how to adapt the ideas and objective functions of this book to his or her particular circumstance.

CHOOSING THE THEORETICAL DISTRIBUTION

The theoretical distributions offer several advantages over using the empirical distributions. Following are four of these advantages:

1. *The theoretical distributions offer closed form solutions for many formulas and statistics.* This can be a mathematical convenience.

2. *The properties are well known.* Distributions such as the normal and log normal can be characterized by their respective mean and variance.

3. *Tables and analytical tools are widely available.* They are usually included in software packages such as Excel and R.

4. *Working with the theoretical distributions is much less computer intensive than working with the empirical distribution.* Savings in computer time can be on the order of thousandfold when compared to robust resampling methods.

Offsetting these advantage are four disadvantages to using the theoretical distributions:

1. *The tails of relative return distributions tend to be too fat.* This implies the existence of outliers in the data, or at least a nonstationary variance per the GARCH models.

2. *The usual statistical tests will tend to be biased when estimating significance.* In particular, tests such as the t test will tend to find significance somewhat more than 5 percent of the time at the 5 percent level. *Thus, all results are at least slightly suspect.*

3. *The existence of the fat tails in stock returns and other speculative markets is widely known.* Anyone who seeks to sell his or her results or services to others will undoubtedly encounter at least mild resistance to the use of the standard theoretical distributions.

4. *The theoretical normal family of distributions has difficulties when we attempt to apply them to skewed distributions or extremely exotic distributions.* A good example of this would be options and spreads involving either options or futures. Other examples of highly skewed distributions would include complex strategies involving stop losses and profit targets. Any model that includes options or stop loss and profit target strategies is almost certainly nonnormal and should not use the theoretical distributions.

THE EMPIRICAL DISTRIBUTION

The empirical distribution is the actual distribution that we observe in the data. The goal is to make as few assumptions about the data as possible with respect to distribution. We also seek to avoid any assumption about coterminal or lagged correlations in the data. Ideally, we also wish to avoid assumptions with respect to coterminal or lagged intermarket relationships.

Using resampling methods, we are essentially asking the question, "If all we know about the data is contained in the data, then what are the chances that this sample could have arisen by chance?" Ideally, we make no assumptions about the distribution, other than this is the data. This question is then answered by resampling the data perhaps 100 to 1,000 times. Each time the data is resampled, we use slightly smaller samples than the entire data set. Thus, to the extent that the actual distribution of the data is skewed or has fat tails, the resampling will exhibit similar properties as well.

We can summarize the advantages of using the empirical distributions as follows:

- The portfolio modeler makes minimal assumptions about the nature of the underlying probability distribution.
- The use of robust methods is nonparametric. It does not rely on a proper estimation of the usual parameters of the normal distribution.
- Robust methods directly provide the necessary quantiles of the distribution of the sample means, standard deviations, and other desired statistics. They provide a straightforward way to test for significance and derive confidence intervals and p values. In order to interpret the data, one does not even need a statistics book. The percentiles of the data itself will give the required p values.
- Robust methods require no knowledge of the mathematical properties of the normal or log normal distributions, because they are not used. Rather, the skill set to perform robust resampling requires only knowledge of how to calculate the desired statistic and how to sort the multiple resampled statistics.
- Robust methods can be applied to extremely skewed and exotic distributions, such as the distribution of option and spread returns. In contrast, the theoretical distributions do not apply at all in any straightforward fashion to these kinds of trading instruments. The only way one could model options with a theoretical distribution would be to use the underlying asset as a lognormal and then work through the complicated mathematics of the distribution implied by the Black–Scholes model.
- The Black-Scholes model is predicated on the concept of a log-normal distribution of price changes in the underlying stock. The result would be a new exotic theoretical distribution. However, it would be neither normal nor lognormal, but rather, highly

skewed. Any analysis of the distribution would have to be derived by the user using higher math. Clearly, the empirical distribution is a far superior choice.

There are three major drawbacks of using the empirical distribution:

1. The entire distribution must be saved. It is no longer possible to simply summarize the data by the mean and standard deviation, knowing that these will adequately define the underlying normal or log normal distribution.

2. Considerably more computer time will be spent performing the resampling procedures hundreds to thousand of times, as compared to the closed form statistical calculations of the standard distributions. Fortunately, computing power is becoming still cheaper, so this disadvantage diminishes with time.

3. Using robust methods can sometimes confuse the underlying intuition that one can obtain from a thoughtful understanding of the normal and log normal distribution.

The latter disadvantage is one of the reasons that this book has discussed both the theoretical and the empirical distributions. The theoretical has offered us intuition and insights into how markets work that may be simpler to understand than a robust number-crunching exercise. Yet, both techniques will yield the right answer.

You should now have the tools and knowledge to make an intelligent choice between the theoretical and empirical. In general, the empirical methods will give better answers. *Occasionally, the empirical distribution together with robust methods may be the only model that will give a reasonably accurate answer.*

SELECTING SHARPE VERSUS A LOG LOG OBJECTIVE FUNCTION

Sometimes the organization in which one works will dictate an objective function. Perhaps more to the point, the quarterly or annual bonus may be tied to a certain performance metric. In such a circumstance, the choice of an investment objective function becomes abundantly clear to the portfolio manager.

However, for those who have more freedom to choose their performance metric, we will discuss the merits of the two most common. First, the Sharpe Ratio is ubiquitous in portfolio performance evaluation. It serves as a de facto standard in the capital management industry. It is an accepted metric and is generally welcome and understood in almost any context in the investment world. The ratio measures the excess return accruing to a portfolio per unit of risk.

By contrast, the log log objective function helps to maximize the long-term compounded utility of wealth to the manager and potentially to the client. The inherent advantages of this should not be ignored. They are significant. For the manager or individual

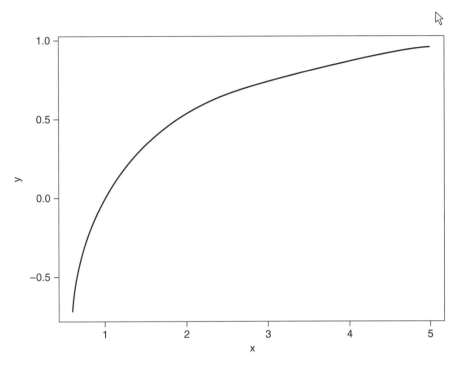

Figure 9.1 Iterated Log Function

who is interested in achieving a very high compounded return while still maintaining an acceptable risk profile, this measure is to be preferred.

It should be emphasized that the iterated log function is a conservative function (see Figure 9.1). The two log functions offer double concavity that is a more conservative risk measurement than that offered by a single log function as in the maximal compounded return formula. In one sense, the iterated log function represents using the log function itself as a measure of risk.

Interested readers are invited to compare the form of the various log functions used here to similar formulas given by Shannon in his famous work on information theory. In a like fashion, you should note that the formulas are quite similar to those given by Hamilton with respect to the concept of entropy in thermodynamics.

MODEL SIMULATION

Generally, the best practices for performing model simulation involve trying to replicate the underlying process of the market. When we model multiple securities or investments, we can model on the actual data itself in its original order. However, we can also randomly resample from our data set in order to establish confidence bands for the statistics of interest. Naturally, random resampling offers the best method to model our portfolio and trading techniques in an assumption and distribution free manner.

There are three primary ways to perform robust resampling of multivariate data:

1. *The simplest form of random resampling is to select a sub-sample of our data without any constraints.* Under this regime, each stock i from each period t has an equal probability to be selected. Implicit in this schema is the assumption that stock returns are independent of one another within the period and unrelated from period to period. Of course, we know that stock returns are highly correlated with one another within the same period. This simple form of sampling ignores that fact and this is likely to lead to spurious results that do not reflect the realities of the markets. This method is not recommended except perhaps as a cross check on the assumptions.

2. *To avoid the problems induced by contemporaneous correlations between assets we can and should restrict our resampling to observations from the same period.* Under this form of resampling, we would select all stocks within period t. However, the period t itself would be selected randomly. This type of resampling can generally be recommended, and it is often quite good. It does effectively capture the existing correlations and coincident co-movements between stocks.

    The major drawback to this technique is that it ignores any sequential correlations or cross market correlations that may exist from one period to the subsequent period. However, generally these correlations are quite small and can often be ignored.

    Another area of concern is the situation in which there exist nonlinear serial relationships. It is possible for no significant simple linear correlations to exist, but nonlinear relationships still remain from period to period. A good example of this is the GARCH class of models. From these we know that there is often a serial correlation between periods of high volatility and the next period. It is the volatility that is positively correlated without respect to direction of returns.

    This can be the case even though there is no simple linear correlation that would allow one to make money. Evidence in support of the GARCH models can be seen simply by looking at the correlation between the net return squared for this period and the net return squared for the next period. The squared terms are large for both large positive and large negative numbers. The original direction of the change is lost when the return data are squared.

3. The third technique for resampling is to *randomize the samples by start date, but continue the analysis sequentially from there for a predetermined number of time periods.* As an example, we could randomly select period t and all stocks from that period and continue our analysis for 20 days from there. Alternatively, we could

perform our analysis from time t backward for a similar window of, say, 20 days. This technique will preserve both the same period correlation structure of the data as well as any linear or nonlinear relationships hidden in the data. Generally speaking, this procedure is the best choice of the three.

However, remember that using overlapping periods in the analysis can cause problems when not using robust statistics. Thus, the best practice is to perform the robust resampling using a larger sample than normal. If the sample size is 1,000, then perhaps it should be 10,000 samples. Obviously, the issue involves the availability of computing resources, as well as other practical issues. If performed correctly, this form of resampling is the best and requires the fewest assumptions in order to implement.

PROFESSIONAL MONEY MANAGER VERSUS PRIVATE INVESTOR

Unfortunately, there is a built-in conflict of interest between the money manager and the individual or ultimate investor. Examples of this abound. A case in point would be the manager whose incentive compensation is based on hitting a certain threshold performance level. Suppose the level is 10 percent. Once that level is reached, the manager has every incentive to cut risk and attempt to coast to the finish line for that period with the goal safely in hand. It can be demonstrated that when the market is up after three quarters, many fund managers actually reduce risk. From their standpoint, they may figure, "Why risk a good performance year right at the end?" So they reduce their risk in order to preserve gains.

In another scenario, the manager who has locked in his bonus threshold for the year may decide to play it safe. He no longer has any incentive to take risks. In fact, added risk can only be punished.

Suppose that the situation is slightly different. The manager has achieved a 9 percent gain for the period as the end approaches. His bonus increases if the return can be improved to 10 percent. Perhaps a compensation structure such as this might induce the manager to take larger risks as the end of the period nears. He is hoping that the wilder swings of the increased risk will carry him over the top to his desired goal.

It is important to define what the appropriate goal for the portfolio is. It is the opinion of the author that any professional manager's compensation should be based on and compatible with the putative goals of the investors. To the extent that this does not occur then there arises the possibility of a conflict of interest. However, one must recognize that the realities of marketing are ever present and inescapable. Attracting and retaining clients is essential to every capital management business. Thus, it is fair to say that a little of each must be part of the mix.

We also observe that the ideal professional manager will be compensated by a formula that reflects the underlying goals of his investors. In this light, the use of the log log utility function described in earlier chapters has much to recommend it.

In particular, the iterated log formula is likely to be more in tune with the long-term goals of the investors. It properly weights the long-term compounded return and offers the added value of maximizing the utility of wealth in a fashion that most investors would choose for their own portfolios. The iterated log function also offers a conservative concave risk-averse function to properly reduce risk.

About the CD-ROM

INTRODUCTION

This appendix provides you with information on the contents of the CD that accompanies this book. For the latest and greatest information, please refer to the ReadMe file located at the root of the CD.

SYSTEM REQUIREMENTS

- A computer with a processor running at 120 Mhz or faster
- At least 32 MB of total RAM installed on your computer; for best performance, we recommend at least 64 MB
- A CD-ROM drive

NOTE: Many popular spreadsheet programs are capable of reading Excel files. However, users should be aware that a slight amount of formatting might be lost when using a program other than Microsoft Excel.

Using the CD with Windows

To install the items from the CD to your hard drive, follow these steps:

1. Insert the CD into your computer's CD-ROM drive.
2. The CD-ROM interface will appear. The interface provides a simple point-and-click way to explore the contents of the CD.

If the opening screen of the CD-ROM does not appear automatically, follow these steps to access the CD:

1. Click the Start button on the left end of the taskbar and then choose Run from the menu that pops up.

2. In the dialog box that appears, type $d:\backslash$**start.exe.** (If your CD-ROM drive is not drive d, fill in the appropriate letter in place of d.) This brings up the CD Interface described in the preceding set of steps.

WHAT'S ON THE CD

The following sections provide a summary of the software and other materials you'll find on the CD. The CD contains program examples which are intended to illustrate the subjects presented in the book. The examples are written in either Excel or the statistical programming language R.

Content

The CD is organized into two major categories:

1. The *Programs* - which includes the Excel and R language programs which relate to the subjects covered in the text. There are numerous program and application examples which illustrate the points discussed. In addition the code for many of the graphics and figures used in the text is included as well to provide additional concrete examples.

2. *Data* - This includes both sample empirical data as well as simulated stock prices for randomized models.

The programs may be run from either the CD-ROM or the hard drive once the user has copied the files over to the hard drive. Generally it will prove more convenient to run them from the hard drive.

Using the Programs

Excel   For the purposes of this section it is assumed that the user has already installed Excel. For help on this the reader is referred to the documentation which came with the software package.

Running the Excel spread sheets from within Excel is performed by loading the appropriate file from the folder. It is assumed that the use has basic knowledge of the operation of Excel, so this will not be discussed further here.

To understand the spread sheets does not require knowledge of Visual Basic for Applications. It is not used. Only fundamental spread sheet knowledge is assumed. The purpose of the examples is to introduce the user to some of the more advanced features of Excel and to illustrate how they might be used for modeling applications. Special emphasis is on the optimization and statistical techniques discussed in the book.

R Language   R is an open source statistical language which offers powerful functions with only a few user written commands. R offers math and statistical functions as well as powerful data manipulation and graphical plotting routines.

Readers who have not installed R may wish to refer to the accompanying section entitled Installing R. It describes how to download R and install it.

There are also several resources and references listed in the Installing R section. So even if the user has already installed the R package it may prove helpful to review this section as well.

To Run the Programs on this CD-ROM

In order to run the programs on this CD-ROM the user should first copy the entire contents of this CD onto his C drive in the folder called c:/Optimal which is short hand for Optimal Portfolio Modeling, the name of the book.

This procedure may be carried out by entering the following command in the command line on your Windows machine.

xcopy D:*.* C:\Optimal*.* \S

The above assumes that your D: drive is your CD-ROM drive.

There is a short cut to a batch file on this CD-ROM which will perform the same function. To execute this just double click on the file named 'Install' in the main directory of the CD-ROM.

About Chapter 1: Loading Data

The files on this CD-ROM pertaining to Chapter 1 are really more tutorials on how to load data into Excel and R. The instructions contained in the text files show how to download free stock price history data from Yahoo.

The Excel spread sheet in Chapter 1 is an example of what the data should look like as of the date the spread sheet was written.

Your spread should look similar but will be updated to the current date on which you download your data.

The R program will download the data for a sample stock symbol. In order to download a different symbol just edit the symbol.

In order to run the R code contained in the text file with extension .txt you simply copy and paste the code from the text file into the R Gui environment. Some packages may require loading of various library packages. If for some reason your environment does not have the required package loaded simply click Packages then Load Package from the R menu. From there you will see a list of available packages. simply select the one which is required and the download will proceed automatically.

About the Programs

The programs are intended to show particular examples of very simple concepts which often arise in portfolio modeling. Each is meant to be short and very understandable if one is willing to read the code.

About the Figure Programs

The programs in this folder are examples of how the figures in the book were created. As such they are a very useful tutorial on how to handle certain types of data and functions discussed in the text. They also serve as illustrations of how to produce graphics output with a minimum of effort in both Excel and R. As before the emphasis is on brevity and ease of understanding.

UPDATES TO THE CD-ROM

When and if there are updates to the CD-ROM and the programs associated with this text the author intends to publish them at his web site. The URL for the update page is:

http://www.pmcdonnell.com/OptimalPortfolioModeling

Readers are encouraged to check there periodically for software updates and bug fixes.

CUSTOMER CARE

If you have trouble with the CD-ROM, please call the Wiley Product Technical Support phone number at (800) 762-2974. Outside the United States, call 1(317) 572-3994. You can also contact Wiley Product Technical Support at **http://support.wiley.com**. John Wiley & Sons will provide technical support only for installation and other general quality control items. For technical support on the applications themselves, consult the program's vendor or author.

To place additional orders or to request information about other Wiley products, please call (877) 762-2974.

Table of Values of the Normal Distribution

Probability	Normal	Probability	Normal
0.005	−2.57583	0.120	−1.17499
0.010	−2.32634	0.125	−1.15035
0.015	−2.17009	0.130	−1.12639
0.020	−2.05375	0.135	−1.10306
0.025	−1.95996	0.140	−1.08032
0.030	−1.88079	0.145	−1.05812
0.035	−1.81191	0.150	−1.03643
0.040	−1.75069	0.155	−1.01522
0.045	−1.69540	0.160	−0.99446
0.050	−1.64485	0.165	−0.97411
0.055	−1.59819	0.170	−0.95416
0.060	−1.55477	0.175	−0.93459
0.065	−1.51410	0.180	−0.91537
0.070	−1.47579	0.185	−0.89647
0.075	−1.43953	0.190	−0.87790
0.080	−1.40507	0.195	−0.85962
0.085	−1.37220	0.200	−0.84162
0.090	−1.34075	0.205	−0.82389
0.095	−1.31058	0.210	−0.80642
0.100	−1.28155	0.215	−0.78919
0.105	−1.25357	0.220	−0.77219
0.110	−1.22653	0.225	−0.75541
0.115	−1.20036	0.230	−0.73885

(*continued*)

Probability	Normal	Probability	Normal
0.235	−0.72248	0.455	−0.11304
0.240	−0.70630	0.460	−0.10043
0.245	−0.69031	0.465	−0.08784
0.250	−0.67449	0.470	−0.07527
0.255	−0.65884	0.475	−0.06271
0.260	−0.64334	0.480	−0.05015
0.265	−0.62801	0.485	−0.03761
0.270	−0.61281	0.490	−0.02507
0.275	−0.59776	0.495	−0.01253
0.280	−0.58284	0.500	0.00000
0.285	−0.56805	0.505	0.01253
0.290	−0.55338	0.510	0.02507
0.295	−0.53884	0.515	0.03761
0.300	−0.52440	0.520	0.05015
0.305	−0.51007	0.525	0.06271
0.310	−0.49585	0.530	0.07527
0.315	−0.48173	0.535	0.08784
0.320	−0.46770	0.540	0.10043
0.325	−0.45376	0.545	0.11304
0.330	−0.43991	0.550	0.12566
0.335	−0.42615	0.555	0.13830
0.340	−0.41246	0.560	0.15097
0.345	−0.39886	0.565	0.16366
0.350	−0.38532	0.570	0.17637
0.355	−0.37186	0.575	0.18912
0.360	−0.35846	0.580	0.20189
0.365	−0.34513	0.585	0.21470
0.370	−0.33185	0.590	0.22755
0.375	−0.31864	0.595	0.24043
0.380	−0.30548	0.600	0.25335
0.385	−0.29238	0.605	0.26631
0.390	−0.27932	0.610	0.27932
0.395	−0.26631	0.615	0.29238
0.400	−0.25335	0.620	0.30548
0.405	−0.24043	0.625	0.31864
0.410	−0.22755	0.630	0.33185
0.415	−0.21470	0.635	0.34513
0.420	−0.20189	0.640	0.35846
0.425	−0.18912	0.645	0.37186
0.430	−0.17637	0.650	0.38532
0.435	−0.16366	0.655	0.39886
0.440	−0.15097	0.660	0.41246
0.445	−0.13830	0.665	0.42615
0.450	−0.12566	0.670	0.43991

Probability	Normal	Probability	Normal
0.675	0.45376	0.840	0.99446
0.680	0.46770	0.845	1.01522
0.685	0.48173	0.850	1.03643
0.690	0.49585	0.855	1.05812
0.695	0.51007	0.860	1.08032
0.700	0.52440	0.865	1.10306
0.705	0.53884	0.870	1.12639
0.710	0.55338	0.875	1.15035
0.715	0.56805	0.880	1.17499
0.720	0.58284	0.885	1.20036
0.725	0.59776	0.890	1.22653
0.730	0.61281	0.895	1.25357
0.735	0.62801	0.900	1.28155
0.740	0.64334	0.905	1.31058
0.745	0.65884	0.910	1.34075
0.750	0.67449	0.915	1.37220
0.755	0.69031	0.920	1.40507
0.760	0.70630	0.925	1.43953
0.765	0.72248	0.930	1.47579
0.770	0.73885	0.935	1.51410
0.775	0.75541	0.940	1.55477
0.780	0.77219	0.945	1.59819
0.785	0.78919	0.950	1.64485
0.790	0.80642	0.955	1.69540
0.795	0.82389	0.960	1.75069
0.800	0.84162	0.965	1.81191
0.805	0.85962	0.970	1.88079
0.810	0.87790	0.975	1.95996
0.815	0.89647	0.980	2.05375
0.820	0.91537	0.985	2.17009
0.825	0.93459	0.990	2.32634
0.830	0.95416	0.995	2.57583
0.835	0.97411		

The table was produced on a spreadsheet that is available on the CD-ROM accompanying this volume. It illustrates the use of the normsinv( ) function to provide the cumulative values of the normal distribution function.

Readers will note that the distribution from .005 to .500 is the mirror image of the distribution from .500 to .995. This property illustrates the reflection principle in a very intuitive way.

Installing R

Those readers who have not installed the statistical language R can do so with the information provided in this section.

The R Project home page offers many helpful links to R resources and is generally considered the reference source of choice for most information on R. The Web site may be referenced from the following URL link:

```
http://www.r-project.org/
```

The latest copy of the R language can be downloaded at no charge from the following Web page:

```
http://www.r-project.org/
```

Simply select a download mirror site near you for the fastest possible download. Users located in the United States will need to scroll way down the page to locate the various download sites based in the United States.

Installation and administration of your R installation is discussed in a downloadable document available from the Web site just given.

The latest copy of the R language manual is available at the following Web page:

```
http://cran.r-project.org/doc/manuals/R-lang.pdf
```

Introduction to R

T his appendix provides an introduction to the statistical and graphics language R. R is a freely available language that is based on the commercial language S. Programs written in either language are virtually identical to programs written in the other.

Therefore, users can usually run S programs unchanged in the free R environment. In the same fashion, R programs will usually run unchanged in an S environment.

The developers of R have created the language as a labor of love. The software is freely available, and the developers have worked to provide the benefits of R to the world without asking any compensation. It is a quintessential example of freely available software at its best.

The following document provides an introduction to programming in the R language. It is provided as a way to contribute to the R community and as a way to spread the message about R.

The document itself is presented as a verbatim copy of the original. Full credit is due to the authors. In doing so, we have relied on and reproduced the permissions of the authors given in the first few sentences.

An Introduction to R

Notes on R: A Programming Environment for Data Analysis and Graphics
Version 2.5.1 (2007-06-27)

W. N. Venables, D. M. Smith
and the R Development Core Team

ISBN 3-900051-12-7

i

Table of Contents

Preface

This introduction to R is derived from an original set of notes describing the S and S-Plus environments written by Bill Venables and David M. Smith (Insightful Corporation). We have made a number of small changes to reflect differences between the R and S programs, and expanded some of the material.

We would like to extend warm thanks to Bill Venables (and David Smith) for granting permission to distribute this modified version of the notes in this way, and for being a supporter of R from way back.

Comments and corrections are always welcome. Please address email correspondence to R-core@R-project.org.

Suggestions to the reader

Most R novices will start with the introductory session in Appendix A. This should give some familiarity with the style of R sessions and more importantly some instant feedback on what actually happens.

Many users will come to R mainly for its graphical facilities. In this case, Chapter 12 [Graphics], page 62 on the graphics facilities can be read at almost any time and need not wait until all the preceding sections have been digested.

1 Introduction and preliminaries

1.1 The R environment

R is an integrated suite of software facilities for data manipulation, calculation and graphical display. Among other things it has

- an effective data handling and storage facility,
- a suite of operators for calculations on arrays, in particular matrices,
- a large, coherent, integrated collection of intermediate tools for data analysis,
- graphical facilities for data analysis and display either directly at the computer or on hard-copy, and
- a well developed, simple and effective programming language (called 'S') which includes conditionals, loops, user defined recursive functions and input and output facilities. (Indeed most of the system supplied functions are themselves written in the S language.)

The term "environment" is intended to characterize it as a fully planned and coherent system, rather than an incremental accretion of very specific and inflexible tools, as is frequently the case with other data analysis software.

R is very much a vehicle for newly developing methods of interactive data analysis. It has developed rapidly, and has been extended by a large collection of *packages*. However, most programs written in R are essentially ephemeral, written for a single piece of data analysis.

1.2 Related software and documentation

R can be regarded as an implementation of the S language which was developed at Bell Laboratories by Rick Becker, John Chambers and Allan Wilks, and also forms the basis of the S-PLUS systems.

The evolution of the S language is characterized by four books by John Chambers and coauthors. For R, the basic reference is *The New S Language: A Programming Environment for Data Analysis and Graphics* by Richard A. Becker, John M. Chambers and Allan R. Wilks. The new features of the 1991 release of S are covered in *Statistical Models in S* edited by John M. Chambers and Trevor J. Hastie. The formal methods and classes of the **methods** package are based on those described in *Programming with Data* by John M. Chambers. See Appendix F [References], page 94, for precise references.

There are now a number of books which describe how to use R for data analysis and statistics, and documentation for S/S-PLUS can typically be used with R, keeping the differences between the S implementations in mind. See section "What documentation exists for R?" in *The R statistical system FAQ*.

1.3 R and statistics

Our introduction to the R environment did not mention *statistics*, yet many people use R as a statistics system. We prefer to think of it of an environment within which many classical and modern statistical techniques have been implemented. A few of these built into the base R environment, but many are supplied as *packages*. There are about 25 packages supplied with R (called "standard" and "recommended" packages) and many more are available through the CRAN family of Internet sites (via http://CRAN.R-project.org) and elsewhere. More details on packages are given later (see Chapter 13 [Packages], page 76).

Most classical statistics and much of the latest methodology is available for use with R, but users may need to be prepared to do a little work to find it.

There is an important difference in philosophy between S (and hence R) and the other main statistical systems. In S a statistical analysis is normally done as a series of steps, with intermediate results being stored in objects. Thus whereas SAS and SPSS will give copious output from a regression or discriminant analysis, R will give minimal output and store the results in a fit object for subsequent interrogation by further R functions.

1.4 R and the window system

The most convenient way to use R is at a graphics workstation running a windowing system. This guide is aimed at users who have this facility. In particular we will occasionally refer to the use of R on an X window system although the vast bulk of what is said applies generally to any implementation of the R environment.

Most users will find it necessary to interact directly with the operating system on their computer from time to time. In this guide, we mainly discuss interaction with the operating system on UNIX machines. If you are running R under Windows or MacOS you will need to make some small adjustments.

Setting up a workstation to take full advantage of the customizable features of R is a straight-forward if somewhat tedious procedure, and will not be considered further here. Users in difficulty should seek local expert help.

1.5 Using R interactively

When you use the R program it issues a prompt when it expects input commands. The default prompt is '>', which on UNIX might be the same as the shell prompt, and so it may appear that nothing is happening. However, as we shall see, it is easy to change to a different R prompt if you wish. We will assume that the UNIX shell prompt is '$'.

In using R under UNIX the suggested procedure for the first occasion is as follows:

1. Create a separate sub-directory, say 'work', to hold data files on which you will use R for this problem. This will be the working directory whenever you use R for this particular problem.

   ```
   $ mkdir work
   $ cd work
   ```

2. Start the R program with the command

   ```
   $ R
   ```

3. At this point R commands may be issued (see later).

4. To quit the R program the command is

   ```
   > q()
   ```

   At this point you will be asked whether you want to save the data from your R session. On some systems this will bring up a dialog box, and on others you will receive a text prompt to which you can respond *yes*, *no* or *cancel* (a single letter abbreviation will do) to save the data before quitting, quit without saving, or return to the R session. Data which is saved will be available in future R sessions.

Further R sessions are simple.

1. Make 'work' the working directory and start the program as before:

   ```
   $ cd work
   $ R
   ```

2. Use the R program, terminating with the q() command at the end of the session.

To use R under Windows the procedure to follow is basically the same. Create a folder as the working directory, and set that in the 'Start In' field in your R shortcut. Then launch R by double clicking on the icon.

Chapter 1: Introduction and preliminaries 4

1.6 An introductory session

Readers wishing to get a feel for R at a computer before proceeding are strongly advised to work through the introductory session given in Appendix A [A sample session], page 78.

1.7 Getting help with functions and features

R has an inbuilt help facility similar to the `man` facility of UNIX. To get more information on any specific named function, for example `solve`, the command is

```
> help(solve)
```

An alternative is

```
> ?solve
```

For a feature specified by special characters, the argument must be enclosed in double or single quotes, making it a "character string": This is also necessary for a few words with syntactic meaning including `if`, `for` and `function`.

```
> help("[[")
```

Either form of quote mark may be used to escape the other, as in the string `"It's important"`. Our convention is to use double quote marks for preference.

On most R installations help is available in HTML format by running

```
> help.start()
```

which will launch a Web browser that allows the help pages to be browsed with hyperlinks. On UNIX, subsequent help requests are sent to the HTML-based help system. The 'Search Engine and Keywords' link in the page loaded by `help.start()` is particularly useful as it is contains a high-level concept list which searches though available functions. It can be a great way to get your bearings quickly and to understand the breadth of what R has to offer.

The `help.search` command allows searching for help in various ways: try `?help.search` for details and examples.

The examples on a help topic can normally be run by

```
> example(topic)
```

Windows versions of R have other optional help systems: use

```
> ?help
```

for further details.

1.8 R commands, case sensitivity, etc.

Technically R is an *expression language* with a very simple syntax. It is *case sensitive* as are most UNIX based packages, so `A` and `a` are different symbols and would refer to different variables. The set of symbols which can be used in R names depends on the operating system and country within which R is being run (technically on the *locale* in use). Normally all alphanumeric symbols are allowed[1] (and in some countries this includes accented letters) plus '.' and '_', with the restriction that a name must start with '.' or a letter, and if it starts with '.' the second character must not be a digit.

Elementary commands consist of either *expressions* or *assignments*. If an expression is given as a command, it is evaluated, printed (unless specifically made invisible), and the value is lost. An assignment also evaluates an expression and passes the value to a variable but the result is not automatically printed.

Commands are separated either by a semi-colon ('`;`'), or by a newline. Elementary commands can be grouped together into one compound expression by braces ('`{`' and '`}`'). *Comments* can

---

[1] For portable R code (including that to be used in R packages) only A–Za–z0–9 should be used.

be put almost[2] anywhere, starting with a hashmark ('#'), everything to the end of the line is a comment.

If a command is not complete at the end of a line, R will give a different prompt, by default

+

on second and subsequent lines and continue to read input until the command is syntactically complete. This prompt may be changed by the user. We will generally omit the continuation prompt and indicate continuation by simple indenting.

Command lines entered at the console are limited[3] to about 1024 bytes (not characters).

1.9 Recall and correction of previous commands

Under many versions of UNIX and on Windows, R provides a mechanism for recalling and re-executing previous commands. The vertical arrow keys on the keyboard can be used to scroll forward and backward through a *command history*. Once a command is located in this way, the cursor can be moved within the command using the horizontal arrow keys, and characters can be removed with the (DEL) key or added with the other keys. More details are provided later: see Appendix C [The command-line editor], page 87.

The recall and editing capabilities under UNIX are highly customizable. You can find out how to do this by reading the manual entry for the **readline** library.

Alternatively, the Emacs text editor provides more general support mechanisms (via ESS, *Emacs Speaks Statistics*) for working interactively with R. See section "R and Emacs" in *The R statistical system FAQ*.

1.10 Executing commands from or diverting output to a file

If commands[4] are stored in an external file, say 'commands.R' in the working directory 'work', they may be executed at any time in an R session with the command

```
> source("commands.R")
```

For Windows **Source** is also available on the **File** menu. The function sink,

```
> sink("record.lis")
```

will divert all subsequent output from the console to an external file, 'record.lis'. The command

```
> sink()
```

restores it to the console once again.

1.11 Data permanency and removing objects

The entities that R creates and manipulates are known as *objects*. These may be variables, arrays of numbers, character strings, functions, or more general structures built from such components.

During an R session, objects are created and stored by name (we discuss this process in the next session). The R command

```
> objects()
```

(alternatively, ls()) can be used to display the names of (most of) the objects which are currently stored within R. The collection of objects currently stored is called the *workspace*.

To remove objects the function rm is available:

---

[2] **not** inside strings, nor within the argument list of a function definition
[3] some of the consoles will not allow you to enter more, and amongst those which do some will silently discard the excess and some will use it as the start of the next line.
[4] of unlimited length.

Chapter 1: Introduction and preliminaries   6

> ```
> rm(x, y, z, ink, junk, temp, foo, bar)
> ```

All objects created during an R sessions can be stored permanently in a file for use in future R sessions. At the end of each R session you are given the opportunity to save all the currently available objects. If you indicate that you want to do this, the objects are written to a file called '.RData'[5] in the current directory, and the command lines used in the session are saved to a file called '.Rhistory'.

When R is started at later time from the same directory it reloads the workspace from this file. At the same time the associated commands history is reloaded.

It is recommended that you should use separate working directories for analyses conducted with R. It is quite common for objects with names x and y to be created during an analysis. Names like this are often meaningful in the context of a single analysis, but it can be quite hard to decide what they might be when the several analyses have been conducted in the same directory.

---

[5] The leading "dot" in this file name makes it *invisible* in normal file listings in UNIX.

2 Simple manipulations; numbers and vectors

2.1 Vectors and assignment

R operates on named *data structures*. The simplest such structure is the numeric *vector*, which is a single entity consisting of an ordered collection of numbers. To set up a vector named x, say, consisting of five numbers, namely 10.4, 5.6, 3.1, 6.4 and 21.7, use the R command

```
> x <- c(10.4, 5.6, 3.1, 6.4, 21.7)
```

This is an *assignment* statement using the *function* c() which in this context can take an arbitrary number of vector *arguments* and whose value is a vector got by concatenating its arguments end to end.[1]

A number occurring by itself in an expression is taken as a vector of length one.

Notice that the assignment operator ('<-'), which consists of the two characters '<' ("less than") and '-' ("minus") occurring strictly side-by-side and it 'points' to the object receiving the value of the expression. In most contexts the '=' operator can be used as a alternative.

Assignment can also be made using the function assign(). An equivalent way of making the same assignment as above is with:

```
> assign("x", c(10.4, 5.6, 3.1, 6.4, 21.7))
```

The usual operator, <-, can be thought of as a syntactic short-cut to this.

Assignments can also be made in the other direction, using the obvious change in the assignment operator. So the same assignment could be made using

```
> c(10.4, 5.6, 3.1, 6.4, 21.7) -> x
```

If an expression is used as a complete command, the value is printed *and lost*[2]. So now if we were to use the command

```
> 1/x
```

the reciprocals of the five values would be printed at the terminal (and the value of x, of course, unchanged).

The further assignment

```
> y <- c(x, 0, x)
```

would create a vector y with 11 entries consisting of two copies of x with a zero in the middle place.

2.2 Vector arithmetic

Vectors can be used in arithmetic expressions, in which case the operations are performed element by element. Vectors occurring in the same expression need not all be of the same length. If they are not, the value of the expression is a vector with the same length as the longest vector which occurs in the expression. Shorter vectors in the expression are *recycled* as often as need be (perhaps fractionally) until they match the length of the longest vector. In particular a constant is simply repeated. So with the above assignments the command

```
> v <- 2*x + y + 1
```

generates a new vector v of length 11 constructed by adding together, element by element, 2*x repeated 2.2 times, y repeated just once, and 1 repeated 11 times.

The elementary arithmetic operators are the usual +, -, *, / and ^ for raising to a power. In addition all of the common arithmetic functions are available. log, exp, sin, cos, tan, sqrt,

---

[1] With other than vector types of argument, such as list mode arguments, the action of c() is rather different. See Section 6.2.1 [Concatenating lists], page 27.

[2] Actually, it is still available as .Last.value before any other statements are executed.

and so on, all have their usual meaning. `max` and `min` select the largest and smallest elements of a vector respectively. `range` is a function whose value is a vector of length two, namely `c(min(x),` `max(x))`. `length(x)` is the number of elements in `x`, `sum(x)` gives the total of the elements in `x`, and `prod(x)` their product.

Two statistical functions are `mean(x)` which calculates the sample mean, which is the same as `sum(x)/length(x)`, and `var(x)` which gives

```
sum((x-mean(x))^2)/(length(x)-1)
```

or sample variance. If the argument to `var()` is an n-by-p matrix the value is a p-by-p sample covariance matrix got by regarding the rows as independent p-variate sample vectors.

`sort(x)` returns a vector of the same size as `x` with the elements arranged in increasing order; however there are other more flexible sorting facilities available (see `order()` or `sort.list()` which produce a permutation to do the sorting).

Note that `max` and `min` select the largest and smallest values in their arguments, even if they are given several vectors. The *parallel* maximum and minimum functions `pmax` and `pmin` return a vector (of length equal to their longest argument) that contains in each element the largest (smallest) element in that position in any of the input vectors.

For most purposes the user will not be concerned if the "numbers" in a numeric vector are integers, reals or even complex. Internally calculations are done as double precision real numbers, or double precision complex numbers if the input data are complex.

To work with complex numbers, supply an explicit complex part. Thus

```
sqrt(-17)
```

will give `NaN` and a warning, but

```
sqrt(-17+0i)
```

will do the computations as complex numbers.

2.3 Generating regular sequences

R has a number of facilities for generating commonly used sequences of numbers. For example `1:30` is the vector `c(1, 2, ..., 29, 30)`. The colon operator has high priority within an expression, so, for example `2*1:15` is the vector `c(2, 4, ..., 28, 30)`. Put `n <- 10` and compare the sequences `1:n-1` and `1:(n-1)`.

The construction `30:1` may be used to generate a sequence backwards.

The function `seq()` is a more general facility for generating sequences. It has five arguments, only some of which may be specified in any one call. The first two arguments, if given, specify the beginning and end of the sequence, and if these are the only two arguments given the result is the same as the colon operator. That is `seq(2,10)` is the same vector as `2:10`.

Parameters to `seq()`, and to many other R functions, can also be given in named form, in which case the order in which they appear is irrelevant. The first two parameters may be named `from=value` and `to=value`; thus `seq(1,30)`, `seq(from=1, to=30)` and `seq(to=30, from=1)` are all the same as `1:30`. The next two parameters to `seq()` may be named `by=value` and `length=value`, which specify a step size and a length for the sequence respectively. If neither of these is given, the default `by=1` is assumed.

For example

```
> seq(-5, 5, by=.2) -> s3
```

generates in `s3` the vector `c(-5.0, -4.8, -4.6, ..., 4.6, 4.8, 5.0)`. Similarly

```
> s4 <- seq(length=51, from=-5, by=.2)
```

generates the same vector in `s4`.

Chapter 2: Simple manipulations; numbers and vectors

9

The fifth parameter may be named `along=`*vector*, which if used must be the only parameter, and creates a sequence `1, 2, ..., length(`*vector*`)`, or the empty sequence if the vector is empty (as it can be).

A related function is `rep()` which can be used for replicating an object in various complicated ways. The simplest form is

```
> s5 <- rep(x, times=5)
```

which will put five copies of `x` end-to-end in `s5`. Another useful version is

```
> s6 <- rep(x, each=5)
```

which repeats each element of `x` five times before moving on to the next.

2.4 Logical vectors

As well as numerical vectors, R allows manipulation of logical quantities. The elements of a logical vector can have the values `TRUE`, `FALSE`, and `NA` (for "not available", see below). The first two are often abbreviated as `T` and `F`, respectively. Note however that `T` and `F` are just variables which are set to `TRUE` and `FALSE` by default, but are not reserved words and hence can be overwritten by the user. Hence, you should always use `TRUE` and `FALSE`.

Logical vectors are generated by *conditions*. For example

```
> temp <- x > 13
```

sets `temp` as a vector of the same length as `x` with values `FALSE` corresponding to elements of `x` where the condition is *not* met and `TRUE` where it is.

The logical operators are `<, <=, >, >=, ==` for exact equality and `!=` for inequality. In addition if `c1` and `c2` are logical expressions, then `c1 & c2` is their intersection (*"and"*), `c1 | c2` is their union (*"or"*), and `!c1` is the negation of `c1`.

Logical vectors may be used in ordinary arithmetic, in which case they are *coerced* into numeric vectors, `FALSE` becoming 0 and `TRUE` becoming 1. However there are situations where logical vectors and their coerced numeric counterparts are not equivalent, for example see the next subsection.

2.5 Missing values

In some cases the components of a vector may not be completely known. When an element or value is "not available" or a "missing value" in the statistical sense, a place within a vector may be reserved for it by assigning it the special value `NA`. In general any operation on an `NA` becomes an `NA`. The motivation for this rule is simply that if the specification of an operation is incomplete, the result cannot be known and hence is not available.

The function `is.na(x)` gives a logical vector of the same size as `x` with value `TRUE` if and only if the corresponding element in `x` is `NA`.

```
> z <- c(1:3,NA);  ind <- is.na(z)
```

Notice that the logical expression `x == NA` is quite different from `is.na(x)` since `NA` is not really a value but a marker for a quantity that is not available. Thus `x == NA` is a vector of the same length as `x` *all* of whose values are `NA` as the logical expression itself is incomplete and hence undecidable.

Note that there is a second kind of "missing" values which are produced by numerical computation, the so-called *Not a Number*, `NaN`, values. Examples are

```
> 0/0
```

or

Chapter 2: Simple manipulations; numbers and vectors   10

```
> Inf - Inf
```
which both give NaN since the result cannot be defined sensibly.

In summary, is.na(xx) is TRUE *both* for NA and NaN values. To differentiate these, is.nan(xx) is only TRUE for NaNs.

Missing values are sometimes printed as <NA>, when character vectors are printed without quotes.

2.6 Character vectors

Character quantities and character vectors are used frequently in R, for example as plot labels. Where needed they are denoted by a sequence of characters delimited by the double quote character, e.g., "x-values", "New iteration results".

Character strings are entered using either double (") or single (') quotes, but are printed using double quotes (or sometimes without quotes). They use C-style escape sequences, using \ as the escape character, so \\ is entered and printed as \\, and inside double quotes " is entered as \". Other useful escape sequences are \n, newline, \t, tab and \b, backspace.

Character vectors may be concatenated into a vector by the c() function; examples of their use will emerge frequently.

The paste() function takes an arbitrary number of arguments and concatenates them one by one into character strings. Any numbers given among the arguments are coerced into character strings in the evident way, that is, in the same way they would be if they were printed. The arguments are by default separated in the result by a single blank character, but this can be changed by the named parameter, sep=*string*, which changes it to *string*, possibly empty.

For example
```
> labs <- paste(c("X","Y"), 1:10, sep="")
```
makes labs into the character vector
```
c("X1", "Y2", "X3", "Y4", "X5", "Y6", "X7", "Y8", "X9", "Y10")
```
Note particularly that recycling of short lists takes place here too; thus c("X", "Y") is repeated 5 times to match the sequence 1:10.[3]

2.7 Index vectors; selecting and modifying subsets of a data set

Subsets of the elements of a vector may be selected by appending to the name of the vector an *index vector* in square brackets. More generally any expression that evaluates to a vector may have subsets of its elements similarly selected by appending an index vector in square brackets immediately after the expression.

Such index vectors can be any of four distinct types.

1. **A logical vector.** In this case the index vector must be of the same length as the vector from which elements are to be selected. Values corresponding to TRUE in the index vector are selected and those corresponding to FALSE are omitted. For example
   ```
   > y <- x[!is.na(x)]
   ```
   creates (or re-creates) an object y which will contain the non-missing values of x, in the same order. Note that if x has missing values, y will be shorter than x. Also
   ```
   > (x+1)[(!is.na(x)) & x>0] -> z
   ```
   creates an object z and places in it the values of the vector x+1 for which the corresponding value in x was both non-missing and positive.

---

[3] paste(..., collapse=*ss*) joins the arguments into a single character string putting *ss* in between. There are more tools for character manipulation, see the help for sub and substring.

Chapter 2: Simple manipulations; numbers and vectors 11

2. **A vector of positive integral quantities**. In this case the values in the index vector must lie in the set {1, 2, ..., `length(x)`}. The corresponding elements of the vector are selected and concatenated, *in that order*, in the result. The index vector can be of any length and the result is of the same length as the index vector. For example `x[6]` is the sixth component of x and

   > x[1:10]

selects the first 10 elements of x (assuming `length(x)` is not less than 10). Also

   > c("x","y")[rep(c(1,2,2,1), times=4)]

(an admittedly unlikely thing to do) produces a character vector of length 16 consisting of "x", "y", "y", "x" repeated four times.

3. **A vector of negative integral quantities**. Such an index vector specifies the values to be *excluded* rather than included. Thus

   > y <- x[-(1:5)]

gives y all but the first five elements of x.

4. **A vector of character strings**. This possibility only applies where an object has a `names` attribute to identify its components. In this case a sub-vector of the names vector may be used in the same way as the positive integral labels in item 2 further above.

   > fruit <- c(5, 10, 1, 20)
   > names(fruit) <- c("orange", "banana", "apple", "peach")
   > lunch <- fruit[c("apple","orange")]

The advantage is that alphanumeric *names* are often easier to remember than *numeric indices*. This option is particularly useful in connection with data frames, as we shall see later.

An indexed expression can also appear on the receiving end of an assignment, in which case the assignment operation is performed *only on those elements of the vector*. The expression must be of the form `vector[index_vector]` as having an arbitrary expression in place of the vector name does not make much sense here.

The vector assigned must match the length of the index vector, and in the case of a logical index vector it must again be the same length as the vector it is indexing.

For example

   > x[is.na(x)] <- 0

replaces any missing values in x by zeros and

   > y[y < 0] <- -y[y < 0]

has the same effect as

   > y <- abs(y)

2.8 Other types of objects

Vectors are the most important type of object in R, but there are several others which we will meet more formally in later sections.

- *matrices* or more generally *arrays* are multi-dimensional generalizations of vectors. In fact, they *are* vectors that can be indexed by two or more indices and will be printed in special ways. See Chapter 5 [Arrays and matrices], page 18.

- *factors* provide compact ways to handle categorical data. See Chapter 4 [Factors], page 16.

- *lists* are a general form of vector in which the various elements need not be of the same type, and are often themselves vectors or lists. Lists provide a convenient way to return the results of a statistical computation. See Section 6.1 [Lists], page 26.

Chapter 2: Simple manipulations; numbers and vectors   12

- *data frames* are matrix-like structures, in which the columns can be of different types. Think of data frames as 'data matrices' with one row per observational unit but with (possibly) both numerical and categorical variables. Many experiments are best described by data frames: the treatments are categorical but the response is numeric. See Section 6.3 [Data frames], page 27.
- *functions* are themselves objects in R which can be stored in the project's workspace. This provides a simple and convenient way to extend R. See Chapter 10 [Writing your own functions], page 42.

3 Objects, their modes and attributes

3.1 Intrinsic attributes: mode and length

The entities R operates on are technically known as *objects*. Examples are vectors of numeric (real) or complex values, vectors of logical values and vectors of character strings. These are known as "atomic" structures since their components are all of the same type, or *mode*, namely *numeric*[1], *complex*, *logical*, *character* and *raw*.

Vectors must have their values *all of the same mode*. Thus any given vector must be unambiguously either *logical*, *numeric*, *complex*, *character* or *raw*. (The only apparent exception to this rule is the special "value" listed as NA for quantities not available, but in fact there are several types of NA). Note that a vector can be empty and still have a mode. For example the empty character string vector is listed as `character(0)` and the empty numeric vector as `numeric(0)`.

R also operates on objects called *lists*, which are of mode *list*. These are ordered sequences of objects which individually can be of any mode. *lists* are known as "recursive" rather than atomic structures since their components can themselves be lists in their own right.

The other recursive structures are those of mode *function* and *expression*. Functions are the objects that form part of the R system along with similar user written functions, which we discuss in some detail later. Expressions as objects form an advanced part of R which will not be discussed in this guide, except indirectly when we discuss *formulae* used with modeling in R.

By the *mode* of an object we mean the basic type of its fundamental constituents. This is a special case of a "property" of an object. Another property of every object is its *length*. The functions `mode(object)` and `length(object)` can be used to find out the mode and length of any defined structure[2].

Further properties of an object are usually provided by `attributes(object)`, see Section 3.3 [Getting and setting attributes], page 14. Because of this, *mode* and *length* are also called "intrinsic attributes" of an object.

For example, if z is a complex vector of length 100, then in an expression `mode(z)` is the character string `"complex"` and `length(z)` is 100.

R caters for changes of mode almost anywhere it could be considered sensible to do so, (and a few where it might not be). For example with

```
> z <- 0:9
```

we could put

```
> digits <- as.character(z)
```

after which `digits` is the character vector c("0", "1", "2", ..., "9"). A further *coercion*, or change of mode, reconstructs the numerical vector again:

```
> d <- as.integer(digits)
```

Now d and z are the same.[3] There is a large collection of functions of the form `as.something()` for either coercion from one mode to another, or for investing an object with some other attribute it may not already possess. The reader should consult the different help files to become familiar with them.

---

[1] *numeric* mode is actually an amalgam of two distinct modes, namely *integer* and *double* precision, as explained in the manual.

[2] Note however that `length(object)` does not always contain intrinsic useful information, e.g., when *object* is a function.

[3] In general, coercion from numeric to character and back again will not be exactly reversible, because of roundoff errors in the character representation.

3.2 Changing the length of an object

An "empty" object may still have a mode. For example

```
> e <- numeric()
```

makes e an empty vector structure of mode numeric. Similarly `character()` is a empty character vector, and so on. Once an object of any size has been created, new components may be added to it simply by giving it an index value outside its previous range. Thus

```
> e[3] <- 17
```

now makes e a vector of length 3, (the first two components of which are at this point both NA). This applies to any structure at all, provided the mode of the additional component(s) agrees with the mode of the object in the first place.

This automatic adjustment of lengths of an object is used often, for example in the `scan()` function for input. (see Section 7.2 [The scan() function], page 31.)

Conversely to truncate the size of an object requires only an assignment to do so. Hence if alpha is an object of length 10, then

```
> alpha <- alpha[2 * 1:5]
```

makes it an object of length 5 consisting of just the former components with even index. (The old indices are not retained, of course.) We can then retain just the first three values by

```
> length(alpha) <- 3
```

and vectors can be extended (by missing values) in the same way.

3.3 Getting and setting attributes

The function `attributes(object)` returns a list of all the non-intrinsic attributes currently defined for that object. The function `attr(object, name)` can be used to select a specific attribute. These functions are rarely used, except in rather special circumstances when some new attribute is being created for some particular purpose, for example to associate a creation date or an operator with an R object. The concept, however, is very important.

Some care should be exercised when assigning or deleting attributes since they are an integral part of the object system used in R.

When it is used on the left hand side of an assignment it can be used either to associate a new attribute with *object* or to change an existing one. For example

```
> attr(z, "dim") <- c(10,10)
```

allows R to treat z as if it were a 10-by-10 matrix.

3.4 The class of an object

All objects in R have a *class*, reported by the function class. For simple vectors this is just the mode, for example "numeric", "logical", "character" or "list", but "matrix", "array", "factor" and "data.frame" are other possible values.

A special attribute known as the *class* of the object is used to allow for an object-oriented style[4] of programming in R. For example if an object has class "data.frame", it will be printed in a certain way, the `plot()` function will display it graphically in a certain way, and other so-called generic functions such as `summary()` will react to it as an argument in a way sensitive to its class.

To remove temporarily the effects of class, use the function `unclass()`. For example if winter has the class "data.frame" then

---

[4] A different style using 'formal' or 'S4' classes is provided in package methods.

Chapter 3: Objects, their modes and attributes   15


```
> winter
```
will print it in data frame form, which is rather like a matrix, whereas
```
> unclass(winter)
```
will print it as an ordinary list. Only in rather special situations do you need to use this facility, but one is when you are learning to come to terms with the idea of class and generic functions.

Generic functions and classes will be discussed further in Section 10.9 [Object orientation], page 48, but only briefly.

4 Ordered and unordered factors

A *factor* is a vector object used to specify a discrete classification (grouping) of the components of other vectors of the same length. R provides both *ordered* and *unordered* factors. While the "real" application of factors is with model formulae (see Section 11.1.1 [Contrasts], page 52), we here look at a specific example.

4.1 A specific example

Suppose, for example, we have a sample of 30 tax accountants from all the states and territories of Australia[1] and their individual state of origin is specified by a character vector of state mnemonics as

```
> state <- c("tas", "sa",  "qld", "nsw", "nsw", "nt",  "wa",  "wa",
             "qld", "vic", "nsw", "vic", "qld", "qld", "sa",  "tas",
             "sa",  "nt",  "wa",  "vic", "qld", "nsw", "nsw", "wa",
             "sa",  "act", "nsw", "vic", "vic", "act")
```

Notice that in the case of a character vector, "sorted" means sorted in alphabetical order.

A *factor* is similarly created using the `factor()` function:

```
> statef <- factor(state)
```

The `print()` function handles factors slightly differently from other objects:

```
> statef
 [1] tas sa  qld nsw nsw nt  wa  wa  qld vic nsw vic qld qld sa
[16] tas sa  nt  wa  vic qld nsw nsw wa  sa  act nsw vic vic act
Levels:  act nsw nt qld sa tas vic wa
```

To find out the levels of a factor the function `levels()` can be used.

```
> levels(statef)
[1] "act" "nsw" "nt"  "qld" "sa"  "tas" "vic" "wa"
```

4.2 The function `tapply()` and ragged arrays

To continue the previous example, suppose we have the incomes of the same tax accountants in another vector (in suitably large units of money)

```
> incomes <- c(60, 49, 40, 61, 64, 60, 59, 54, 62, 69, 70, 42, 56,
               61, 61, 61, 58, 51, 48, 65, 49, 49, 41, 48, 52, 46,
               59, 46, 58, 43)
```

To calculate the sample mean income for each state we can now use the special function `tapply()`:

```
> incmeans <- tapply(incomes, statef, mean)
```

giving a means vector with the components labelled by the levels

```
    act    nsw     nt    qld     sa    tas    vic     wa
 44.500 57.333 55.500 53.600 55.000 60.500 56.000 52.250
```

The function `tapply()` is used to apply a function, here `mean()`, to each group of components of the first argument, here `incomes`, defined by the levels of the second component, here `statef`[2],

---

[1] Readers should note that there are eight states and territories in Australia, namely the Australian Capital Territory, New South Wales, the Northern Territory, Queensland, South Australia, Tasmania, Victoria and Western Australia.

[2] Note that `tapply()` also works in this case when its second argument is not a factor, e.g., '`tapply(incomes, state)`', and this is true for quite a few other functions, since arguments are *coerced* to factors when necessary (using `as.factor()`).

as if they were separate vector structures. The result is a structure of the same length as the levels attribute of the factor containing the results. The reader should consult the help document for more details.

Suppose further we needed to calculate the standard errors of the state income means. To do this we need to write an R function to calculate the standard error for any given vector. Since there is an builtin function `var()` to calculate the sample variance, such a function is a very simple one liner, specified by the assignment:

```
> stderr <- function(x) sqrt(var(x)/length(x))
```

(Writing functions will be considered later in Chapter 10 [Writing your own functions], page 42, and in this case was unnecessary as R also has a builtin function `sd()`.) After this assignment, the standard errors are calculated by

```
> incster <- tapply(incomes, statef, stderr)
```

and the values calculated are then

```
> incster
 act    nsw   nt    qld     sa  tas    vic      wa
 1.5 4.3102 4.5 4.1061 2.7386 0.5 5.244 2.6575
```

As an exercise you may care to find the usual 95% confidence limits for the state mean incomes. To do this you could use `tapply()` once more with the `length()` function to find the sample sizes, and the `qt()` function to find the percentage points of the appropriate t-distributions. (You could also investigate R's facilities for t-tests.)

The function `tapply()` can also be used to handle more complicated indexing of a vector by multiple categories. For example, we might wish to split the tax accountants by both state and sex. However in this simple instance (just one factor) what happens can be thought of as follows. The values in the vector are collected into groups corresponding to the distinct entries in the factor. The function is then applied to each of these groups individually. The value is a vector of function results, labelled by the `levels` attribute of the factor.

The combination of a vector and a labelling factor is an example of what is sometimes called a *ragged array*, since the subclass sizes are possibly irregular. When the subclass sizes are all the same the indexing may be done implicitly and much more efficiently, as we see in the next section.

4.3 Ordered factors

The levels of factors are stored in alphabetical order, or in the order they were specified to `factor` if they were specified explicitly.

Sometimes the levels will have a natural ordering that we want to record and want our statistical analysis to make use of. The `ordered()` function creates such ordered factors but is otherwise identical to `factor`. For most purposes the only difference between ordered and unordered factors is that the former are printed showing the ordering of the levels, but the contrasts generated for them in fitting linear models are different.

5 Arrays and matrices

5.1 Arrays

An array can be considered as a multiply subscripted collection of data entries, for example numeric. R allows simple facilities for creating and handling arrays, and in particular the special case of matrices.

A dimension vector is a vector of non-negative integers. If its length is k then the array is k-dimensional, e.g. a matrix is a 2-dimensional array. The dimensions are indexed from one up to the values given in the dimension vector.

A vector can be used by R as an array only if it has a dimension vector as its *dim* attribute. Suppose, for example, z is a vector of 1500 elements. The assignment

```
> dim(z) <- c(3,5,100)
```

gives it the *dim* attribute that allows it to be treated as a 3 by 5 by 100 array.

Other functions such as matrix() and array() are available for simpler and more natural looking assignments, as we shall see in Section 5.4 [The array() function], page 20.

The values in the data vector give the values in the array in the same order as they would occur in FORTRAN, that is "column major order," with the first subscript moving fastest and the last subscript slowest.

For example if the dimension vector for an array, say a, is c(3,4,2) then there are $3 \times 4 \times 2 = 24$ entries in a and the data vector holds them in the order a[1,1,1], a[2,1,1], ..., a[2,4,2], a[3,4,2].

Arrays can be one-dimensional: such arrays are usually treated in the same way as vectors (including when printing), but the exceptions can cause confusion.

5.2 Array indexing. Subsections of an array

Individual elements of an array may be referenced by giving the name of the array followed by the subscripts in square brackets, separated by commas.

More generally, subsections of an array may be specified by giving a sequence of *index vectors* in place of subscripts; however *if any index position is given an empty index vector, then the full range of that subscript is taken.*

Continuing the previous example, a[2,,] is a 4×2 array with dimension vector c(4,2) and data vector containing the values

```
c(a[2,1,1], a[2,2,1], a[2,3,1], a[2,4,1],
  a[2,1,2], a[2,2,2], a[2,3,2], a[2,4,2])
```

in that order. a[,,] stands for the entire array, which is the same as omitting the subscripts entirely and using a alone.

For any array, say Z, the dimension vector may be referenced explicitly as dim(Z) (on either side of an assignment).

Also, if an array name is given with just *one subscript or index vector*, then the corresponding values of the data vector only are used; in this case the dimension vector is ignored. This is not the case, however, if the single index is not a vector but itself an array, as we next discuss.

Chapter 5: Arrays and matrices 19

5.3 Index matrices

As well as an index vector in any subscript position, a matrix may be used with a single *index matrix* in order either to assign a vector of quantities to an irregular collection of elements in the array, or to extract an irregular collection as a vector.

A matrix example makes the process clear. In the case of a doubly indexed array, an index matrix may be given consisting of two columns and as many rows as desired. The entries in the index matrix are the row and column indices for the doubly indexed array. Suppose for example we have a 4 by 5 array X and we wish to do the following:

- Extract elements X[1,3], X[2,2] and X[3,1] as a vector structure, and
- Replace these entries in the array X by zeroes.

In this case we need a 3 by 2 subscript array, as in the following example.

```
> x <- array(1:20, dim=c(4,5))    # Generate a 4 by 5 array.
> x
     [,1] [,2] [,3] [,4] [,5]
[1,]    1    5    9   13   17
[2,]    2    6   10   14   18
[3,]    3    7   11   15   19
[4,]    4    8   12   16   20
> i <- array(c(1:3,3:1), dim=c(3,2))
> i                               # i is a 3 by 2 index array.
     [,1] [,2]
[1,]    1    3
[2,]    2    2
[3,]    3    1
> x[i]                            # Extract those elements
[1] 9 6 3
> x[i] <- 0                       # Replace those elements by zeros.
> x
     [,1] [,2] [,3] [,4] [,5]
[1,]    1    5    0   13   17
[2,]    2    0   10   14   18
[3,]    0    7   11   15   19
[4,]    4    8   12   16   20
>
```

Negative indices are not allowed in index matrices. NA and zero values are allowed: rows in the index matrix containing a zero are ignored, and rows containing an NA produce an NA in the result.

As a less trivial example, suppose we wish to generate an (unreduced) design matrix for a block design defined by factors blocks (b levels) and varieties (v levels). Further suppose there are n plots in the experiment. We could proceed as follows:

```
> Xb <- matrix(0, n, b)
> Xv <- matrix(0, n, v)
> ib <- cbind(1:n, blocks)
> iv <- cbind(1:n, varieties)
> Xb[ib] <- 1
> Xv[iv] <- 1
> X <- cbind(Xb, Xv)
```

To construct the incidence matrix, N say, we could use

```
> N <- crossprod(Xb, Xv)
```

Chapter 5: Arrays and matrices 20

However a simpler direct way of producing this matrix is to use `table()`:

```
> N <- table(blocks, varieties)
```

Index matrices must be numerical: any other form of matrix (e.g. a logical or character matrix) supplied as a matrix is treated as an indexing vector.

5.4 The `array()` function

As well as giving a vector structure a `dim` attribute, arrays can be constructed from vectors by the `array` function, which has the form

```
> Z <- array(data_vector, dim_vector)
```

For example, if the vector h contains 24 or fewer, numbers then the command

```
> Z <- array(h, dim=c(3,4,2))
```

would use h to set up 3 by 4 by 2 array in Z. If the size of h is exactly 24 the result is the same as

```
> dim(Z) <- c(3,4,2)
```

However if h is shorter than 24, its values are recycled from the beginning again to make it up to size 24 (see Section 5.4.1 [The recycling rule], page 20). As an extreme but common example

```
> Z <- array(0, c(3,4,2))
```

makes Z an array of all zeros.

At this point `dim(Z)` stands for the dimension vector `c(3,4,2)`, and `Z[1:24]` stands for the data vector as it was in h, and `Z[]` with an empty subscript or Z with no subscript stands for the entire array as an array.

Arrays may be used in arithmetic expressions and the result is an array formed by element-by-element operations on the data vector. The `dim` attributes of operands generally need to be the same, and this becomes the dimension vector of the result. So if A, B and C are all similar arrays, then

```
> D <- 2*A*B + C + 1
```

makes D a similar array with its data vector being the result of the given element-by-element operations. However the precise rule concerning mixed array and vector calculations has to be considered a little more carefully.

5.4.1 Mixed vector and array arithmetic. The recycling rule

The precise rule affecting element by element mixed calculations with vectors and arrays is somewhat quirky and hard to find in the references. From experience we have found the following to be a reliable guide.

- The expression is scanned from left to right.
- Any short vector operands are extended by recycling their values until they match the size of any other operands.
- As long as short vectors and arrays *only* are encountered, the arrays must all have the same `dim` attribute or an error results.
- Any vector operand longer than a matrix or array operand generates an error.
- If array structures are present and no error or coercion to vector has been precipitated, the result is an array structure with the common `dim` attribute of its array operands.

5.5 The outer product of two arrays

An important operation on arrays is the *outer product*. If a and b are two numeric arrays, their outer product is an array whose dimension vector is obtained by concatenating their two dimension vectors (order is important), and whose data vector is got by forming all possible products of elements of the data vector of a with those of b. The outer product is formed by the special operator %o%:

```
> ab <- a %o% b
```

An alternative is

```
> ab <- outer(a, b, "*")
```

The multiplication function can be replaced by an arbitrary function of two variables. For example if we wished to evaluate the function $f(x; y) = \cos(y)/(1 + x^2)$ over a regular grid of values with x- and y-coordinates defined by the R vectors x and y respectively, we could proceed as follows:

```
> f <- function(x, y) cos(y)/(1 + x^2)
> z <- outer(x, y, f)
```

In particular the outer product of two ordinary vectors is a doubly subscripted array (that is a matrix, of rank at most 1). Notice that the outer product operator is of course non-commutative. Defining your own R functions will be considered further in Chapter 10 [Writing your own functions], page 42.

An example: Determinants of 2 by 2 single-digit matrices

As an artificial but cute example, consider the determinants of 2 by 2 matrices $[a, b; c, d]$ where each entry is a non-negative integer in the range $0, 1, \ldots, 9$, that is a digit.

The problem is to find the determinants, $ad - bc$, of all possible matrices of this form and represent the frequency with which each value occurs as a *high density* plot. This amounts to finding the probability distribution of the determinant if each digit is chosen independently and uniformly at random.

A neat way of doing this uses the `outer()` function twice:

```
> d <- outer(0:9, 0:9)
> fr <- table(outer(d, d, "-"))
> plot(as.numeric(names(fr)), fr, type="h",
        xlab="Determinant", ylab="Frequency")
```

Notice the coercion of the **names** attribute of the frequency table to numeric in order to recover the range of the determinant values. The "obvious" way of doing this problem with **for** loops, to be discussed in Chapter 9 [Loops and conditional execution], page 40, is so inefficient as to be impractical.

It is also perhaps surprising that about 1 in 20 such matrices is singular.

5.6 Generalized transpose of an array

The function `aperm(a, perm)` may be used to permute an array, a. The argument **perm** must be a permutation of the integers $\{1, \ldots, k\}$, where k is the number of subscripts in a. The result of the function is an array of the same size as a but with old dimension given by **perm[j]** becoming the new j-th dimension. The easiest way to think of this operation is as a generalization of transposition for matrices. Indeed if A is a matrix, (that is, a doubly subscripted array) then B given by

```
> B <- aperm(A, c(2,1))
```

is just the transpose of A. For this special case a simpler function `t()` is available, so we could have used B <- t(A).

Chapter 5: Arrays and matrices 22

5.7 Matrix facilities

As noted above, a matrix is just an array with two subscripts. However it is such an important special case it needs a separate discussion. R contains many operators and functions that are available only for matrices. For example t(X) is the matrix transpose function, as noted above. The functions nrow(A) and ncol(A) give the number of rows and columns in the matrix A respectively.

5.7.1 Matrix multiplication

The operator %*% is used for matrix multiplication. An n by 1 or 1 by n matrix may of course be used as an n-vector if in the context such is appropriate. Conversely, vectors which occur in matrix multiplication expressions are automatically promoted either to row or column vectors, whichever is multiplicatively coherent, if possible, (although this is not always unambiguously possible, as we see later).

If, for example, A and B are square matrices of the same size, then

```
> A * B
```

is the matrix of element by element products and

```
> A %*% B
```

is the matrix product. If x is a vector, then

```
> x %*% A %*% x
```

is a quadratic form.[1]

The function crossprod() forms "crossproducts", meaning that crossprod(X, y) is the same as t(X) %*% y but the operation is more efficient. If the second argument to crossprod() is omitted it is taken to be the same as the first.

The meaning of diag() depends on its argument. diag(v), where v is a vector, gives a diagonal matrix with elements of the vector as the diagonal entries. On the other hand diag(M), where M is a matrix, gives the vector of main diagonal entries of M. This is the same convention as that used for diag() in MATLAB. Also, somewhat confusingly, if k is a single numeric value then diag(k) is the k by k identity matrix!

5.7.2 Linear equations and inversion

Solving linear equations is the inverse of matrix multiplication. When after

```
> b <- A %*% x
```

only A and b are given, the vector x is the solution of that linear equation system. In R,

```
> solve(A,b)
```

solves the system, returning x (up to some accuracy loss). Note that in linear algebra, formally $x = A^{-1}b$ where A^{-1} denotes the *inverse* of A, which can be computed by

```
solve(A)
```

but rarely is needed. Numerically, it is both inefficient and potentially unstable to compute x <- solve(A) %*% b instead of solve(A,b).

The quadratic form $x'A^{-1}x$ which is used in multivariate computations, should be computed by something like[2] x %*% solve(A,x), rather than computing the inverse of A.

---

[1] Note that x %*% x is ambiguous, as it could mean either $x'x$ or xx', where x is the column form. In such cases the smaller matrix seems implicitly to be the interpretation adopted, so the scalar $x'x$ is in this case the result. The matrix xx' may be calculated either by cbind(x) %*% x or x %*% rbind(x) since the result of rbind() or cbind() is always a matrix. However, the best way to compute $x'x$ or xx' is crossprod(x) or x %o% x respectively.

[2] Even better would be to form a matrix square root B with $A = BB'$ and find the squared length of the solution of $By = x$, perhaps using the Cholesky or eigendecomposition of A.

5.7.3 Eigenvalues and eigenvectors

The function `eigen(Sm)` calculates the eigenvalues and eigenvectors of a symmetric matrix `Sm`. The result of this function is a list of two components named `values` and `vectors`. The assignment

> `> ev <- eigen(Sm)`

will assign this list to `ev`. Then `ev$val` is the vector of eigenvalues of `Sm` and `ev$vec` is the matrix of corresponding eigenvectors. Had we only needed the eigenvalues we could have used the assignment:

> `> evals <- eigen(Sm)$values`

`evals` now holds the vector of eigenvalues and the second component is discarded. If the expression

> `> eigen(Sm)`

is used by itself as a command the two components are printed, with their names. For large matrices it is better to avoid computing the eigenvectors if they are not needed by using the expression

> `> evals <- eigen(Sm, only.values = TRUE)$values`

5.7.4 Singular value decomposition and determinants

The function `svd(M)` takes an arbitrary matrix argument, `M`, and calculates the singular value decomposition of `M`. This consists of a matrix of orthonormal columns `U` with the same column space as `M`, a second matrix of orthonormal columns `V` whose column space is the row space of `M` and a diagonal matrix of positive entries `D` such that `M = U %*% D %*% t(V)`. `D` is actually returned as a vector of the diagonal elements. The result of `svd(M)` is actually a list of three components named `d`, `u` and `v`, with evident meanings.

If `M` is in fact square, then, it is not hard to see that

> `> absdetM <- prod(svd(M)$d)`

calculates the absolute value of the determinant of `M`. If this calculation were needed often with a variety of matrices it could be defined as an R function

> `> absdet <- function(M) prod(svd(M)$d)`

after which we could use `absdet()` as just another R function. As a further trivial but potentially useful example, you might like to consider writing a function, say `tr()`, to calculate the trace of a square matrix. [Hint: You will not need to use an explicit loop. Look again at the `diag()` function.]

R has a builtin function `det` to calculate a determinant, including the sign, and another, `determinant`, to give the sign and modulus (optionally on log scale),

5.7.5 Least squares fitting and the QR decomposition

The function `lsfit()` returns a list giving results of a least squares fitting procedure. An assignment such as

> `> ans <- lsfit(X, y)`

gives the results of a least squares fit where `y` is the vector of observations and `X` is the design matrix. See the help facility for more details, and also for the follow-up function `ls.diag()` for, among other things, regression diagnostics. Note that a grand mean term is automatically included and need not be included explicitly as a column of `X`. Further note that you almost always will prefer using `lm(.)` (see Section 11.2 [Linear models], page 53) to `lsfit()` for regression modelling.

Another closely related function is `qr()` and its allies. Consider the following assignments

```
> Xplus <- qr(X)
> b <- qr.coef(Xplus, y)
> fit <- qr.fitted(Xplus, y)
> res <- qr.resid(Xplus, y)
```

These compute the orthogonal projection of y onto the range of X in fit, the projection onto the orthogonal complement in res and the coefficient vector for the projection in b, that is, b is essentially the result of the MATLAB 'backslash' operator.

It is not assumed that X has full column rank. Redundancies will be discovered and removed as they are found.

This alternative is the older, low-level way to perform least squares calculations. Although still useful in some contexts, it would now generally be replaced by the statistical models features, as will be discussed in Chapter 11 [Statistical models in R], page 50.

5.8 Forming partitioned matrices, cbind() and rbind()

As we have already seen informally, matrices can be built up from other vectors and matrices by the functions cbind() and rbind(). Roughly cbind() forms matrices by binding together matrices horizontally, or column-wise, and rbind() vertically, or row-wise.

In the assignment

```
> X <- cbind(arg_1, arg_2, arg_3, ...)
```

the arguments to cbind() must be either vectors of any length, or matrices with the same column size, that is the same number of rows. The result is a matrix with the concatenated arguments arg_1, arg_2, ... forming the columns.

If some of the arguments to cbind() are vectors they may be shorter than the column size of any matrices present, in which case they are cyclically extended to match the matrix column size (or the length of the longest vector if no matrices are given).

The function rbind() does the corresponding operation for rows. In this case any vector argument, possibly cyclically extended, are of course taken as row vectors.

Suppose X1 and X2 have the same number of rows. To combine these by columns into a matrix X, together with an initial column of 1s we can use

```
> X <- cbind(1, X1, X2)
```

The result of rbind() or cbind() always has matrix status. Hence cbind(x) and rbind(x) are possibly the simplest ways explicitly to allow the vector x to be treated as a column or row matrix respectively.

5.9 The concatenation function, c(), with arrays

It should be noted that whereas cbind() and rbind() are concatenation functions that respect dim attributes, the basic c() function does not, but rather clears numeric objects of all dim and dimnames attributes. This is occasionally useful in its own right.

The official way to coerce an array back to a simple vector object is to use as.vector()

```
> vec <- as.vector(X)
```

However a similar result can be achieved by using c() with just one argument, simply for this side-effect:

```
> vec <- c(X)
```

There are slight differences between the two, but ultimately the choice between them is largely a matter of style (with the former being preferable).

5.10 Frequency tables from factors

Recall that a factor defines a partition into groups. Similarly a pair of factors defines a two way cross classification, and so on. The function `table()` allows frequency tables to be calculated from equal length factors. If there are k factor arguments, the result is a k-way array of frequencies.

Suppose, for example, that `statef` is a factor giving the state code for each entry in a data vector. The assignment

```
> statefr <- table(statef)
```

gives in `statefr` a table of frequencies of each state in the sample. The frequencies are ordered and labelled by the `levels` attribute of the factor. This simple case is equivalent to, but more convenient than,

```
> statefr <- tapply(statef, statef, length)
```

Further suppose that `incomef` is a factor giving a suitably defined "income class" for each entry in the data vector, for example with the `cut()` function:

```
> factor(cut(incomes, breaks = 35+10*(0:7))) -> incomef
```

Then to calculate a two-way table of frequencies:

```
> table(incomef,statef)
         statef
incomef   act nsw nt qld sa tas vic wa
  (35,45]   1   1  0   1  0   0   1  0
  (45,55]   1   1  1   1  2   0   1  3
  (55,65]   0   3  1   3  2   2   2  1
  (65,75]   0   1  0   0  0   0   1  0
```

Extension to higher-way frequency tables is immediate.

6 Lists and data frames

6.1 Lists

An R *list* is an object consisting of an ordered collection of objects known as its *components*.

There is no particular need for the components to be of the same mode or type, and, for example, a list could consist of a numeric vector, a logical value, a matrix, a complex vector, a character array, a function, and so on. Here is a simple example of how to make a list:

```
> Lst <- list(name="Fred", wife="Mary", no.children=3,
              child.ages=c(4,7,9))
```

Components are always *numbered* and may always be referred to as such. Thus if `Lst` is the name of a list with four components, these may be individually referred to as `Lst[[1]]`, `Lst[[2]]`, `Lst[[3]]` and `Lst[[4]]`. If, further, `Lst[[4]]` is a vector subscripted array then `Lst[[4]][1]` is its first entry.

If `Lst` is a list, then the function `length(Lst)` gives the number of (top level) components it has.

Components of lists may also be *named*, and in this case the component may be referred to either by giving the component name as a character string in place of the number in double square brackets, or, more conveniently, by giving an expression of the form

```
> name$component_name
```

for the same thing.

This is a very useful convention as it makes it easier to get the right component if you forget the number.

So in the simple example given above:

`Lst$name` is the same as `Lst[[1]]` and is the string `"Fred"`,

`Lst$wife` is the same as `Lst[[2]]` and is the string `"Mary"`,

`Lst$child.ages[1]` is the same as `Lst[[4]][1]` and is the number 4.

Additionally, one can also use the names of the list components in double square brackets, i.e., `Lst[["name"]]` is the same as `Lst$name`. This is especially useful, when the name of the component to be extracted is stored in another variable as in

```
> x <- "name"; Lst[[x]]
```

It is very important to distinguish `Lst[[1]]` from `Lst[1]`. '`[[...]]`' is the operator used to select a single element, whereas '`[...]`' is a general subscripting operator. Thus the former is the *first object in the list* `Lst`, and if it is a named list the name is *not* included. The latter is a *sublist of the list* `Lst` *consisting of the first entry only. If it is a named list, the names are transferred to the sublist.*

The names of components may be abbreviated down to the minimum number of letters needed to identify them uniquely. Thus `Lst$coefficients` may be minimally specified as `Lst$coe` and `Lst$covariance` as `Lst$cov`.

The vector of names is in fact simply an attribute of the list like any other and may be handled as such. Other structures besides lists may, of course, similarly be given a *names* attribute also.

6.2 Constructing and modifying lists

New lists may be formed from existing objects by the function `list()`. An assignment of the form

```
> Lst <- list(name_1=object_1, ..., name_m=object_m)
```

sets up a list Lst of m components using $object\_1, \ldots, object\_m$ for the components and giving them names as specified by the argument names, (which can be freely chosen). If these names are omitted, the components are numbered only. The components used to form the list are *copied* when forming the new list and the originals are not affected.

Lists, like any subscripted object, can be extended by specifying additional components. For example

```
> Lst[5] <- list(matrix=Mat)
```

6.2.1 Concatenating lists

When the concatenation function c() is given list arguments, the result is an object of mode list also, whose components are those of the argument lists joined together in sequence.

```
> list.ABC <- c(list.A, list.B, list.C)
```

Recall that with vector objects as arguments the concatenation function similarly joined together all arguments into a single vector structure. In this case all other attributes, such as dim attributes, are discarded.

6.3 Data frames

A *data frame* is a list with class "data.frame". There are restrictions on lists that may be made into data frames, namely

- The components must be vectors (numeric, character, or logical), factors, numeric matrices, lists, or other data frames.
- Matrices, lists, and data frames provide as many variables to the new data frame as they have columns, elements, or variables, respectively.
- Numeric vectors, logicals and factors are included as is, and character vectors are coerced to be factors, whose levels are the unique values appearing in the vector.
- Vector structures appearing as variables of the data frame must all have the *same length*, and matrix structures must all have the same *row size*.

A data frame may for many purposes be regarded as a matrix with columns possibly of differing modes and attributes. It may be displayed in matrix form, and its rows and columns extracted using matrix indexing conventions.

6.3.1 Making data frames

Objects satisfying the restrictions placed on the columns (components) of a data frame may be used to form one using the function data.frame:

```
> accountants <- data.frame(home=statef, loot=incomes, shot=incomef)
```

A list whose components conform to the restrictions of a data frame may be *coerced* into a data frame using the function as.data.frame()

The simplest way to construct a data frame from scratch is to use the read.table() function to read an entire data frame from an external file. This is discussed further in Chapter 7 [Reading data from files], page 30.

6.3.2 attach() and detach()

The $ notation, such as accountants$statef, for list components is not always very convenient. A useful facility would be somehow to make the components of a list or data frame temporarily visible as variables under their component name, without the need to quote the list name explicitly each time.

Chapter 6: Lists and data frames 28

The `attach()` function takes a 'database' such as a list or data frame as its argument. Thus suppose `lentils` is a data frame with three variables `lentils$u`, `lentils$v`, `lentils$w`. The attach

```
> attach(lentils)
```

places the data frame in the search path at position 2, and provided there are no variables u, v or w in position 1, u, v and w are available as variables from the data frame in their own right. At this point an assignment such as

```
> u <- v+w
```

does not replace the component u of the data frame, but rather masks it with another variable u in the working directory at position 1 on the search path. To make a permanent change to the data frame itself, the simplest way is to resort once again to the $ notation:

```
> lentils$u <- v+w
```

However the new value of component u is not visible until the data frame is detached and attached again.

To detach a data frame, use the function

```
> detach()
```

More precisely, this statement detaches from the search path the entity currently at position 2. Thus in the present context the variables u, v and w would be no longer visible, except under the list notation as `lentils$u` and so on. Entities at positions greater than 2 on the search path can be detached by giving their number to `detach`, but it is much safer to always use a name, for example by `detach(lentils)` or `detach("lentils")`

> **Note:** In R lists and data frames can only be attached at position 2 or above, and what is attached is a *copy* of the original object. You can alter the attached values *via* `assign`, but the original list or data frame is unchanged.

6.3.3 Working with data frames

A useful convention that allows you to work with many different problems comfortably together in the same working directory is

- gather together all variables for any well defined and separate problem in a data frame under a suitably informative name;
- when working with a problem attach the appropriate data frame at position 2, and use the working directory at level 1 for operational quantities and temporary variables;
- before leaving a problem, add any variables you wish to keep for future reference to the data frame using the $ form of assignment, and then `detach()`;
- finally remove all unwanted variables from the working directory and keep it as clean of left-over temporary variables as possible.

In this way it is quite simple to work with many problems in the same directory, all of which have variables named x, y and z, for example.

6.3.4 Attaching arbitrary lists

`attach()` is a generic function that allows not only directories and data frames to be attached to the search path, but other classes of object as well. In particular any object of mode `"list"` may be attached in the same way:

```
> attach(any.old.list)
```

Anything that has been attached can be detached by `detach`, by position number or, preferably, by name.

6.3.5 Managing the search path

The function `search` shows the current search path and so is a very useful way to keep track of which data frames and lists (and packages) have been attached and detached. Initially it gives

```
> search()
[1] ".GlobalEnv"    "Autoloads"      "package:base"
```

where `.GlobalEnv` is the workspace.[1]

After `lentils` is attached we have

```
> search()
[1] ".GlobalEnv"    "lentils"      "Autoloads"      "package:base"
> ls(2)
[1] "u" "v" "w"
```

and as we see `ls` (or `objects`) can be used to examine the contents of any position on the search path.

Finally, we detach the data frame and confirm it has been removed from the search path.

```
> detach("lentils")
> search()
[1] ".GlobalEnv"    "Autoloads"      "package:base"
```

---

[1] See the on-line help for `autoload` for the meaning of the second term.

7 Reading data from files

Large data objects will usually be read as values from external files rather than entered during an R session at the keyboard. R input facilities are simple and their requirements are fairly strict and even rather inflexible. There is a clear presumption by the designers of R that you will be able to modify your input files using other tools, such as file editors or Perl[1] to fit in with the requirements of R. Generally this is very simple.

If variables are to be held mainly in data frames, as we strongly suggest they should be, an entire data frame can be read directly with the **read.table()** function. There is also a more primitive input function, **scan()**, that can be called directly.

For more details on importing data into R and also exporting data, see the *R Data Import/Export* manual.

7.1 The read.table() function

To read an entire data frame directly, the external file will normally have a special form.

- The first line of the file should have a *name* for each variable in the data frame.
- Each additional line of the file has as its first item a *row label* and the values for each variable.

If the file has one fewer item in its first line than in its second, this arrangement is presumed to be in force. So the first few lines of a file to be read as a data frame might look as follows.

```
Input file form with names and row labels:

      Price    Floor    Area   Rooms   Age   Cent.heat
01    52.00    111.0     830     5     6.2      no
02    54.75    128.0     710     5     7.5      no
03    57.50    101.0    1000     5     4.2      no
04    57.50    131.0     690     6     8.8      no
05    59.75     93.0     900     5     1.9      yes
...
```

By default numeric items (except row labels) are read as numeric variables and non-numeric variables, such as Cent.heat in the example, as factors. This can be changed if necessary.

The function read.table() can then be used to read the data frame directly

```
> HousePrice <- read.table("houses.data")
```

Often you will want to omit including the row labels directly and use the default labels. In this case the file may omit the row label column as in the following.

```
Input file form without row labels:

Price    Floor    Area   Rooms   Age   Cent.heat
52.00    111.0     830     5     6.2      no
54.75    128.0     710     5     7.5      no
57.50    101.0    1000     5     4.2      no
57.50    131.0     690     6     8.8      no
59.75     93.0     900     5     1.9      yes
...
```

---

[1] Under UNIX, the utilities Sed or Awk can be used.

The data frame may then be read as

```
> HousePrice <- read.table("houses.data", header=TRUE)
```

where the `header=TRUE` option specifies that the first line is a line of headings, and hence, by implication from the form of the file, that no explicit row labels are given.

7.2 The scan() function

Suppose the data vectors are of equal length and are to be read in parallel. Further suppose that there are three vectors, the first of mode character and the remaining two of mode numeric, and the file is 'input.dat'. The first step is to use scan() to read in the three vectors as a list, as follows

```
> inp <- scan("input.dat", list("",0,0))
```

The second argument is a dummy list structure that establishes the mode of the three vectors to be read. The result, held in `inp`, is a list whose components are the three vectors read in. To separate the data items into three separate vectors, use assignments like

```
> label <- inp[[1]]; x <- inp[[2]]; y <- inp[[3]]
```

More conveniently, the dummy list can have named components, in which case the names can be used to access the vectors read in. For example

```
> inp <- scan("input.dat", list(id="", x=0, y=0))
```

If you wish to access the variables separately they may either be re-assigned to variables in the working frame:

```
> label <- inp$id; x <- inp$x; y <- inp$y
```

or the list may be attached at position 2 of the search path (see Section 6.3.4 [Attaching arbitrary lists], page 28).

If the second argument is a single value and not a list, a single vector is read in, all components of which must be of the same mode as the dummy value.

```
> X <- matrix(scan("light.dat", 0), ncol=5, byrow=TRUE)
```

There are more elaborate input facilities available and these are detailed in the manuals.

7.3 Accessing builtin datasets

Around 100 datasets are supplied with R (in package **datasets**), and others are available in packages (including the recommended packages supplied with R). To see the list of datasets currently available use

```
data()
```

As from R version 2.0.0 all the datasets supplied with R are available directly by name. However, many packages still use the earlier convention in which `data` was also used to load datasets into R, for example

```
data(infert)
```

and this can still be used with the standard packages (as in this example). In most cases this will load an R object of the same name. However, in a few cases it loads several objects, so see the on-line help for the object to see what to expect.

7.3.1 Loading data from other R packages

To access data from a particular package, use the `package` argument, for example

```
data(package="rpart")
data(Puromycin, package="datasets")
```

If a package has been attached by `library`, its datasets are automatically included in the search.

User-contributed packages can be a rich source of datasets.

7.4 Editing data

When invoked on a data frame or matrix, `edit` brings up a separate spreadsheet-like environment for editing. This is useful for making small changes once a data set has been read. The command

```
> xnew <- edit(xold)
```

will allow you to edit your data set `xold`, and on completion the changed object is assigned to `xnew`. If you want to alter the original dataset `xold`, the simplest way is to use `fix(xold)`, which is equivalent to `xold <- edit(xold)`.

Use

```
> xnew <- edit(data.frame())
```

to enter new data via the spreadsheet interface.

8 Probability distributions

8.1 R as a set of statistical tables

One convenient use of R is to provide a comprehensive set of statistical tables. Functions are provided to evaluate the cumulative distribution function $P(X \leq x)$, the probability density function and the quantile function (given q, the smallest x such that $P(X \leq x) > q$), and to simulate from the distribution.

Distribution	R name	additional arguments
beta	beta	shape1, shape2, ncp
binomial	binom	size, prob
Cauchy	cauchy	location, scale
chi-squared	chisq	df, ncp
exponential	exp	rate
F	f	df1, df2, ncp
gamma	gamma	shape, scale
geometric	geom	prob
hypergeometric	hyper	m, n, k
log-normal	lnorm	meanlog, sdlog
logistic	logis	location, scale
negative binomial	nbinom	size, prob
normal	norm	mean, sd
Poisson	pois	lambda
Student's t	t	df, ncp
uniform	unif	min, max
Weibull	weibull	shape, scale
Wilcoxon	wilcox	m, n

Prefix the name given here by 'd' for the density, 'p' for the CDF, 'q' for the quantile function and 'r' for simulation (*random* deviates). The first argument is x for d*xxx*, q for p*xxx*, p for q*xxx* and n for r*xxx* (except for **rhyper** and **rwilcox**, for which it is **nn**). In not quite all cases is the non-centrality parameter **ncp** are currently available: see the on-line help for details.

The p*xxx* and q*xxx* functions all have logical arguments **lower.tail** and **log.p** and the d*xxx* ones have **log**. This allows, e.g., getting the cumulative (or "integrated") *hazard* function, $H(t) = -\log(1 - F(t))$, by

    - pxxx(t, ..., lower.tail = FALSE, log.p = TRUE)

or more accurate log-likelihoods (by d*xxx*(..., log = TRUE)), directly.

In addition there are functions **ptukey** and **qtukey** for the distribution of the studentized range of samples from a normal distribution.

Here are some examples

```
> ## 2-tailed p-value for t distribution
> 2*pt(-2.43, df = 13)
> ## upper 1% point for an F(2, 7) distribution
> qf(0.01, 2, 7, lower.tail = FALSE)
```

8.2 Examining the distribution of a set of data

Given a (univariate) set of data we can examine its distribution in a large number of ways. The simplest is to examine the numbers. Two slightly different summaries are given by **summary** and **fivenum** and a display of the numbers by **stem** (a "stem and leaf" plot).

Chapter 8: Probability distributions   34

```
> attach(faithful)
> summary(eruptions)
   Min. 1st Qu.  Median    Mean 3rd Qu.    Max.
  1.600   2.163   4.000   3.488   4.454   5.100
> fivenum(eruptions)
[1] 1.6000 2.1585 4.0000 4.4585 5.1000
> stem(eruptions)

  The decimal point is 1 digit(s) to the left of the |

  16 | 070355555588
  18 | 000022233333335577777777888822335777888
  20 | 00002223378800035778
  22 | 0002335578023578
  24 | 00228
  26 | 23
  28 | 080
  30 | 7
  32 | 2337
  34 | 250077
  36 | 0000823577
  38 | 2333335582225577
  40 | 0000003357788888002233555577778
  42 | 03335555778800233333555577778
  44 | 02222335557780000000023333357778888
  46 | 00002333577000000023578
  48 | 00000022335800333
  50 | 0370
```

A stem-and-leaf plot is like a histogram, and R has a function `hist` to plot histograms.

```
> hist(eruptions)
## make the bins smaller, make a plot of density
> hist(eruptions, seq(1.6, 5.2, 0.2), prob=TRUE)
> lines(density(eruptions, bw=0.1))
> rug(eruptions) # show the actual data points
```

More elegant density plots can be made by `density`, and we added a line produced by `density` in this example. The bandwidth `bw` was chosen by trial-and-error as the default gives

Chapter 8: Probability distributions   35

too much smoothing (it usually does for "interesting" densities). (Better automated methods of bandwidth choice are available, and in this example `bw = "SJ"` gives a good result.)

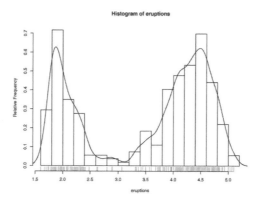

We can plot the empirical cumulative distribution function by using the function `ecdf`.

```
> plot(ecdf(eruptions), do.points=FALSE, verticals=TRUE)
```

This distribution is obviously far from any standard distribution. How about the right-hand mode, say eruptions of longer than 3 minutes? Let us fit a normal distribution and overlay the fitted CDF.

```
> long <- eruptions[eruptions > 3]
> plot(ecdf(long), do.points=FALSE, verticals=TRUE)
> x <- seq(3, 5.4, 0.01)
> lines(x, pnorm(x, mean=mean(long), sd=sqrt(var(long))), lty=3)
```

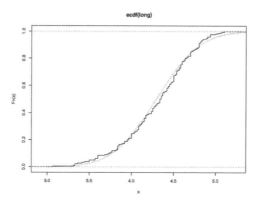

Quantile-quantile (Q-Q) plots can help us examine this more carefully.

```
par(pty="s")        # arrange for a square figure region
qqnorm(long); qqline(long)
```

Chapter 8: Probability distributions   36

which shows a reasonable fit but a shorter right tail than one would expect from a normal distribution. Let us compare this with some simulated data from a t distribution

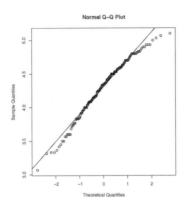

```
x <- rt(250, df = 5)
qqnorm(x); qqline(x)
```

which will usually (if it is a random sample) show longer tails than expected for a normal. We can make a Q-Q plot against the generating distribution by

```
qqplot(qt(ppoints(250), df = 5), x, xlab = "Q-Q plot for t dsn")
qqline(x)
```

Finally, we might want a more formal test of agreement with normality (or not). R provides the Shapiro-Wilk test

```
> shapiro.test(long)

        Shapiro-Wilk normality test

data:  long
W = 0.9793, p-value = 0.01052
```

and the Kolmogorov-Smirnov test

```
> ks.test(long, "pnorm", mean = mean(long), sd = sqrt(var(long)))

        One-sample Kolmogorov-Smirnov test

data:  long
D = 0.0661, p-value = 0.4284
alternative hypothesis: two.sided
```

(Note that the distribution theory is not valid here as we have estimated the parameters of the normal distribution from the same sample.)

8.3 One- and two-sample tests

So far we have compared a single sample to a normal distribution. A much more common operation is to compare aspects of two samples. Note that in R, all "classical" tests including the ones used below are in package **stats** which is normally loaded.

Consider the following sets of data on the latent heat of the fusion of ice (cal/gm) from Rice (1995, p.490)

```
Method A: 79.98 80.04 80.02 80.04 80.03 80.03 80.04 79.97
          80.05 80.03 80.02 80.00 80.02
Method B: 80.02 79.94 79.98 79.97 79.97 80.03 79.95 79.97
```
Boxplots provide a simple graphical comparison of the two samples.
```
A <- scan()
79.98 80.04 80.02 80.04 80.03 80.03 80.04 79.97
80.05 80.03 80.02 80.00 80.02

B <- scan()
80.02 79.94 79.98 79.97 79.97 80.03 79.95 79.97

boxplot(A, B)
```
which indicates that the first group tends to give higher results than the second.

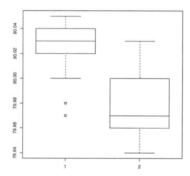

To test for the equality of the means of the two examples, we can use an *unpaired* t-test by
```
> t.test(A, B)

        Welch Two Sample t-test

data:  A and B
t = 3.2499, df = 12.027, p-value = 0.00694
alternative hypothesis: true difference in means is not equal to 0
95 percent confidence interval:
 0.01385526 0.07018320
sample estimates:
mean of x mean of y
 80.02077  79.97875
```
which does indicate a significant difference, assuming normality. By default the R function does not assume equality of variances in the two samples (in contrast to the similar S-PLUS t.test function). We can use the F test to test for equality in the variances, provided that the two samples are from normal populations.
```
> var.test(A, B)

        F test to compare two variances
```

Chapter 8: Probability distributions   38

```
data:  A and B
F = 0.5837, num df = 12, denom df =  7, p-value = 0.3938
alternative hypothesis: true ratio of variances is not equal to 1
95 percent confidence interval:
 0.1251097 2.1052687
sample estimates:
ratio of variances
          0.5837405
```

which shows no evidence of a significant difference, and so we can use the classical *t*-test that assumes equality of the variances.

```
> t.test(A, B, var.equal=TRUE)

        Two Sample t-test

data:  A and B
t = 3.4722, df = 19, p-value = 0.002551
alternative hypothesis: true difference in means is not equal to 0
95 percent confidence interval:
 0.01669058 0.06734788
sample estimates:
mean of x mean of y
 80.02077  79.97875
```

All these tests assume normality of the two samples. The two-sample Wilcoxon (or Mann-Whitney) test only assumes a common continuous distribution under the null hypothesis.

```
> wilcox.test(A, B)

        Wilcoxon rank sum test with continuity correction

data:  A and B
W = 89, p-value = 0.007497
alternative hypothesis: true location shift is not equal to 0

Warning message:
Cannot compute exact p-value with ties in: wilcox.test(A, B)
```

Note the warning: there are several ties in each sample, which suggests strongly that these data are from a discrete distribution (probably due to rounding).

There are several ways to compare graphically the two samples. We have already seen a pair of boxplots. The following

```
> plot(ecdf(A), do.points=FALSE, verticals=TRUE, xlim=range(A, B))
> plot(ecdf(B), do.points=FALSE, verticals=TRUE, add=TRUE)
```

will show the two empirical CDFs, and qqplot will perform a Q-Q plot of the two samples. The Kolmogorov-Smirnov test is of the maximal vertical distance between the two ecdf's, assuming a common continuous distribution:

```
> ks.test(A, B)

        Two-sample Kolmogorov-Smirnov test

data:  A and B
D = 0.5962, p-value = 0.05919
```

Chapter 8: Probability distributions 39

```
    alternative hypothesis: two-sided

Warning message:
cannot compute correct p-values with ties in: ks.test(A, B)
```

9 Grouping, loops and conditional execution

9.1 Grouped expressions

R is an expression language in the sense that its only command type is a function or expression which returns a result. Even an assignment is an expression whose result is the value assigned, and it may be used wherever any expression may be used; in particular multiple assignments are possible.

Commands may be grouped together in braces, {*expr_1* ; ...; *expr_m*}, in which case the value of the group is the result of the last expression in the group evaluated. Since such a group is also an expression it may, for example, be itself included in parentheses and used a part of an even larger expression, and so on.

9.2 Control statements

9.2.1 Conditional execution: if statements

The language has available a conditional construction of the form

> if (*expr_1*) *expr_2* else *expr_3*

where *expr_1* must evaluate to a single logical value and the result of the entire expression is then evident.

The "short-circuit" operators && and || are often used as part of the condition in an if statement. Whereas & and | apply element-wise to vectors, && and || apply to vectors of length one, and only evaluate their second argument if necessary.

There is a vectorized version of the if/else construct, the ifelse function. This has the form ifelse(condition, a, b) and returns a vector of the length of its longest argument, with elements a[i] if condition[i] is true, otherwise b[i].

9.2.2 Repetitive execution: for loops, repeat and while

There is also a for loop construction which has the form

> for (*name* in *expr_1*) *expr_2*

where *name* is the loop variable. *expr_1* is a vector expression, (often a sequence like 1:20), and *expr_2* is often a grouped expression with its sub-expressions written in terms of the dummy *name*. *expr_2* is repeatedly evaluated as *name* ranges through the values in the vector result of *expr_1*.

As an example, suppose ind is a vector of class indicators and we wish to produce separate plots of y versus x within classes. One possibility here is to use coplot(),[1] which will produce an array of plots corresponding to each level of the factor. Another way to do this, now putting all plots on the one display, is as follows:

```
> xc <- split(x, ind)
> yc <- split(y, ind)
> for (i in 1:length(yc)) {
    plot(xc[[i]], yc[[i]]);
    abline(lsfit(xc[[i]], yc[[i]]))
  }
```

(Note the function split() which produces a list of vectors obtained by splitting a larger vector according to the classes specified by a factor. This is a useful function, mostly used in connection with boxplots. See the help facility for further details.)

---

[1] to be discussed later, or use xyplot from package **lattice**.

Chapter 9: Grouping, loops and conditional execution   41

Warning: for() loops are used in R code much less often than in compiled languages. Code that takes a 'whole object' view is likely to be both clearer and faster in R.

Other looping facilities include the

```
> repeat expr
```

statement and the

```
> while (condition) expr
```

statement.

The break statement can be used to terminate any loop, possibly abnormally. This is the only way to terminate repeat loops.

The next statement can be used to discontinue one particular cycle and skip to the "next".

Control statements are most often used in connection with *functions* which are discussed in Chapter 10 [Writing your own functions], page 42, and where more examples will emerge.

10 Writing your own functions

As we have seen informally along the way, the R language allows the user to create objects of mode *function*. These are true R functions that are stored in a special internal form and may be used in further expressions and so on. In the process, the language gains enormously in power, convenience and elegance, and learning to write useful functions is one of the main ways to make your use of R comfortable and productive.

It should be emphasized that most of the functions supplied as part of the R system, such as `mean()`, `var()`, `postscript()` and so on, are themselves written in R and thus do not differ materially from user written functions.

A function is defined by an assignment of the form

```
> name <- function(arg_1, arg_2, ...) expression
```

The *expression* is an R expression, (usually a grouped expression), that uses the arguments, *arg_i*, to calculate a value. The value of the expression is the value returned for the function.

A call to the function then usually takes the form `name(expr_1, expr_2, ...)` and may occur anywhere a function call is legitimate.

10.1 Simple examples

As a first example, consider a function to calculate the two sample t-statistic, showing "all the steps". This is an artificial example, of course, since there are other, simpler ways of achieving the same end.

The function is defined as follows:

```
> twosam <- function(y1, y2) {
    n1  <- length(y1); n2  <- length(y2)
    yb1 <- mean(y1);   yb2 <- mean(y2)
    s1  <- var(y1);    s2  <- var(y2)
    s <- ((n1-1)*s1 + (n2-1)*s2)/(n1+n2-2)
    tst <- (yb1 - yb2)/sqrt(s*(1/n1 + 1/n2))
    tst
  }
```

With this function defined, you could perform two sample t-tests using a call such as

```
> tstat <- twosam(data$male, data$female); tstat
```

As a second example, consider a function to emulate directly the MATLAB backslash command, which returns the coefficients of the orthogonal projection of the vector y onto the column space of the matrix, X. (This is ordinarily called the least squares estimate of the regression coefficients.) This would ordinarily be done with the `qr()` function; however this is sometimes a bit tricky to use directly and it pays to have a simple function such as the following to use it safely.

Thus given a n by 1 vector y and an n by p matrix X then $X y$ is defined as $(X'X)^- X'y$, where $(X'X)^-$ is a generalized inverse of $X'X$.

```
> bslash <- function(X, y) {
  X <- qr(X)
  qr.coef(X, y)
}
```

After this object is created it may be used in statements such as

```
> regcoeff <- bslash(Xmat, yvar)
```

and so on.

The classical R function `lsfit()` does this job quite well, and more[1]. It in turn uses the functions `qr()` and `qr.coef()` in the slightly counterintuitive way above to do this part of the calculation. Hence there is probably some value in having just this part isolated in a simple to use function if it is going to be in frequent use. If so, we may wish to make it a matrix binary operator for even more convenient use.

10.2 Defining new binary operators

Had we given the `bslash()` function a different name, namely one of the form

    %anything%

it could have been used as a *binary operator* in expressions rather than in function form. Suppose, for example, we choose ! for the internal character. The function definition would then start as

```
> "%!%" <- function(X, y) { ... }
```

(Note the use of quote marks.) The function could then be used as X %!% y. (The backslash symbol itself is not a convenient choice as it presents special problems in this context.)

The matrix multiplication operator, `%*%`, and the outer product matrix operator `%o%` are other examples of binary operators defined in this way.

10.3 Named arguments and defaults

As first noted in Section 2.3 [Generating regular sequences], page 8, if arguments to called functions are given in the "*name=object*" form, they may be given in any order. Furthermore the argument sequence may begin in the unnamed, positional form, and specify named arguments after the positional arguments.

Thus if there is a function `fun1` defined by

```
> fun1 <- function(data, data.frame, graph, limit) {
    [function body omitted]
  }
```

then the function may be invoked in several ways, for example

```
> ans <- fun1(d, df, TRUE, 20)
> ans <- fun1(d, df, graph=TRUE, limit=20)
> ans <- fun1(data=d, limit=20, graph=TRUE, data.frame=df)
```

are all equivalent.

In many cases arguments can be given commonly appropriate default values, in which case they may be omitted altogether from the call when the defaults are appropriate. For example, if `fun1` were defined as

```
> fun1 <- function(data, data.frame, graph=TRUE, limit=20) { ... }
```

it could be called as

```
> ans <- fun1(d, df)
```

which is now equivalent to the three cases above, or as

```
> ans <- fun1(d, df, limit=10)
```

which changes one of the defaults.

It is important to note that defaults may be arbitrary expressions, even involving other arguments to the same function; they are not restricted to be constants as in our simple example here.

---

[1] See also the methods described in Chapter 11 [Statistical models in R], page 50

10.4 The '...' argument

Another frequent requirement is to allow one function to pass on argument settings to another. For example many graphics functions use the function `par()` and functions like `plot()` allow the user to pass on graphical parameters to `par()` to control the graphical output. (See Section 12.4.1 [The par() function], page 67, for more details on the `par()` function.) This can be done by including an extra argument, literally '...', of the function, which may then be passed on. An outline example is given below.

```
fun1 <- function(data, data.frame, graph=TRUE, limit=20, ...) {
  [omitted statements]
  if (graph)
    par(pch="*", ...)
  [more omissions]
}
```

10.5 Assignments within functions

Note that *any ordinary assignments done within the function are local and temporary and are lost after exit from the function.* Thus the assignment X <- qr(X) does not affect the value of the argument in the calling program.

To understand completely the rules governing the scope of R assignments the reader needs to be familiar with the notion of an evaluation *frame*. This is a somewhat advanced, though hardly difficult, topic and is not covered further here.

If global and permanent assignments are intended within a function, then either the "superassignment" operator, `<<-` or the function `assign()` can be used. See the `help` document for details. S-PLUS users should be aware that `<<-` has different semantics in R. These are discussed further in Section 10.7 [Scope], page 46.

10.6 More advanced examples

10.6.1 Efficiency factors in block designs

As a more complete, if a little pedestrian, example of a function, consider finding the efficiency factors for a block design. (Some aspects of this problem have already been discussed in Section 5.3 [Index matrices], page 19.)

A block design is defined by two factors, say `blocks` (b levels) and `varieties` (v levels). If R and K are the v by v and b by b *replications* and *block size* matrices, respectively, and N is the b by v incidence matrix, then the efficiency factors are defined as the eigenvalues of the matrix

$$E = I_v - R^{-1/2}N'K^{-1}NR^{-1/2} = I_v - A'A,$$

where $A = K^{-1/2}NR^{-1/2}$. One way to write the function is given below.

```
> bdeff <- function(blocks, varieties) {
    blocks <- as.factor(blocks)             # minor safety move
    b <- length(levels(blocks))
    varieties <- as.factor(varieties)       # minor safety move
    v <- length(levels(varieties))
    K <- as.vector(table(blocks))           # remove dim attr
    R <- as.vector(table(varieties))        # remove dim attr
    N <- table(blocks, varieties)
    A <- 1/sqrt(K) * N * rep(1/sqrt(R), rep(b, v))
    sv <- svd(A)
    list(eff=1 - sv$d^2, blockcv=sv$u, varietycv=sv$v)
```

```
  }
```

It is numerically slightly better to work with the singular value decomposition on this occasion rather than the eigenvalue routines.

The result of the function is a list giving not only the efficiency factors as the first component, but also the block and variety canonical contrasts, since sometimes these give additional useful qualitative information.

10.6.2 Dropping all names in a printed array

For printing purposes with large matrices or arrays, it is often useful to print them in close block form without the array names or numbers. Removing the `dimnames` attribute will not achieve this effect, but rather the array must be given a `dimnames` attribute consisting of empty strings. For example to print a matrix, `X`

```
> temp <- X
> dimnames(temp) <- list(rep("", nrow(X)), rep("", ncol(X)))
> temp; rm(temp)
```

This can be much more conveniently done using a function, `no.dimnames()`, shown below, as a "wrap around" to achieve the same result. It also illustrates how some effective and useful user functions can be quite short.

```
no.dimnames <- function(a) {
  ## Remove all dimension names from an array for compact printing.
  d <- list()
  l <- 0
  for(i in dim(a)) {
    d[[l <- l + 1]] <- rep("", i)
  }
  dimnames(a) <- d
  a
}
```

With this function defined, an array may be printed in close format using

```
> no.dimnames(X)
```

This is particularly useful for large integer arrays, where patterns are the real interest rather than the values.

10.6.3 Recursive numerical integration

Functions may be recursive, and may themselves define functions within themselves. Note, however, that such functions, or indeed variables, are not inherited by called functions in higher evaluation frames as they would be if they were on the search path.

The example below shows a naive way of performing one-dimensional numerical integration. The integrand is evaluated at the end points of the range and in the middle. If the one-panel trapezium rule answer is close enough to the two panel, then the latter is returned as the value. Otherwise the same process is recursively applied to each panel. The result is an adaptive integration process that concentrates function evaluations in regions where the integrand is farthest from linear. There is, however, a heavy overhead, and the function is only competitive with other algorithms when the integrand is both smooth and very difficult to evaluate.

The example is also given partly as a little puzzle in R programming.

```
area <- function(f, a, b, eps = 1.0e-06, lim = 10) {
  fun1 <- function(f, a, b, fa, fb, a0, eps, lim, fun) {
    ## function 'fun1' is only visible inside 'area'
    d <- (a + b)/2
```

```
      h <- (b - a)/4
      fd <- f(d)
      a1 <- h * (fa + fd)
      a2 <- h * (fd + fb)
      if(abs(a0 - a1 - a2) < eps || lim == 0)
        return(a1 + a2)
      else {
        return(fun(f, a, d, fa, fd, a1, eps, lim - 1, fun) +
               fun(f, d, b, fd, fb, a2, eps, lim - 1, fun))
      }
    }
    fa <- f(a)
    fb <- f(b)
    a0 <- ((fa + fb) * (b - a))/2
    fun1(f, a, b, fa, fb, a0, eps, lim, fun1)
  }
```

10.7 Scope

The discussion in this section is somewhat more technical than in other parts of this document. However, it details one of the major differences between S-PLUS and R.

The symbols which occur in the body of a function can be divided into three classes; formal parameters, local variables and free variables. The formal parameters of a function are those occurring in the argument list of the function. Their values are determined by the process of *binding* the actual function arguments to the formal parameters. Local variables are those whose values are determined by the evaluation of expressions in the body of the functions. Variables which are not formal parameters or local variables are called free variables. Free variables become local variables if they are assigned to. Consider the following function definition.

```
    f <- function(x) {
      y <- 2*x
      print(x)
      print(y)
      print(z)
    }
```

In this function, x is a formal parameter, y is a local variable and z is a free variable.

In R the free variable bindings are resolved by first looking in the environment in which the function was created. This is called *lexical scope*. First we define a function called cube.

```
    cube <- function(n) {
      sq <- function() n*n
      n*sq()
    }
```

The variable n in the function sq is not an argument to that function. Therefore it is a free variable and the scoping rules must be used to ascertain the value that is to be associated with it. Under static scope (S-PLUS) the value is that associated with a global variable named n. Under lexical scope (R) it is the parameter to the function cube since that is the active binding for the variable n at the time the function sq was defined. The difference between evaluation in R and evaluation in S-PLUS is that S-PLUS looks for a global variable called n while R first looks for a variable called n in the environment created when cube was invoked.

```
    ## first evaluation in S
    S> cube(2)
    Error in sq(): Object "n" not found
```

```
Dumped
S> n <- 3
S> cube(2)
[1] 18
## then the same function evaluated in R
R> cube(2)
[1] 8
```

Lexical scope can also be used to give functions *mutable state*. In the following example we show how R can be used to mimic a bank account. A functioning bank account needs to have a balance or total, a function for making withdrawals, a function for making deposits and a function for stating the current balance. We achieve this by creating the three functions within `account` and then returning a list containing them. When `account` is invoked it takes a numerical argument `total` and returns a list containing the three functions. Because these functions are defined in an environment which contains `total`, they will have access to its value.

The special assignment operator, `<<-`, is used to change the value associated with `total`. This operator looks back in enclosing environments for an environment that contains the symbol `total` and when it finds such an environment it replaces the value, in that environment, with the value of right hand side. If the global or top-level environment is reached without finding the symbol `total` then that variable is created and assigned to there. For most users `<<-` creates a global variable and assigns the value of the right hand side to it[2]. Only when `<<-` has been used in a function that was returned as the value of another function will the special behavior described here occur.

```
open.account <- function(total) {
  list(
    deposit = function(amount) {
      if(amount <= 0)
        stop("Deposits must be positive!\n")
      total <<- total + amount
      cat(amount, "deposited.  Your balance is", total, "\n\n")
    },
    withdraw = function(amount) {
      if(amount > total)
        stop("You don't have that much money!\n")
      total <<- total - amount
      cat(amount, "withdrawn.  Your balance is", total, "\n\n")
    },
    balance = function() {
      cat("Your balance is", total, "\n\n")
    }
  )
}

ross <- open.account(100)
robert <- open.account(200)

ross$withdraw(30)
ross$balance()
robert$balance()
```

---

[2] In some sense this mimics the behavior in S-PLUS since in S-PLUS this operator always creates or assigns to a global variable.

```
ross$deposit(50)
ross$balance()
ross$withdraw(500)
```

10.8 Customizing the environment

Users can customize their environment in several different ways. There is a site initialization file and every directory can have its own special initialization file. Finally, the special functions .First and .Last can be used.

The location of the site initialization file is taken from the value of the R_PROFILE environment variable. If that variable is unset, the file 'Rprofile.site' in the R home subdirectory 'etc' is used. This file should contain the commands that you want to execute every time R is started under your system. A second, personal, profile file named '.Rprofile'[3] can be placed in any directory. If R is invoked in that directory then that file will be sourced. This file gives individual users control over their workspace and allows for different startup procedures in different working directories. If no '.Rprofile' file is found in the startup directory, then R looks for a '.Rprofile' file in the user's home directory and uses that (if it exists).

Any function named .First() in either of the two profile files or in the '.RData' image has a special status. It is automatically performed at the beginning of an R session and may be used to initialize the environment. For example, the definition in the example below alters the prompt to $ and sets up various other useful things that can then be taken for granted in the rest of the session.

Thus, the sequence in which files are executed is, 'Rprofile.site', '.Rprofile', '.RData' and then .First(). A definition in later files will mask definitions in earlier files.

```
> .First <- function() {
    options(prompt="$ ", continue="+\t")   # $ is the prompt
    options(digits=5, length=999)          # custom numbers and printout
    x11()                                  # for graphics
    par(pch = "+")                         # plotting character
    source(file.path(Sys.getenv("HOME"), "R", "mystuff.R"))
                                           # my personal functions
    library(MASS)                          # attach a package
}
```

Similarly a function .Last(), if defined, is (normally) executed at the very end of the session. An example is given below.

```
> .Last <- function() {
    graphics.off()                         # a small safety measure.
    cat(paste(date(),"\nAdios\n"))         # Is it time for lunch?
}
```

10.9 Classes, generic functions and object orientation

The class of an object determines how it will be treated by what are known as *generic* functions. Put the other way round, a generic function performs a task or action on its arguments *specific to the class of the argument itself*. If the argument lacks any class attribute, or has a class not catered for specifically by the generic function in question, there is always a *default action* provided.

An example makes things clearer. The class mechanism offers the user the facility of designing and writing generic functions for special purposes. Among the other generic functions are plot()

---

[3] So it is hidden under UNIX.

for displaying objects graphically, summary() for summarizing analyses of various types, and anova() for comparing statistical models.

The number of generic functions that can treat a class in a specific way can be quite large. For example, the functions that can accommodate in some fashion objects of class "data.frame" include

```
[       [[<-     any     as.matrix
[<-     mean     plot    summary
```

A currently complete list can be got by using the methods() function:

```
> methods(class="data.frame")
```

Conversely the number of classes a generic function can handle can also be quite large. For example the plot() function has a default method and variants for objects of classes "data.frame", "density", "factor", and more. A complete list can be got again by using the methods() function:

```
> methods(plot)
```

For many generic functions the function body is quite short, for example

```
> coef
function (object, ...)
UseMethod("coef")
```

The presence of UseMethod indicates this is a generic function. To see what methods are available we can use methods()

```
> methods(coef)
[1] coef.aov*          coef.Arima*       coef.default*     coef.listof*
[5] coef.nls*          coef.summary.nls*

      Non-visible functions are asterisked
```

In this example there are six methods, none of which can be seen by typing its name. We can read these by either of

```
> getAnywhere("coef.aov")
A single object matching 'coef.aov' was found
It was found in the following places
  registered S3 method for coef from namespace stats
  namespace:stats
with value

function (object, ...)
{
    z <- object$coef
    z[!is.na(z)]
}

> getS3method("coef", "aov")
function (object, ...)
{
    z <- object$coef
    z[!is.na(z)]
}
```

The reader is referred to the *R Language Definition* for a more complete discussion of this mechanism.

11 Statistical models in R

This section presumes the reader has some familiarity with statistical methodology, in particular with regression analysis and the analysis of variance. Later we make some rather more ambitious presumptions, namely that something is known about generalized linear models and nonlinear regression.

The requirements for fitting statistical models are sufficiently well defined to make it possible to construct general tools that apply in a broad spectrum of problems.

R provides an interlocking suite of facilities that make fitting statistical models very simple. As we mention in the introduction, the basic output is minimal, and one needs to ask for the details by calling extractor functions.

11.1 Defining statistical models; formulae

The template for a statistical model is a linear regression model with independent, homoscedastic errors

$$y_i = \sum_{j=0}^{p} \beta_j x_{ij} + e_i, \qquad e_i \sim \mathrm{NID}(0, \sigma^2), \qquad i = 1, \dots, n$$

In matrix terms this would be written

$$y = X\beta + e$$

where the y is the response vector, X is the *model matrix* or *design matrix* and has columns $x_0, x_1, \dots, x_p$, the determining variables. Very often x_0 will be a column of ones defining an *intercept* term.

Examples

Before giving a formal specification, a few examples may usefully set the picture.

Suppose y, x, x0, x1, x2, . . . are numeric variables, X is a matrix and A, B, C, . . . are factors. The following formulae on the left side below specify statistical models as described on the right.

y ~ x
y ~ 1 + x   Both imply the same simple linear regression model of y on x. The first has an implicit intercept term, and the second an explicit one.

y ~ 0 + x
y ~ -1 + x
y ~ x - 1   Simple linear regression of y on x through the origin (that is, without an intercept term).

log(y) ~ x1 + x2
              Multiple regression of the transformed variable, $\log(y)$, on $x1$ and $x2$ (with an implicit intercept term).

y ~ poly(x,2)
y ~ 1 + x + I(x^2)
              Polynomial regression of y on x of degree 2. The first form uses orthogonal polynomials, and the second uses explicit powers, as basis.

y ~ X + poly(x,2)
              Multiple regression y with model matrix consisting of the matrix X as well as polynomial terms in x to degree 2.

Chapter 11: Statistical models in R   51

y ˜ A   Single classification analysis of variance model of y, with classes determined by A.

y ˜ A + x   Single classification analysis of covariance model of y, with classes determined by
             A, and with covariate x.

y ˜ A*B
y ˜ A + B + A:B
y ˜ B %in% A
y ˜ A/B   Two factor non-additive model of y on A and B. The first two specify the same
             crossed classification and the second two specify the same nested classification. In
             abstract terms all four specify the same model subspace.

y ˜ (A + B + C)^2
y ˜ A*B*C - A:B:C
             Three factor experiment but with a model containing main effects and two factor
             interactions only. Both formulae specify the same model.

y ˜ A * x
y ˜ A/x
y ˜ A/(1 + x) - 1
             Separate simple linear regression models of y on x within the levels of A, with
             different codings. The last form produces explicit estimates of as many different
             intercepts and slopes as there are levels in A.

y ˜ A*B + Error(C)
             An experiment with two treatment factors, A and B, and error strata determined
             by factor C. For example a split plot experiment, with whole plots (and hence also
             subplots), determined by factor C.

The operator ˜ is used to define a *model formula* in R. The form, for an ordinary linear
model, is

    response ˜ op_1 term_1 op_2 term_2 op_3 term_3 ...

where

response   is a vector or matrix, (or expression evaluating to a vector or matrix) defining the
             response variable(s).

op_i   is an operator, either + or -, implying the inclusion or exclusion of a term in the
             model, (the first is optional).

term_i   is either

             • a vector or matrix expression, or 1,

             • a factor, or

             • a *formula expression* consisting of factors, vectors or matrices connected by
               formula operators.

             In all cases each term defines a collection of columns either to be added to or
             removed from the model matrix. A 1 stands for an intercept column and is by
             default included in the model matrix unless explicitly removed.

The *formula operators* are similar in effect to the Wilkinson and Rogers notation used by
such programs as Glim and Genstat. One inevitable change is that the operator '.' becomes ':'
since the period is a valid name character in R.

The notation is summarized below (based on Chambers & Hastie, 1992, p.29):

Y ˜ M Y is modeled as M.

M_1 + M_2   Include M_1 and M_2.

Chapter 11: Statistical models in R 52

M_1 - M_2 Include *M_1* leaving out terms of *M_2*.

M_1 : M_2 The tensor product of *M_1* and *M_2*. If both terms are factors, then the "subclasses" factor.

M_1 %in% M_2
　　　　Similar to *M_1:M_2*, but with a different coding.

*M_1 * M_2* *M_1 + M_2 + M_1:M_2*.

M_1 / M_2 *M_1 + M_2 %in% M_1*.

M^n All terms in *M* together with "interactions" up to order *n*

I(M) Insulate *M*. Inside *M* all operators have their normal arithmetic meaning, and that term appears in the model matrix.

Note that inside the parentheses that usually enclose function arguments all operators have their normal arithmetic meaning. The function I() is an identity function used to allow terms in model formulae to be defined using arithmetic operators.

Note particularly that the model formulae specify the *columns of the model matrix*, the specification of the parameters being implicit. This is not the case in other contexts, for example in specifying nonlinear models.

11.1.1 Contrasts

We need at least some idea how the model formulae specify the columns of the model matrix. This is easy if we have continuous variables, as each provides one column of the model matrix (and the intercept will provide a column of ones if included in the model).

What about a k-level factor A? The answer differs for unordered and ordered factors. For *unordered* factors $k - 1$ columns are generated for the indicators of the second, ..., kth levels of the factor. (Thus the implicit parameterization is to contrast the response at each level with that at the first.) For *ordered* factors the $k - 1$ columns are the orthogonal polynomials on $1, \ldots, k$, omitting the constant term.

Although the answer is already complicated, it is not the whole story. First, if the intercept is omitted in a model that contains a factor term, the first such term is encoded into k columns giving the indicators for all the levels. Second, the whole behavior can be changed by the options setting for contrasts. The default setting in R is

```
options(contrasts = c("contr.treatment", "contr.poly"))
```

The main reason for mentioning this is that R and S have different defaults for unordered factors, S using Helmert contrasts. So if you need to compare your results to those of a textbook or paper which used S-PLUS, you will need to set

```
options(contrasts = c("contr.helmert", "contr.poly"))
```

This is a deliberate difference, as treatment contrasts (R's default) are thought easier for newcomers to interpret.

We have still not finished, as the contrast scheme to be used can be set for each term in the model using the functions contrasts and C.

We have not yet considered interaction terms: these generate the products of the columns introduced for their component terms.

Although the details are complicated, model formulae in R will normally generate the models that an expert statistician would expect, provided that marginality is preserved. Fitting, for example, a model with an interaction but not the corresponding main effects will in general lead to surprising results, and is for experts only.

11.2 Linear models

The basic function for fitting ordinary multiple models is `lm()`, and a streamlined version of the call is as follows:

```
> fitted.model <- lm(formula, data = data.frame)
```

For example

```
> fm2 <- lm(y ~ x1 + x2, data = production)
```

would fit a multiple regression model of y on $x1$ and $x2$ (with implicit intercept term).

The important (but technically optional) parameter `data = production` specifies that any variables needed to construct the model should come first from the `production` *data frame*. *This is the case regardless of whether data frame* `production` *has been attached on the search path or not.*

11.3 Generic functions for extracting model information

The value of `lm()` is a fitted model object; technically a list of results of class `"lm"`. Information about the fitted model can then be displayed, extracted, plotted and so on by using generic functions that orient themselves to objects of class `"lm"`. These include

add1	deviance	formula	predict	step
alias	drop1	kappa	print	summary
anova	effects	labels	proj	vcov
coef	family	plot	residuals	

A brief description of the most commonly used ones is given below.

`anova(object_1, object_2)`
> Compare a submodel with an outer model and produce an analysis of variance table.

`coef(object)`
> Extract the regression coefficient (matrix).
>
> Long form: `coefficients(object)`.

`deviance(object)`
> Residual sum of squares, weighted if appropriate.

`formula(object)`
> Extract the model formula.

`plot(object)`
> Produce four plots, showing residuals, fitted values and some diagnostics.

`predict(object, newdata=data.frame)`
> The data frame supplied must have variables specified with the same labels as the original. The value is a vector or matrix of predicted values corresponding to the determining variable values in *data.frame*.

`print(object)`
> Print a concise version of the object. Most often used implicitly.

`residuals(object)`
> Extract the (matrix of) residuals, weighted as appropriate.
>
> Short form: `resid(object)`.

`step(object)`
> Select a suitable model by adding or dropping terms and preserving hierarchies. The model with the smallest value of AIC (Akaike's An Information Criterion) discovered in the stepwise search is returned.

```
summary(object)
```
        Print a comprehensive summary of the results of the regression analysis.

```
vcov(object)
```
        Returns the variance-covariance matrix of the main parameters of a fitted model object.

11.4 Analysis of variance and model comparison

The model fitting function `aov(formula, data=data.frame)` operates at the simplest level in a very similar way to the function `lm()`, and most of the generic functions listed in the table in Section 11.3 [Generic functions for extracting model information], page 53 apply.

It should be noted that in addition `aov()` allows an analysis of models with multiple error strata such as split plot experiments, or balanced incomplete block designs with recovery of inter-block information. The model formula

    response ~ mean.formula + Error(*strata.formula*)

specifies a multi-stratum experiment with error strata defined by the *strata.formula*. In the simplest case, *strata.formula* is simply a factor, when it defines a two strata experiment, namely between and within the levels of the factor.

For example, with all determining variables factors, a model formula such as that in:

```
> fm <- aov(yield ~ v + n*p*k + Error(farms/blocks), data=farm.data)
```

would typically be used to describe an experiment with mean model v + n*p*k and three error strata, namely "between farms", "within farms, between blocks" and "within blocks".

11.4.1 ANOVA tables

Note also that the analysis of variance table (or tables) are for a sequence of fitted models. The sums of squares shown are the decrease in the residual sums of squares resulting from an inclusion of *that term* in the model at *that place* in the sequence. Hence only for orthogonal experiments will the order of inclusion be inconsequential.

For multistratum experiments the procedure is first to project the response onto the error strata, again in sequence, and to fit the mean model to each projection. For further details, see Chambers & Hastie (1992).

A more flexible alternative to the default full ANOVA table is to compare two or more models directly using the `anova()` function.

```
> anova(fitted.model.1, fitted.model.2, ...)
```

The display is then an ANOVA table showing the differences between the fitted models when fitted in sequence. The fitted models being compared would usually be an hierarchical sequence, of course. This does not give different information to the default, but rather makes it easier to comprehend and control.

11.5 Updating fitted models

The `update()` function is largely a convenience function that allows a model to be fitted that differs from one previously fitted usually by just a few additional or removed terms. Its form is

```
> new.model <- update(old.model, new.formula)
```

In the *new.formula* the special name consisting of a period, '.', only, can be used to stand for "the corresponding part of the old model formula". For example,

```
> fm05 <- lm(y ~ x1 + x2 + x3 + x4 + x5, data = production)
> fm6  <- update(fm05, . ~ . + x6)
> smf6 <- update(fm6, sqrt(.) ~ .)
```

would fit a five variate multiple regression with variables (presumably) from the data frame `production`, fit an additional model including a sixth regressor variable, and fit a variant on the model where the response had a square root transform applied.

Note especially that if the `data=` argument is specified on the original call to the model fitting function, this information is passed on through the fitted model object to `update()` and its allies.

The name '`.`' can also be used in other contexts, but with slightly different meaning. For example

```
> fmfull <- lm(y ~ . , data = production)
```

would fit a model with response y and regressor variables *all other variables in the data frame* `production`.

Other functions for exploring incremental sequences of models are `add1()`, `drop1()` and `step()`. The names of these give a good clue to their purpose, but for full details see the on-line help.

11.6 Generalized linear models

Generalized linear modeling is a development of linear models to accommodate both non-normal response distributions and transformations to linearity in a clean and straightforward way. A generalized linear model may be described in terms of the following sequence of assumptions:

- There is a response, y, of interest and stimulus variables x_1, x_2, ..., whose values influence the distribution of the response.

- The stimulus variables influence the distribution of y through *a single linear function, only.* This linear function is called the *linear predictor*, and is usually written

$$\eta = \beta_1 x_1 + \beta_2 x_2 + \cdots + \beta_p x_p,$$

hence x_i has no influence on the distribution of y if and only if $\beta_i = 0$.

- The distribution of y is of the form

$$f_Y(y; \mu, \varphi) = \exp\left[\frac{A}{\varphi}\left\{y\lambda(\mu) - \gamma\left(\lambda(\mu)\right)\right\} + \tau(y, \varphi)\right]$$

where φ is a *scale parameter* (possibly known), and is constant for all observations, A represents a prior weight, assumed known but possibly varying with the observations, and μ is the mean of y. So it is assumed that the distribution of y is determined by its mean and possibly a scale parameter as well.

- The mean, μ, is a smooth invertible function of the linear predictor:

$$\mu = m(\eta), \qquad \eta = m^{-1}(\mu) = \ell(\mu)$$

and this inverse function, $\ell()$, is called the *link function*.

These assumptions are loose enough to encompass a wide class of models useful in statistical practice, but tight enough to allow the development of a unified methodology of estimation and inference, at least approximately. The reader is referred to any of the current reference works on the subject for full details, such as McCullagh & Nelder (1989) or Dobson (1990).

11.6.1 Families

The class of generalized linear models handled by facilities supplied in R includes *gaussian*, *binomial*, *poisson*, *inverse gaussian* and *gamma* response distributions and also *quasi-likelihood* models where the response distribution is not explicitly specified. In the latter case the *variance function* must be specified as a function of the mean, but in other cases this function is implied by the response distribution.

Each response distribution admits a variety of link functions to connect the mean with the linear predictor. Those automatically available are shown in the following table:

Family name	Link functions
binomial	logit, probit, log, cloglog
gaussian	identity, log, inverse
Gamma	identity, inverse, log
inverse.gaussian	1/mu^2, identity, inverse, log
poisson	identity, log, sqrt
quasi	logit, probit, cloglog, identity, inverse, log, 1/mu^2, sqrt

The combination of a response distribution, a link function and various other pieces of information that are needed to carry out the modeling exercise is called the *family* of the generalized linear model.

11.6.2 The glm() function

Since the distribution of the response depends on the stimulus variables through a single linear function *only*, the same mechanism as was used for linear models can still be used to specify the linear part of a generalized model. The family has to be specified in a different way.

The R function to fit a generalized linear model is glm() which uses the form

```
> fitted.model <- glm(formula, family=family.generator, data=data.frame)
```

The only new feature is the *family.generator*, which is the instrument by which the family is described. It is the name of a function that generates a list of functions and expressions that together define and control the model and estimation process. Although this may seem a little complicated at first sight, its use is quite simple.

The names of the standard, supplied family generators are given under "Family Name" in the table in Section 11.6.1 [Families], page 56. Where there is a choice of links, the name of the link may also be supplied with the family name, in parentheses as a parameter. In the case of the **quasi** family, the variance function may also be specified in this way.

Some examples make the process clear.

The gaussian family

A call such as

```
> fm <- glm(y ~ x1 + x2, family = gaussian, data = sales)
```

achieves the same result as

```
> fm <- lm(y ~ x1+x2, data=sales)
```

but much less efficiently. Note how the gaussian family is not automatically provided with a choice of links, so no parameter is allowed. If a problem requires a gaussian family with a nonstandard link, this can usually be achieved through the **quasi** family, as we shall see later.

The binomial family

Consider a small, artificial example, from Silvey (1970).

On the Aegean island of Kalythos the male inhabitants suffer from a congenital eye disease, the effects of which become more marked with increasing age. Samples of islander males of various ages were tested for blindness and the results recorded. The data is shown below:

Age:	20	35	45	55	70
No. tested:	50	50	50	50	50
No. blind:	6	17	26	37	44

The problem we consider is to fit both logistic and probit models to this data, and to estimate for each model the LD50, that is the age at which the chance of blindness for a male inhabitant is 50%.

If y is the number of blind at age x and n the number tested, both models have the form

$$y \sim B(n, F(\beta_0 + \beta_1 x))$$

where for the probit case, $F(z) = \Phi(z)$ is the standard normal distribution function, and in the logit case (the default), $F(z) = e^z/(1 + e^z)$. In both cases the LD50 is

$$LD50 = -\beta_0/\beta_1$$

that is, the point at which the argument of the distribution function is zero.

The first step is to set the data up as a data frame

```
> kalythos <- data.frame(x = c(20,35,45,55,70), n = rep(50,5),
                         y = c(6,17,26,37,44))
```

To fit a binomial model using glm() there are three possibilities for the response:

- If the response is a *vector* it is assumed to hold *binary* data, and so must be a 0/1 vector.
- If the response is a *two-column matrix* it is assumed that the first column holds the number of successes for the trial and the second holds the number of failures.
- If the response is a *factor*, its first level is taken as failure (0) and all other levels as 'success' (1).

Here we need the second of these conventions, so we add a matrix to our data frame:

```
> kalythos$Ymat <- cbind(kalythos$y, kalythos$n - kalythos$y)
```

To fit the models we use

```
> fmp <- glm(Ymat ~ x, family = binomial(link=probit), data = kalythos)
> fml <- glm(Ymat ~ x, family = binomial, data = kalythos)
```

Since the logit link is the default the parameter may be omitted on the second call. To see the results of each fit we could use

```
> summary(fmp)
> summary(fml)
```

Both models fit (all too) well. To find the LD50 estimate we can use a simple function:

```
> ld50 <- function(b) -b[1]/b[2]
> ldp <- ld50(coef(fmp)); ldl <- ld50(coef(fml)); c(ldp, ldl)
```

The actual estimates from this data are 43.663 years and 43.601 years respectively.

Poisson models

With the Poisson family the default link is the `log`, and in practice the major use of this family is to fit surrogate Poisson log-linear models to frequency data, whose actual distribution is often multinomial. This is a large and important subject we will not discuss further here. It even forms a major part of the use of non-gaussian generalized models overall.

Occasionally genuinely Poisson data arises in practice and in the past it was often analyzed as gaussian data after either a log or a square-root transformation. As a graceful alternative to the latter, a Poisson generalized linear model may be fitted as in the following example:

```
> fmod <- glm(y ~ A + B + x, family = poisson(link=sqrt),
              data = worm.counts)
```

Quasi-likelihood models

For all families the variance of the response will depend on the mean and will have the scale parameter as a multiplier. The form of dependence of the variance on the mean is a characteristic of the response distribution; for example for the poisson distribution $\text{Var}[y] = \mu$.

For quasi-likelihood estimation and inference the precise response distribution is not specified, but rather only a link function and the form of the variance function as it depends on the mean. Since quasi-likelihood estimation uses formally identical techniques to those for the gaussian distribution, this family provides a way of fitting gaussian models with non-standard link functions or variance functions, incidentally.

For example, consider fitting the non-linear regression

$$y = \frac{\theta_1 z_1}{z_2 - \theta_2} + e$$

which may be written alternatively as

$$y = \frac{1}{\beta_1 x_1 + \beta_2 x_2} + e$$

where $x_1 = z_2/z_1$, $x_2 = -1/z_1$, $\beta_1 = 1/\theta_1$ and $\beta_2 = \theta_2/\theta_1$. Supposing a suitable data frame to be set up we could fit this non-linear regression as

```
> nlfit <- glm(y ~ x1 + x2 - 1,
               family = quasi(link=inverse, variance=constant),
               data = biochem)
```

The reader is referred to the manual and the help document for further information, as needed.

11.7 Nonlinear least squares and maximum likelihood models

Certain forms of nonlinear model can be fitted by Generalized Linear Models (glm()). But in the majority of cases we have to approach the nonlinear curve fitting problem as one of nonlinear optimization. R's nonlinear optimization routines are optim(), nlm() and (from R 2.2.0) nlminb(), which provide the functionality (and more) of S-PLUS's ms() and nlminb(). We seek the parameter values that minimize some index of lack-of-fit, and they do this by trying out various parameter values iteratively. Unlike linear regression for example, there is no guarantee that the procedure will converge on satisfactory estimates. All the methods require initial guesses about what parameter values to try, and convergence may depend critically upon the quality of the starting values.

11.7.1 Least squares

One way to fit a nonlinear model is by minimizing the sum of the squared errors (SSE) or residuals. This method makes sense if the observed errors could have plausibly arisen from a normal distribution.

Here is an example from Bates & Watts (1988), page 51. The data are:

```
> x <- c(0.02, 0.02, 0.06, 0.06, 0.11, 0.11, 0.22, 0.22, 0.56, 0.56,
         1.10, 1.10)
> y <- c(76, 47, 97, 107, 123, 139, 159, 152, 191, 201, 207, 200)
```

The model to be fitted is:

```
> fn <- function(p) sum((y - (p[1] * x)/(p[2] + x))^2)
```

In order to do the fit we need initial estimates of the parameters. One way to find sensible starting values is to plot the data, guess some parameter values, and superimpose the model curve using those values.

```
> plot(x, y)
> xfit <- seq(.02, 1.1, .05)
> yfit <- 200 * xfit/(0.1 + xfit)
> lines(spline(xfit, yfit))
```

We could do better, but these starting values of 200 and 0.1 seem adequate. Now do the fit:

```
> out <- nlm(fn, p = c(200, 0.1), hessian = TRUE)
```

After the fitting, out$minimum is the SSE, and out$estimate are the least squares estimates of the parameters. To obtain the approximate standard errors (SE) of the estimates we do:

```
> sqrt(diag(2*out$minimum/(length(y) - 2) * solve(out$hessian)))
```

The 2 in the line above represents the number of parameters. A 95% confidence interval would be the parameter estimate ± 1.96 SE. We can superimpose the least squares fit on a new plot:

```
> plot(x, y)
> xfit <- seq(.02, 1.1, .05)
> yfit <- 212.68384222 * xfit/(0.06412146 + xfit)
> lines(spline(xfit, yfit))
```

The standard package **stats** provides much more extensive facilities for fitting non-linear models by least squares. The model we have just fitted is the Michaelis-Menten model, so we can use

```
> df <- data.frame(x=x, y=y)
> fit <- nls(y ~ SSmicmen(x, Vm, K), df)
> fit
Nonlinear regression model
  model:  y ~ SSmicmen(x, Vm, K)
   data:  df
           Vm              K
212.68370711    0.06412123
 residual sum-of-squares:  1195.449
> summary(fit)

Formula: y ~ SSmicmen(x, Vm, K)

Parameters:
     Estimate Std. Error t value Pr(>|t|)
Vm 2.127e+02  6.947e+00  30.615 3.24e-11
K  6.412e-02  8.281e-03   7.743 1.57e-05

Residual standard error: 10.93 on 10 degrees of freedom

Correlation of Parameter Estimates:
     Vm
K 0.7651
```

11.7.2 Maximum likelihood

Maximum likelihood is a method of nonlinear model fitting that applies even if the errors are not normal. The method finds the parameter values which maximize the log likelihood, or

Chapter 11: Statistical models in R 60

equivalently which minimize the negative log-likelihood. Here is an example from Dobson (1990), pp. 108–111. This example fits a logistic model to dose-response data, which clearly could also be fit by `glm()`. The data are:

```
> x <- c(1.6907, 1.7242, 1.7552, 1.7842, 1.8113,
         1.8369, 1.8610, 1.8839)
> y <- c( 6, 13, 18, 28, 52, 53, 61, 60)
> n <- c(59, 60, 62, 56, 63, 59, 62, 60)
```

The negative log-likelihood to minimize is:

```
> fn <- function(p)
   sum( - (y*(p[1]+p[2]*x) - n*log(1+exp(p[1]+p[2]*x))
          + log(choose(n, y)) ))
```

We pick sensible starting values and do the fit:

```
> out <- nlm(fn, p = c(-50,20), hessian = TRUE)
```

After the fitting, `out$minimum` is the negative log-likelihood, and `out$estimate` are the maximum likelihood estimates of the parameters. To obtain the approximate SEs of the estimates we do:

```
> sqrt(diag(solve(out$hessian)))
```

A 95% confidence interval would be the parameter estimate $\pm$ 1.96 SE.

11.8 Some non-standard models

We conclude this chapter with just a brief mention of some of the other facilities available in R for special regression and data analysis problems.

- **Mixed models.** The recommended **nlme** package provides functions `lme()` and `nlme()` for linear and non-linear mixed-effects models, that is linear and non-linear regressions in which some of the coefficients correspond to random effects. These functions make heavy use of formulae to specify the models.

- **Local approximating regressions.** The `loess()` function fits a nonparametric regression by using a locally weighted regression. Such regressions are useful for highlighting a trend in messy data or for data reduction to give some insight into a large data set.

  Function `loess` is in the standard package **stats**, together with code for projection pursuit regression.

- **Robust regression.** There are several functions available for fitting regression models in a way resistant to the influence of extreme outliers in the data. Function `lqs` in the recommended package **MASS** provides state-of-art algorithms for highly-resistant fits. Less resistant but statistically more efficient methods are available in packages, for example function `rlm` in package **MASS**.

- **Additive models.** This technique aims to construct a regression function from smooth additive functions of the determining variables, usually one for each determining variable. Functions **avas** and **ace** in package **acepack** and functions **bruto** and **mars** in package **mda** provide some examples of these techniques in user-contributed packages to R. An extension is **Generalized Additive Models**, implemented in user-contributed packages **gam** and **mgcv**.

- **Tree-based models.** Rather than seek an explicit global linear model for prediction or interpretation, tree-based models seek to bifurcate the data, recursively, at critical points of the determining variables in order to partition the data ultimately into groups that are as homogeneous as possible within, and as heterogeneous as possible between. The results often lead to insights that other data analysis methods tend not to yield.

  Models are again specified in the ordinary linear model form. The model fitting function is `tree()`, but many other generic functions such as `plot()` and `text()` are well adapted to displaying the results of a tree-based model fit in a graphical way.

Chapter 11: Statistical models in R   61

Tree models are available in R *via* the user-contributed packages **rpart** and **tree**.

12 Graphical procedures

Graphical facilities are an important and extremely versatile component of the R environment. It is possible to use the facilities to display a wide variety of statistical graphs and also to build entirely new types of graph.

The graphics facilities can be used in both interactive and batch modes, but in most cases, interactive use is more productive. Interactive use is also easy because at startup time R initiates a graphics *device driver* which opens a special *graphics window* for the display of interactive graphics. Although this is done automatically, it is useful to know that the command used is X11() under UNIX and windows() under Windows.

Once the device driver is running, R plotting commands can be used to produce a variety of graphical displays and to create entirely new kinds of display.

Plotting commands are divided into three basic groups:

- **High-level** plotting functions create a new plot on the graphics device, possibly with axes, labels, titles and so on.
- **Low-level** plotting functions add more information to an existing plot, such as extra points, lines and labels.
- **Interactive** graphics functions allow you interactively add information to, or extract information from, an existing plot, using a pointing device such as a mouse.

In addition, R maintains a list of *graphical parameters* which can be manipulated to customize your plots.

This manual only describes what are known as 'base' graphics. A separate graphics subsystem in package **grid** coexists with base – it is more powerful but harder to use. There is a recommended package **lattice** which builds on **grid** and provides ways to produce multi-panel plots akin to those in the *Trellis* system in S.

12.1 High-level plotting commands

High-level plotting functions are designed to generate a complete plot of the data passed as arguments to the function. Where appropriate, axes, labels and titles are automatically generated (unless you request otherwise.) High-level plotting commands always start a new plot, erasing the current plot if necessary.

12.1.1 The plot() function

One of the most frequently used plotting functions in R is the plot() function. This is a *generic* function: the type of plot produced is dependent on the type or *class* of the first argument.

plot(x, y)
plot(xy) If x and y are vectors, plot(x, y) produces a scatterplot of y against x. The same effect can be produced by supplying one argument (second form) as either a list containing two elements x and y or a two-column matrix.

plot(x) If x is a time series, this produces a time-series plot. If x is a numeric vector, it produces a plot of the values in the vector against their index in the vector. If x is a complex vector, it produces a plot of imaginary versus real parts of the vector elements.

plot(f)
plot(f, y) f is a factor object, y is a numeric vector. The first form generates a bar plot of f; the second form produces boxplots of y for each level of f.

```
plot(df)
plot(~ expr)
plot(y ~ expr)
```

> df is a data frame, y is any object, $expr$ is a list of object names separated by '+' (e.g., a + b + c). The first two forms produce distributional plots of the variables in a data frame (first form) or of a number of named objects (second form). The third form plots y against every object named in $expr$.

12.1.2 Displaying multivariate data

R provides two very useful functions for representing multivariate data. If X is a numeric matrix or data frame, the command

```
> pairs(X)
```

produces a pairwise scatterplot matrix of the variables defined by the columns of X, that is, every column of X is plotted against every other column of X and the resulting $n(n-1)$ plots are arranged in a matrix with plot scales constant over the rows and columns of the matrix.

When three or four variables are involved a *coplot* may be more enlightening. If a and b are numeric vectors and c is a numeric vector or factor object (all of the same length), then the command

```
> coplot(a ~ b | c)
```

produces a number of scatterplots of a against b for given values of c. If c is a factor, this simply means that a is plotted against b for every level of c. When c is numeric, it is divided into a number of *conditioning intervals* and for each interval a is plotted against b for values of c within the interval. The number and position of intervals can be controlled with `given.values=` argument to `coplot()`—the function `co.intervals()` is useful for selecting intervals. You can also use two *given* variables with a command like

```
> coplot(a ~ b | c + d)
```

which produces scatterplots of a against b for every joint conditioning interval of c and d.

The `coplot()` and `pairs()` function both take an argument `panel=` which can be used to customize the type of plot which appears in each panel. The default is `points()` to produce a scatterplot but by supplying some other low-level graphics function of two vectors x and y as the value of `panel=` you can produce any type of plot you wish. An example panel function useful for coplots is `panel.smooth()`.

12.1.3 Display graphics

Other high-level graphics functions produce different types of plots. Some examples are:

```
qqnorm(x)
qqline(x)
qqplot(x, y)
```

> Distribution-comparison plots. The first form plots the numeric vector x against the expected Normal order scores (a normal scores plot) and the second adds a straight line to such a plot by drawing a line through the distribution and data quartiles. The third form plots the quantiles of x against those of y to compare their respective distributions.

```
hist(x)
hist(x, nclass=n)
hist(x, breaks=b, ...)
```

> Produces a histogram of the numeric vector x. A sensible number of classes is usually chosen, but a recommendation can be given with the `nclass=` argument. Alternatively, the breakpoints can be specified exactly with the `breaks=` argument.

Chapter 12: Graphical procedures   64

If the `probability=TRUE` argument is given, the bars represent relative frequencies instead of counts.

`dotchart(x, ...)`

Constructs a dotchart of the data in `x`. In a dotchart the y-axis gives a labelling of the data in `x` and the x-axis gives its value. For example it allows easy visual selection of all data entries with values lying in specified ranges.

`image(x, y, z, ...)`
`contour(x, y, z, ...)`
`persp(x, y, z, ...)`

Plots of three variables. The `image` plot draws a grid of rectangles using different colours to represent the value of `z`, the `contour` plot draws contour lines to represent the value of `z`, and the `persp` plot draws a 3D surface.

12.1.4 Arguments to high-level plotting functions

There are a number of arguments which may be passed to high-level graphics functions, as follows:

`add=TRUE` Forces the function to act as a low-level graphics function, superimposing the plot on the current plot (some functions only).

`axes=FALSE`

Suppresses generation of axes—useful for adding your own custom axes with the `axis()` function. The default, `axes=TRUE`, means include axes.

`log="x"`
`log="y"`
`log="xy"` Causes the x, y or both axes to be logarithmic. This will work for many, but not all, types of plot.

`type=` The `type=` argument controls the type of plot produced, as follows:

`type="p"` Plot individual points (the default)

`type="l"` Plot lines

`type="b"` Plot points connected by lines (*both*)

`type="o"` Plot points overlaid by lines

`type="h"` Plot vertical lines from points to the zero axis (*high-density*)

`type="s"`
`type="S"` Step-function plots. In the first form, the top of the vertical defines the point; in the second, the bottom.

`type="n"` No plotting at all. However axes are still drawn (by default) and the coordinate system is set up according to the data. Ideal for creating plots with subsequent low-level graphics functions.

`xlab=string`
`ylab=string`

Axis labels for the x and y axes. Use these arguments to change the default labels, usually the names of the objects used in the call to the high-level plotting function.

`main=string`

Figure title, placed at the top of the plot in a large font.

`sub=string`

Sub-title, placed just below the x-axis in a smaller font.

12.2 Low-level plotting commands

Sometimes the high-level plotting functions don't produce exactly the kind of plot you desire. In this case, low-level plotting commands can be used to add extra information (such as points, lines or text) to the current plot.

Some of the more useful low-level plotting functions are:

`points(x, y)`
`lines(x, y)`

> Adds points or connected lines to the current plot. `plot()`'s `type=` argument can also be passed to these functions (and defaults to `"p"` for `points()` and `"l"` for `lines()`.)

`text(x, y, labels, ...)`

> Add text to a plot at points given by `x`, `y`. Normally `labels` is an integer or character vector in which case `labels[i]` is plotted at point (`x[i]`, `y[i]`). The default is `1:length(x)`.

> **Note:** This function is often used in the sequence
>
>   > plot(x, y, type="n"); text(x, y, names)
>
> The graphics parameter `type="n"` suppresses the points but sets up the axes, and the `text()` function supplies special characters, as specified by the character vector `names` for the points.

`abline(a, b)`
`abline(h=y)`
`abline(v=x)`
`abline(lm.obj)`

> Adds a line of slope `b` and intercept `a` to the current plot. `h=y` may be used to specify y-coordinates for the heights of horizontal lines to go across a plot, and `v=x` similarly for the x-coordinates for vertical lines. Also *lm.obj* may be list with a `coefficients` component of length 2 (such as the result of model-fitting functions,) which are taken as an intercept and slope, in that order.

`polygon(x, y, ...)`

> Draws a polygon defined by the ordered vertices in (`x`, `y`) and (optionally) shade it in with hatch lines, or fill it if the graphics device allows the filling of figures.

`legend(x, y, legend, ...)`

> Adds a legend to the current plot at the specified position. Plotting characters, line styles, colors etc., are identified with the labels in the character vector `legend`. At least one other argument v (a vector the same length as `legend`) with the corresponding values of the plotting unit must also be given, as follows:

> `legend( , fill=`v`)`
>> Colors for filled boxes

> `legend( , col=`v`)`
>> Colors in which points or lines will be drawn

> `legend( , lty=`v`)`
>> Line styles

> `legend( , lwd=`v`)`
>> Line widths

> `legend( , pch=`v`)`
>> Plotting characters (character vector)

```
title(main, sub)
```
> Adds a title **main** to the top of the current plot in a large font and (optionally) a sub-title **sub** at the bottom in a smaller font.

```
axis(side, ...)
```
> Adds an axis to the current plot on the side given by the first argument (1 to 4, counting clockwise from the bottom.) Other arguments control the positioning of the axis within or beside the plot, and tick positions and labels. Useful for adding custom axes after calling **plot()** with the **axes=FALSE** argument.

Low-level plotting functions usually require some positioning information (e.g., x and y co-ordinates) to determine where to place the new plot elements. Coordinates are given in terms of *user coordinates* which are defined by the previous high-level graphics command and are chosen based on the supplied data.

Where x and y arguments are required, it is also sufficient to supply a single argument being a list with elements named x and y. Similarly a matrix with two columns is also valid input. In this way functions such as **locator()** (see below) may be used to specify positions on a plot interactively.

12.2.1 Mathematical annotation

In some cases, it is useful to add mathematical symbols and formulae to a plot. This can be achieved in R by specifying an *expression* rather than a character string in any one of **text**, **mtext**, **axis**, or **title**. For example, the following code draws the formula for the Binomial probability function:

```
> text(x, y, expression(paste(bgroup("(", atop(n, x), ")"), p^x, q^{n-x})))
```

More information, including a full listing of the features available can obtained from within R using the commands:

```
> help(plotmath)
> example(plotmath)
> demo(plotmath)
```

12.2.2 Hershey vector fonts

It is possible to specify Hershey vector fonts for rendering text when using the **text** and **contour** functions. There are three reasons for using the Hershey fonts:

- Hershey fonts can produce better output, especially on a computer screen, for rotated and/or small text.
- Hershey fonts provide certain symbols that may not be available in the standard fonts. In particular, there are zodiac signs, cartographic symbols and astronomical symbols.
- Hershey fonts provide cyrillic and japanese (Kana and Kanji) characters.

More information, including tables of Hershey characters can be obtained from within R using the commands:

```
> help(Hershey)
> demo(Hershey)
> help(Japanese)
> demo(Japanese)
```

12.3 Interacting with graphics

R also provides functions which allow users to extract or add information to a plot using a mouse. The simplest of these is the **locator()** function:

`locator(n, type)`

> Waits for the user to select locations on the current plot using the left mouse button. This continues until n (default 512) points have been selected, or another mouse button is pressed. The `type` argument allows for plotting at the selected points and has the same effect as for high-level graphics commands; the default is no plotting. `locator()` returns the locations of the points selected as a list with two components x and y.

`locator()` is usually called with no arguments. It is particularly useful for interactively selecting positions for graphic elements such as legends or labels when it is difficult to calculate in advance where the graphic should be placed. For example, to place some informative text near an outlying point, the command

```
> text(locator(1), "Outlier", adj=0)
```

may be useful. (`locator()` will be ignored if the current device, such as `postscript` does not support interactive pointing.)

`identify(x, y, labels)`

> Allow the user to highlight any of the points defined by x and y (using the left mouse button) by plotting the corresponding component of `labels` nearby (or the index number of the point if `labels` is absent). Returns the indices of the selected points when another button is pressed.

Sometimes we want to identify particular *points* on a plot, rather than their positions. For example, we may wish the user to select some observation of interest from a graphical display and then manipulate that observation in some way. Given a number of (x, y) coordinates in two numeric vectors x and y, we could use the `identify()` function as follows:

```
> plot(x, y)
> identify(x, y)
```

The `identify()` functions performs no plotting itself, but simply allows the user to move the mouse pointer and click the left mouse button near a point. If there is a point near the mouse pointer it will be marked with its index number (that is, its position in the x/y vectors) plotted nearby. Alternatively, you could use some informative string (such as a case name) as a highlight by using the `labels` argument to `identify()`, or disable marking altogether with the `plot = FALSE` argument. When the process is terminated (see above), `identify()` returns the indices of the selected points; you can use these indices to extract the selected points from the original vectors x and y.

12.4 Using graphics parameters

When creating graphics, particularly for presentation or publication purposes, R's defaults do not always produce exactly that which is required. You can, however, customize almost every aspect of the display using *graphics parameters*. R maintains a list of a large number of graphics parameters which control things such as line style, colors, figure arrangement and text justification among many others. Every graphics parameter has a name (such as 'col', which controls colors,) and a value (a color number, for example.)

A separate list of graphics parameters is maintained for each active device, and each device has a default set of parameters when initialized. Graphics parameters can be set in two ways: either permanently, affecting all graphics functions which access the current device; or temporarily, affecting only a single graphics function call.

12.4.1 Permanent changes: The par() function

The `par()` function is used to access and modify the list of graphics parameters for the current graphics device.

par()   Without arguments, returns a list of all graphics parameters and their values for
              the current device.

par(c("col", "lty"))
              With a character vector argument, returns only the named graphics parameters
              (again, as a list.)

par(col=4, lty=2)
              With named arguments (or a single list argument), sets the values of the named
              graphics parameters, and returns the original values of the parameters as a list.

Setting graphics parameters with the par() function changes the value of the parameters
permanently, in the sense that all future calls to graphics functions (on the current device) will
be affected by the new value. You can think of setting graphics parameters in this way as
setting "default" values for the parameters, which will be used by all graphics functions unless
an alternative value is given.

Note that calls to par() *always* affect the global values of graphics parameters, even when
par() is called from within a function. This is often undesirable behavior—usually we want to
set some graphics parameters, do some plotting, and then restore the original values so as not
to affect the user's R session. You can restore the initial values by saving the result of par()
when making changes, and restoring the initial values when plotting is complete.

```
> oldpar <- par(col=4, lty=2)
  ... plotting commands ...
> par(oldpar)
```

To save and restore *all* settable[1] graphical parameters use

```
> oldpar <- par(no.readonly=TRUE)
  ... plotting commands ...
> par(oldpar)
```

12.4.2 Temporary changes: Arguments to graphics functions

Graphics parameters may also be passed to (almost) any graphics function as named arguments.
This has the same effect as passing the arguments to the par() function, except that the changes
only last for the duration of the function call. For example:

```
> plot(x, y, pch="+")
```

produces a scatterplot using a plus sign as the plotting character, without changing the default
plotting character for future plots.

Unfortunately, this is not implemented entirely consistently and it is sometimes necessary to
set and reset graphics parameters using par().

12.5 Graphics parameters list

The following sections detail many of the commonly-used graphical parameters. The R help
documentation for the par() function provides a more concise summary; this is provided as a
somewhat more detailed alternative.

Graphics parameters will be presented in the following form:

name=value
              A description of the parameter's effect. *name* is the name of the parameter, that
              is, the argument name to use in calls to par() or a graphics function. *value* is a
              typical value you might use when setting the parameter.

Note that axes is **not** a graphics parameter but an argument to a few plot methods: see
xaxt and yaxt.

---

[1] Some graphics parameters such as the size of the current device are for information only.

12.5.1 Graphical elements

R plots are made up of points, lines, text and polygons (filled regions.) Graphical parameters exist which control how these *graphical elements* are drawn, as follows:

pch="+"   Character to be used for plotting points. The default varies with graphics drivers, but it is usually 'o'. Plotted points tend to appear slightly above or below the appropriate position unless you use "." as the plotting character, which produces centered points.

pch=4   When pch is given as an integer between 0 and 25 inclusive, a specialized plotting symbol is produced. To see what the symbols are, use the command

```
> legend(locator(1), as.character(0:25), pch = 0:25)
```

Those from 21 to 25 may appear to duplicate earlier symbols, but can be coloured in different ways: see the help on points and its examples.

In addition, pch can be a character or a number in the range 32:255 representing a character in the current font.

lty=2   Line types. Alternative line styles are not supported on all graphics devices (and vary on those that do) but line type 1 is always a solid line, line type 0 is always invisible, and line types 2 and onwards are dotted or dashed lines, or some combination of both.

lwd=2   Line widths. Desired width of lines, in multiples of the "standard" line width. Affects axis lines as well as lines drawn with lines(), etc. Not all devices support this, and some have restrictions on the widths that can be used.

col=2   Colors to be used for points, lines, text, filled regions and images. A number from the current palette (see ?palette) or a named colour.

col.axis
col.lab
col.main
col.sub   The color to be used for axis annotation, x and y labels, main and sub-titles, respectively.

font=2   An integer which specifies which font to use for text. If possible, device drivers arrange so that 1 corresponds to plain text, 2 to bold face, 3 to italic, 4 to bold italic and 5 to a symbol font (which include Greek letters).

font.axis
font.lab
font.main
font.sub   The font to be used for axis annotation, x and y labels, main and sub-titles, respectively.

adj=-0.1   Justification of text relative to the plotting position. 0 means left justify, 1 means right justify and 0.5 means to center horizontally about the plotting position. The actual value is the proportion of text that appears to the left of the plotting position, so a value of -0.1 leaves a gap of 10% of the text width between the text and the plotting position.

cex=1.5   Character expansion. The value is the desired size of text characters (including plotting characters) relative to the default text size.

```
cex.axis
cex.lab
cex.main
cex.sub
```
The character expansion to be used for axis annotation, x and y labels, main and sub-titles, respectively.

12.5.2 Axes and tick marks

Many of R's high-level plots have axes, and you can construct axes yourself with the low-level `axis()` graphics function. Axes have three main components: the *axis line* (line style controlled by the `lty` graphics parameter), the *tick marks* (which mark off unit divisions along the axis line) and the *tick labels* (which mark the units.) These components can be customized with the following graphics parameters.

`lab=c(5, 7, 12)`
The first two numbers are the desired number of tick intervals on the x and y axes respectively. The third number is the desired length of axis labels, in characters (including the decimal point.) Choosing a too-small value for this parameter may result in all tick labels being rounded to the same number!

`las=1` Orientation of axis labels. 0 means always parallel to axis, 1 means always horizontal, and 2 means always perpendicular to the axis.

`mgp=c(3, 1, 0)`
Positions of axis components. The first component is the distance from the axis label to the axis position, in text lines. The second component is the distance to the tick labels, and the final component is the distance from the axis position to the axis line (usually zero). Positive numbers measure outside the plot region, negative numbers inside.

`tck=0.01` Length of tick marks, as a fraction of the size of the plotting region. When `tck` is small (less than 0.5) the tick marks on the x and y axes are forced to be the same size. A value of 1 gives grid lines. Negative values give tick marks outside the plotting region. Use `tck=0.01` and `mgp=c(1,-1.5,0)` for internal tick marks.

```
xaxs="r"
yaxs="i"
```
Axis styles for the x and y axes, respectively. With styles `"i"` (internal) and `"r"` (the default) tick marks always fall within the range of the data, however style `"r"` leaves a small amount of space at the edges. (S has other styles not implemented in R.)

12.5.3 Figure margins

A single plot in R is known as a `figure` and comprises a *plot region* surrounded by margins (possibly containing axis labels, titles, etc.) and (usually) bounded by the axes themselves.

Chapter 12: Graphical procedures   71

A typical figure is

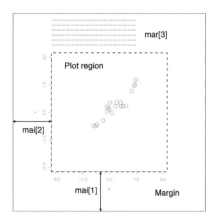

Graphics parameters controlling figure layout include:

`mai=c(1, 0.5, 0.5, 0)`
        Widths of the bottom, left, top and right margins, respectively, measured in inches.

`mar=c(4, 2, 2, 1)`
        Similar to `mai`, except the measurement unit is text lines.

   `mar` and `mai` are equivalent in the sense that setting one changes the value of the other. The default values chosen for this parameter are often too large; the right-hand margin is rarely needed, and neither is the top margin if no title is being used. The bottom and left margins must be large enough to accommodate the axis and tick labels. Furthermore, the default is chosen without regard to the size of the device surface: for example, using the `postscript()` driver with the `height=4` argument will result in a plot which is about 50% margin unless `mar` or `mai` are set explicitly. When multiple figures are in use (see below) the margins are reduced, however this may not be enough when many figures share the same page.

Chapter 12: Graphical procedures   72

12.5.4 Multiple figure environment

R allows you to create an n by m array of figures on a single page. Each figure has its own margins, and the array of figures is optionally surrounded by an *outer margin*, as shown in the following figure.

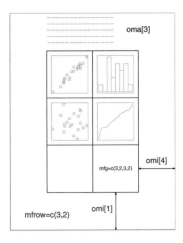

The graphical parameters relating to multiple figures are as follows:

`mfcol=c(3, 2)`
`mfrow=c(2, 4)`

> Set the size of a multiple figure array. The first value is the number of rows; the second is the number of columns. The only difference between these two parameters is that setting `mfcol` causes figures to be filled by column; `mfrow` fills by rows.

> The layout in the Figure could have been created by setting `mfrow=c(3,2)`; the figure shows the page after four plots have been drawn.

> Setting either of these can reduce the base size of symbols and text (controlled by `par("cex")` and the pointsize of the device). In a layout with exactly two rows and columns the base size is reduced by a factor of 0.83: if there are three or more of either rows or columns, the reduction factor is 0.66.

`mfg=c(2, 2, 3, 2)`

> Position of the current figure in a multiple figure environment. The first two numbers are the row and column of the current figure; the last two are the number of rows and columns in the multiple figure array. Set this parameter to jump between figures in the array. You can even use different values for the last two numbers than the *true* values for unequally-sized figures on the same page.

`fig=c(4, 9, 1, 4)/10`

> Position of the current figure on the page. Values are the positions of the left, right, bottom and top edges respectively, as a percentage of the page measured from the bottom left corner. The example value would be for a figure in the bottom right of the page. Set this parameter for arbitrary positioning of figures within a page. If you want to add a figure to a current page, use `new=TRUE` as well (unlike S).

Chapter 12: Graphical procedures   73

```
oma=c(2, 0, 3, 0)
omi=c(0, 0, 0.8, 0)
```
> Size of outer margins. Like `mar` and `mai`, the first measures in text lines and the second in inches, starting with the bottom margin and working clockwise.

Outer margins are particularly useful for page-wise titles, etc. Text can be added to the outer margins with the `mtext()` function with argument `outer=TRUE`. There are no outer margins by default, however, so you must create them explicitly using `oma` or `omi`.

More complicated arrangements of multiple figures can be produced by the `split.screen()` and `layout()` functions, as well as by the **grid** and **lattice** packages.

12.6 Device drivers

R can generate graphics (of varying levels of quality) on almost any type of display or printing device. Before this can begin, however, R needs to be informed what type of device it is dealing with. This is done by starting a *device driver*. The purpose of a device driver is to convert graphical instructions from R ("draw a line," for example) into a form that the particular device can understand.

Device drivers are started by calling a device driver function. There is one such function for every device driver: type `help(Devices)` for a list of them all. For example, issuing the command

```
> postscript()
```

causes all future graphics output to be sent to the printer in PostScript format. Some commonly-used device drivers are:

`X11()`   For use with the X11 window system on Unix-alikes

`windows()`
> For use on Windows

`quartz()`   For use on MacOS X

`postscript()`
> For printing on PostScript printers, or creating PostScript graphics files.

`pdf()`   Produces a PDF file, which can also be included into PDF files.

`png()`   Produces a bitmap PNG file. (Not always available: see its help page.)

`jpeg()`   Produces a bitmap JPEG file, best used for `image` plots. (Not always available: see its help page.)

When you have finished with a device, be sure to terminate the device driver by issuing the command

```
> dev.off()
```

This ensures that the device finishes cleanly; for example in the case of hardcopy devices this ensures that every page is completed and has been sent to the printer. (This will happen automatically at the normal end of a session.)

12.6.1 PostScript diagrams for typeset documents

By passing the `file` argument to the `postscript()` device driver function, you may store the graphics in PostScript format in a file of your choice. The plot will be in landscape orientation unless the `horizontal=FALSE` argument is given, and you can control the size of the graphic with the `width` and `height` arguments (the plot will be scaled as appropriate to fit these dimensions.) For example, the command

Chapter 12: Graphical procedures 74

```
> postscript("file.ps", horizontal=FALSE, height=5, pointsize=10)
```

will produce a file containing PostScript code for a figure five inches high, perhaps for inclusion in a document. It is important to note that if the file named in the command already exists, it will be overwritten. This is the case even if the file was only created earlier in the same R session.

Many usages of PostScript output will be to incorporate the figure in another document. This works best when *encapsulated* PostScript is produced: R always produces conformant output, but only marks the output as such when the `onefile=FALSE` argument is supplied. This unusual notation stems from S-compatibility: it really means that the output will be a single page (which is part of the EPSF specification). Thus to produce a plot for inclusion use something like

```
> postscript("plot1.eps", horizontal=FALSE, onefile=FALSE,
              height=8, width=6, pointsize=10)
```

12.6.2 Multiple graphics devices

In advanced use of R it is often useful to have several graphics devices in use at the same time. Of course only one graphics device can accept graphics commands at any one time, and this is known as the *current device*. When multiple devices are open, they form a numbered sequence with names giving the kind of device at any position.

The main commands used for operating with multiple devices, and their meanings are as follows:

`X11()`   [UNIX]

`windows()`
`win.printer()`
`win.metafile()`
       [Windows]

`quartz()`   [MacOS X]

`postscript()`
`pdf()`
`...`   Each new call to a device driver function opens a new graphics device, thus extending by one the device list. This device becomes the current device, to which graphics output will be sent. (Some platforms may have further devices available.)

`dev.list()`
       Returns the number and name of all active devices. The device at position 1 on the list is always the *null device* which does not accept graphics commands at all.

`dev.next()`
`dev.prev()`
       Returns the number and name of the graphics device next to, or previous to the current device, respectively.

`dev.set(which=k)`
       Can be used to change the current graphics device to the one at position k of the device list. Returns the number and label of the device.

`dev.off(k)`
       Terminate the graphics device at point k of the device list. For some devices, such as `postscript` devices, this will either print the file immediately or correctly complete the file for later printing, depending on how the device was initiated.

```
dev.copy(device, ..., which=k)
dev.print(device, ..., which=k)
```
> Make a copy of the device k. Here `device` is a device function, such as `postscript`, with extra arguments, if needed, specified by '...'. `dev.print` is similar, but the copied device is immediately closed, so that end actions, such as printing hardcopies, are immediately performed.

```
graphics.off()
```
> Terminate all graphics devices on the list, except the null device.

12.7 Dynamic graphics

R does not have builtin capabilities for dynamic or interactive graphics, e.g. rotating point clouds or to "brushing" (interactively highlighting) points. However, extensive dynamic graphics facilities are available in the system GGobi by Swayne, Cook and Buja available from

> http://www.ggobi.org/

and these can be accessed from R via the package **rggobi**, described at http://www.ggobi.org/rggobi.

Also, package **rgl** provides ways to interact with 3D plots, for example of surfaces.

13 Packages

All R functions and datasets are stored in *packages*. Only when a package is loaded are its contents available. This is done both for efficiency (the full list would take more memory and would take longer to search than a subset), and to aid package developers, who are protected from name clashes with other code. The process of developing packages is described in section "Creating R packages" in *Writing R Extensions*. Here, we will describe them from a user's point of view.

To see which packages are installed at your site, issue the command

```
> library()
```

with no arguments. To load a particular package (e.g., the **boot** package containing functions from Davison & Hinkley (1997)), use a command like

```
> library(boot)
```

Users connected to the Internet can use the `install.packages()` and `update.packages()` functions (available through the `Packages` menu in the Windows and RAqua GUIs, see section "Installing packages" in *R Installation and Adminstration*) to install and update packages.

To see which packages are currently loaded, use

```
> search()
```

to display the search list. Some packages may be loaded but not available on the search list (see Section 13.3 [Namespaces], page 76): these will be included in the list given by

```
> loadedNamespaces()
```

To see a list of all available help topics in an installed package, use

```
> help.start()
```

to start the HTML help system, and then navigate to the package listing in the `Reference` section.

13.1 Standard packages

The standard (or *base*) packages are considered part of the R source code. They contain the basic functions that allow R to work, and the datasets and standard statistical and graphical functions that are described in this manual. They should be automatically available in any R installation. See section "R packages" in *R FAQ*, for a complete list.

13.2 Contributed packages and CRAN

There are hundreds of contributed packages for R, written by many different authors. Some of these packages implement specialized statistical methods, others give access to data or hardware, and others are designed to complement textbooks. Some (the *recommended* packages) are distributed with every binary distribution of R. Most are available for download from CRAN (http://CRAN.R-project.org/ and its mirrors), and other repositories such as Bioconductor (http://www.bioconductor.org/). The *R FAQ* contains a list that was current at the time of release, but the collection of available packages changes frequently.

13.3 Namespaces

Packages can have *namespaces*, and currently all of the base and recommended packages do expect the `datasets` package. Namespaces do three things: they allow the package writer to hide functions and data that are meant only for internal use, they prevent functions from breaking when a user (or other package writer) picks a name that clashes with one in the package, and they provide a way to refer to an object within a particular package.

For example, `t()` is the transpose function in R, but users might define their own function named `t`. Namespaces prevent the user's definition from taking precedence, and breaking every function that tries to transpose a matrix.

There are two operators that work with namespaces. The double-colon operator `::` selects definitions from a particular namespace. In the example above, the transpose function will always be available as `base::t`, because it is defined in the `base` package. Only functions that are exported from the package can be retrieved in this way.

The triple-colon operator `:::` may be seen in a few places in R code: it acts like the double-colon operator but also allows access to hidden objects. Users are more likely to use the `getAnywhere()` function, which searches multiple packages.

Packages are often inter-dependent, and loading one may cause others to be automatically loaded. The colon operators described above will also cause automatic loading of the associated package. When packages with namespaces are loaded automatically they are not added to the search list.

Appendix A: A sample session   78

Appendix A A sample session

The following session is intended to introduce to you some features of the R environment by using them. Many features of the system will be unfamiliar and puzzling at first, but this puzzlement will soon disappear.

Login, start your windowing system.

`$ R` Start R as appropriate for your platform.

The R program begins, with a banner.

(Within R, the prompt on the left hand side will not be shown to avoid confusion.)

```
help.start()
```
Start the HTML interface to on-line help (using a web browser available at your machine). You should briefly explore the features of this facility with the mouse.

Iconify the help window and move on to the next part.

```
x <- rnorm(50)
y <- rnorm(x)
```
Generate two pseudo-random normal vectors of x- and y-coordinates.

```
plot(x, y)
```
Plot the points in the plane. A graphics window will appear automatically.

`ls()` See which R objects are now in the R workspace.

`rm(x, y)` Remove objects no longer needed. (Clean up).

`x <- 1:20` Make $x = (1, 2, \ldots, 20)$.

```
w <- 1 + sqrt(x)/2
```
A 'weight' vector of standard deviations.

```
dummy <- data.frame(x=x, y= x + rnorm(x)*w)
dummy
```
Make a *data frame* of two columns, x and y, and look at it.

```
fm <- lm(y ~ x, data=dummy)
summary(fm)
```
Fit a simple linear regression of y on x and look at the analysis.

```
fm1 <- lm(y ~ x, data=dummy, weight=1/w^2)
summary(fm1)
```
Since we know the standard deviations, we can do a weighted regression.

```
attach(dummy)
```
Make the columns in the data frame visible as variables.

```
lrf <- lowess(x, y)
```
Make a nonparametric local regression function.

```
plot(x, y)
```
Standard point plot.

```
lines(x, lrf$y)
```
Add in the local regression.

```
abline(0, 1, lty=3)
```
The true regression line: (intercept 0, slope 1).

```
abline(coef(fm))
```
Unweighted regression line.

```
abline(coef(fm1), col = "red")
```
       Weighted regression line.

```
detach()
```
  Remove data frame from the search path.

```
plot(fitted(fm), resid(fm),
    xlab="Fitted values",
    ylab="Residuals",
    main="Residuals vs Fitted")
```
       A standard regression diagnostic plot to check for heteroscedasticity. Can you see it?

```
qqnorm(resid(fm), main="Residuals Rankit Plot")
```
       A normal scores plot to check for skewness, kurtosis and outliers. (Not very useful here.)

```
rm(fm, fm1, lrf, x, dummy)
```
       Clean up again.

The next section will look at data from the classical experiment of Michaelson and Morley to measure the speed of light. This dataset is available in the `morley` object, but we will read it to illustrate the `read.table` function.

```
filepath <- system.file("data", "morley.tab" , package="datasets")
filepath
```
  Get the path to the data file.

```
file.show(filepath)
```
       Optional. Look at the file.

```
mm <- read.table(filepath)
mm
```
       Read in the Michaelson and Morley data as a data frame, and look at it. There are five experiments (column `Expt`) and each has 20 runs (column `Run`) and `sl` is the recorded speed of light, suitably coded.

```
mm$Expt <- factor(mm$Expt)
mm$Run <- factor(mm$Run)
```
       Change `Expt` and `Run` into factors.

```
attach(mm)
```
       Make the data frame visible at position 3 (the default).

```
plot(Expt, Speed, main="Speed of Light Data", xlab="Experiment No.")
```
       Compare the five experiments with simple boxplots.

```
fm <- aov(Speed ~ Run + Expt, data=mm)
summary(fm)
```
       Analyze as a randomized block, with 'runs' and 'experiments' as factors.

```
fm0 <- update(fm, . ~ . - Run)
anova(fm0, fm)
```
       Fit the sub-model omitting 'runs', and compare using a formal analysis of variance.

```
detach()
rm(fm, fm0)
```
       Clean up before moving on.

We now look at some more graphical features: contour and image plots.

```
x <- seq(-pi, pi, len=50)
y <- x
```
   x is a vector of 50 equally spaced values in $-\pi \leq x \leq \pi$. y is the same.

Appendix A: A sample session 80

```
f <- outer(x, y, function(x, y) cos(y)/(1 + x^2))
```
> f is a square matrix, with rows and columns indexed by x and y respectively, of values of the function $\cos(y)/(1 + x^2)$.

```
oldpar <- par(no.readonly = TRUE)
par(pty="s")
```
> Save the plotting parameters and set the plotting region to "square".

```
contour(x, y, f)
contour(x, y, f, nlevels=15, add=TRUE)
```
> Make a contour map of f; add in more lines for more detail.

```
fa <- (f-t(f))/2
```
> fa is the "asymmetric part" of f. (t() is transpose).

```
contour(x, y, fa, nlevels=15)
```
> Make a contour plot, ...

```
par(oldpar)
```
> ... and restore the old graphics parameters.

```
image(x, y, f)
image(x, y, fa)
```
> Make some high density image plots, (of which you can get hardcopies if you wish), ...

```
objects(); rm(x, y, f, fa)
```
> ... and clean up before moving on.

R can do complex arithmetic, also.

```
th <- seq(-pi, pi, len=100)
z <- exp(1i*th)
```
> 1i is used for the complex number i.

```
par(pty="s")
plot(z, type="l")
```
> Plotting complex arguments means plot imaginary versus real parts. This should be a circle.

```
w <- rnorm(100) + rnorm(100)*1i
```
> Suppose we want to sample points within the unit circle. One method would be to take complex numbers with standard normal real and imaginary parts ...

```
w <- ifelse(Mod(w) > 1, 1/w, w)
```
> ... and to map any outside the circle onto their reciprocal.

```
plot(w, xlim=c(-1,1), ylim=c(-1,1), pch="+",xlab="x", ylab="y")
lines(z)
```
> All points are inside the unit circle, but the distribution is not uniform.

```
w <- sqrt(runif(100))*exp(2*pi*runif(100)*1i)
plot(w, xlim=c(-1,1), ylim=c(-1,1), pch="+", xlab="x", ylab="y")
lines(z)
```
> The second method uses the uniform distribution. The points should now look more evenly spaced over the disc.

```
rm(th, w, z)
```
> Clean up again.

```
q()
```
> Quit the R program. You will be asked if you want to save the R workspace, and for an exploratory session like this, you probably do not want to save it.

Appendix B Invoking R

B.1 Invoking R from the command line

When working in UNIX or at a command line in Windows, the command 'R' can be used both for starting the main R program in the form

> R [*options*] [<*infile*] [>*outfile*],

or, via the R CMD interface, as a wrapper to various R tools (e.g., for processing files in R documentation format or manipulating add-on packages) which are not intended to be called "directly".

You need to ensure that either the environment variable TMPDIR is unset or it points to a valid place to create temporary files and directories.

Most options control what happens at the beginning and at the end of an R session. The startup mechanism is as follows (see also the on-line help for topic 'Startup' for more information, and the section below for some Windows-specific details).

- Unless '--no-environ' was given, R searches for user and site files to process for setting environment variables. The name of the site file is the one pointed to by the environment variable R_ENVIRON; if this is unset, '$R_HOME/etc/Renviron.site' is used (if it exists). The user file searched for is '.Renviron' in the current or in the user's home directory (in that order). These files should contain lines of the form '*name=value*'. (See help(Startup) for a precise description.) Variables you might want to set include R_PAPERSIZE (the default paper size), R_PRINTCMD (the default print command) and R_LIBS (specifies the list of R library trees searched for add-on packages).

- Then R searches for the site-wide startup profile unless the command line option '--no-site-file' was given.   The name of this file is taken from the value of the R_PROFILE environment variable.   If that variable is unset, the default '$R_HOME/etc/Rprofile.site' is used if this exists.

- Then, unless '--no-init-file' was given, R searches for a file called '.Rprofile' in the current directory or in the user's home directory (in that order) and sources it.

- It also loads a saved image from '.RData' if there is one (unless '--no-restore' or '--no-restore-data' was specified).

- Finally, if a function .First exists, it is executed. This function (as well as .Last which is executed at the end of the R session) can be defined in the appropriate startup profiles, or reside in '.RData'.

In addition, there are options for controlling the memory available to the R process (see the on-line help for topic 'Memory' for more information). Users will not normally need to use these unless they are trying to limit the amount of memory used by R.

R accepts the following command-line options.

'--help'
'-h'   Print short help message to standard output and exit successfully.

'--version'
              Print version information to standard output and exit successfully.

'--encoding=*enc*'
              Specify the encoding to be assumed for input from the console or stdin. This needs to be an encoding known to iconv: see its help page.

'RHOME'   Print the path to the R "home directory" to standard output and exit successfully. Apart from the front-end shell script and the man page, R installation puts everything (executables, packages, etc.) into this directory.

'--save'
'--no-save'

> Control whether data sets should be saved or not at the end of the R session. If neither is given in an interactive session, the user is asked for the desired behavior when ending the session with $q()$; in non-interactive use one of these must be specified or implied by some other option (see below).

'--no-environ'

> Do not read any user file to set environment variables.

'--no-site-file'

> Do not read the site-wide profile at startup.

'--no-init-file'

> Do not read the user's profile at startup.

'--restore'
'--no-restore'
'--no-restore-data'

> Control whether saved images (file '.RData' in the directory where R was started) should be restored at startup or not. The default is to restore. ('--no-restore' implies all the specific '--no-restore-*' options.)

'--no-restore-history'

> Control whether the history file (normally file '.Rhistory' in the directory where R was started, but can be set by the environment variable R_HISTFILE) should be restored at startup or not. The default is to restore.

'--no-Rconsole'

> (Windows only) Prevent loading the 'Rconsole' file at startup.

'--vanilla'

> Combine '--no-save', '--no-environ', '--no-site-file', '--no-init-file' and '--no-restore'. Under Windows, this also includes '--no-Rconsole'.

'-f *file*'
'--file=*file*'

> Take input from *file*: '-' means stdin. Implies '--no-save' unless '--save' has been set.

'-e *expression*'

> Use *expression* as an input line. One or more '-e' options can be used, but not together with '-f' or '--file'. Implies '--no-save' unless '--save' has been set. (There is a limit of 10,000 bytes on the total length of expressions used in this way.)

'--no-readline'

> (UNIX only) Turn off command-line editing via **readline**. This is useful when running R from within Emacs using the ESS ("Emacs Speaks Statistics") package. See Appendix C [The command-line editor], page 87, for more information.

'--ess'   (Windows only) Set Rterm up for use by R-inferior-mode in ESS.

'--min-vsize=*N*'
'--max-vsize=*N*'

> Specify the minimum or maximum amount of memory used for variable size objects by setting the "vector heap" size to N bytes. Here, N must either be an integer or an integer ending with 'G', 'M', 'K', or 'k', meaning 'Giga' (2^30), 'Mega' (2^20), (computer) 'Kilo' (2^10), or regular 'kilo' (1000).

'`--min-nsize=`*N*'
'`--max-nsize=`*N*'
> Specify the amount of memory used for fixed size objects by setting the number of "cons cells" to *N*. See the previous option for details on *N*. A cons cell takes 28 bytes on a 32-bit machine, and usually 56 bytes on a 64-bit machine.

'`--max-ppsize=`*N*'
> Specify the maximum size of the pointer protection stack as *N* locations. This defaults to 10000, but can be increased to allow large and complicated calculations to be done. Currently the maximum value accepted is 100000.

'`--max-mem-size=`*N*'
> (Windows only) Specify a limit for the amount of memory to be used both for R objects and working areas. This is set by default to the smaller of 1.5Gb[1] and the amount of physical RAM in the machine, and must be between 32Mb and 3Gb.

'`--quiet`'
'`--silent`'
'`-q`'   Do not print out the initial copyright and welcome messages.

'`--slave`' Make R run as quietly as possible. This option is intended to support programs which use R to compute results for them. It implies '`--quiet`' and '`--no-save`'.

'`--verbose`'
> Print more information about progress, and in particular set R's option `verbose` to `TRUE`. R code uses this option to control the printing of diagnostic messages.

'`--debugger=`*name*'
'`-d `*name*' (UNIX only) Run R through debugger *name*. For most debuggers (the exceptions are `valgrind` and recent versions of `gdb`), further command line options are disregarded, and should instead be given when starting the R executable from inside the debugger.

'`--gui=`*type*'
'`-g `*type*' (UNIX only) Use *type* as graphical user interface (note that this also includes interactive graphics). Currently, possible values for *type* are '`X11`' (the default), provided that '`Tcl/Tk`' support is available, '`Tk`' and '`gnome`' provided that package **gnomeGUI** is installed. (For back-compatibility, '`x11`', '`tk`' and '`GNOME`' are accepted.)

'`--args`' This flag does nothing except cause the rest of the command line to be skipped: this can be useful to retrieve values from it with `commandArgs(TRUE)`.

Note that input and output can be redirected in the usual way (using '`<`' and '`>`'), but the line length limit of 1024 bytes still applies. Warning and error messages are sent to the error channel (`stderr`) except on Windows 9X/ME.

The command `R CMD` allows the invocation of various tools which are useful in conjunction with R, but not intended to be called "directly". The general form is

> `R CMD `*command args*

where *command* is the name of the tool and *args* the arguments passed on to it.

Currently, the following tools are available.

`BATCH`   Run R in batch mode.

`COMPILE`   (UNIX only) Compile files for use with R.

---

[1] 2.5Gb on versions of Windows that support 3Gb per process and have the support enabled: see the '`rw-FAQ`' Q2.9.

Appendix B: Invoking R   84

SHLIB	Build shared library for dynamic loading.
INSTALL	Install add-on packages.
REMOVE	Remove add-on packages.
build	Build (that is, package) add-on packages.
check	Check add-on packages.
LINK	(UNIX only) Front-end for creating executable programs.
Rprof	Post-process R profiling files.
Rdconv	Convert Rd format to various other formats, including HTML, Nroff, LaTeX, plain text, and S documentation format.
Rd2dvi	Convert Rd format to DVI/PDF.
Rd2txt	Convert Rd format to text.
Sd2Rd	Convert S documentation to Rd format.
config	(UNIX only) Obtain configuration information.

Use

```
R CMD command --help
```

to obtain usage information for each of the tools accessible via the R CMD interface.

B.2 Invoking R under Windows

There are two ways to run R under Windows. Within a terminal window (e.g. cmd.exe or command.com or a more capable shell), the methods described in the previous section may be used, invoking by R.exe or more directly by Rterm.exe. (These are principally intended for batch use.) For interactive use, there is a console-based GUI (Rgui.exe).

The startup procedure under Windows is very similar to that under UNIX, but references to the 'home directory' need to be clarified, as this is not always defined on Windows. If the environment variable R_USER is defined, that gives the home directory. Next, if the environment variable HOME is defined, that gives the home directory. After those two user-controllable settings, R tries to find system defined home directories. It first tries to use the Windows "personal" directory (typically C:\Documents and Settings\username\My Documents in Windows XP). If that fails, and environment variables HOMEDRIVE and HOMEPATH are defined (and they normally are under Windows NT/2000/XP) these define the home directory. Failing all those, the home directory is taken to be the starting directory.

You need to ensure that either the environment variables TMPDIR, TMP and TEMP are either unset or one of them points to a valid place to create temporary files and directories.

Environment variables can be supplied as '*name=value*' pairs at the end of the command line.

The following additional command-line options are available when invoking RGui.exe.

'--mdi'
'--sdi'
'--no-mdi'

> Control whether Rgui will operate as an MDI program (with multiple child windows within one main window) or an SDI application (with multiple top-level windows for the console, graphics and pager). The command-line setting overrides the setting in the user's 'Rconsole' file.

Appendix B: Invoking R   85

'--debug'   Enable the "Break to debugger" menu item in Rgui, and trigger a break to the
            debugger during command line processing.

In Windows with R CMD you may also specify your own '*.bat' or '*.exe' file instead of one of
the built-in commands. It will be run with the following environment variables set appropriately:
R_HOME, R_VERSION, R_CMD, R_OSTYPE, PATH, PERL5LIB, and TEXINPUTS. For example, if you
already have 'latex.exe' on your path, then

        R CMD latex.exe mydoc

will run LATEX on 'mydoc.tex', with the path to R's 'share/texmf' macros added to TEXINPUTS.

B.3 Invoking R under Mac OS X

There are two ways to run R under Mac OS X. Within a Terminal.app window by invoking R,
the methods described in the previous sections apply. There is also console-based GUI (R.app)
that by default is installed in the Applications folder on your system. It is a standard double-
clickable Mac OS X application.

The startup procedure under Mac OS X is very similar to that under UNIX. The 'home
directory' is the one inside the R.framework, but the startup and current working directory are
set as the user's home directory unless a different startup directory is given in the Preferences
window accessible from within the GUI.

B.4 Scripting with R

If you just want to run a file 'foo.R' of R commands, the recommended way is to use R CMD
BATCH foo.R. If you want to run this in the background or as a batch job use OS-specific
facilities to do so: for example in most shells R CMD BATCH foo.R & runs a background job.

You can pass parameters to scripts via additional arguments on the command line: for
example

        R CMD BATCH --args arg1 arg2 foo.R &

will pass arguments to a script which can be retrieved as a character vector by

        args <- commandArgs(TRUE)

This is made simpler by the alternative front-end Rscript, which can be invoked by

        Rscript foo.R arg1 arg2

and this can also be used to write executable script files like (at least on Unix-alikes, and in
some Windows shells)

```
#! /path/to/Rscript
args <- commandArgs(TRUE)
...
q(status=<exit status code>)
```

If this is entered into a text file 'runfoo' and this is made executable (by chmod 755 runfoo),
it can be invoked for different arguments by

        runfoo arg1 arg2

For further options see help("Rscript"). If you do not wish to hardcode the path to Rscript
but have it in your path (which is normally the case for an installed R), use

```
#! /usr/bin/env Rscript
...
```

At least in Bourne and bash shells, the #! mechanism does **not** allow extra arguments like #!
/usr/bin/env Rscript --vanilla.

One thing to consider is what stdin() refers to. It is commonplace to write R scripts with
segments like

```
chem <- scan(n=24)
2.90 3.10 3.40 3.40 3.70 3.70 2.80 2.50 2.40 2.40 2.70 2.20
5.28 3.37 3.03 3.03 28.95 3.77 3.40 2.20 3.50 3.60 3.70 3.70
```

and `stdin()` refers to the script file to allow such traditional usage. If you want to refer to the process's 'stdin', use `"stdin"` as a `file` connection, e.g. `scan("stdin", ...)`.

Another way to write executable script files (suggested by Franois Pinard) is to use a *here document* like

```
#!/bin/sh
[environment variables can be set here]
R --slave [other options] <<EOF

    R program goes here...

EOF
```

but here `stdin()` refers to the program source and `"stdin"` will not be usable.

Appendix C The command-line editor

C.1 Preliminaries

When the GNU **readline** library is available at the time R is configured for compilation under UNIX, an inbuilt command line editor allowing recall, editing and re-submission of prior commands is used.

It can be disabled (useful for usage with ESS[1]) using the startup option '`--no-readline`'.

Windows versions of R have somewhat simpler command-line editing: see '`Console`' under the '`Help`' menu of the GUI, and the file '`README.Rterm`' for command-line editing under `Rterm.exe`.

When using R with **readline** capabilities, the functions described below are available.

Many of these use either Control or Meta characters. Control characters, such as `Control-m`, are obtained by holding the (CTRL) down while you press the (m) key, and are written as `C-m` below. Meta characters, such as `Meta-b`, are typed by holding down (META)[2] and pressing (b), and written as `M-b` in the following. If your terminal does not have a (META) key, you can still type Meta characters using two-character sequences starting with `ESC`. Thus, to enter `M-b`, you could type (ESC)(b). The `ESC` character sequences are also allowed on terminals with real Meta keys. Note that case is significant for Meta characters.

C.2 Editing actions

The R program keeps a history of the command lines you type, including the erroneous lines, and commands in your history may be recalled, changed if necessary, and re-submitted as new commands. In Emacs-style command-line editing any straight typing you do while in this editing phase causes the characters to be inserted in the command you are editing, displacing any characters to the right of the cursor. In *vi* mode character insertion mode is started by `M-i` or `M-a`, characters are typed and insertion mode is finished by typing a further (ESC).

Pressing the (RET) command at any time causes the command to be re-submitted.

Other editing actions are summarized in the following table.

C.3 Command-line editor summary

Command recall and vertical motion

`C-p`   Go to the previous command (backwards in the history).

`C-n`   Go to the next command (forwards in the history).

`C-r text`   Find the last command with the *text* string in it.

On most terminals, you can also use the up and down arrow keys instead of `C-p` and `C-n`, respectively.

Horizontal motion of the cursor

`C-a`   Go to the beginning of the command.

`C-e`   Go to the end of the line.

`M-b`   Go back one word.

`M-f`   Go forward one word.

---

[1] The 'Emacs Speaks Statistics' package; see the URL http://ESS.R-project.org

[2] On a PC keyboard this is usually the Alt key, occasionally the 'Windows' key.

Appendix C: The command-line editor   88

C-b   Go back one character.

C-f   Go forward one character.

On most terminals, you can also use the left and right arrow keys instead of C-b and C-f, respectively.

Editing and re-submission

text   Insert *text* at the cursor.

C-f text   Append *text* after the cursor.

(DEL)   Delete the previous character (left of the cursor).

C-d   Delete the character under the cursor.

M-d   Delete the rest of the word under the cursor, and "save" it.

C-k   Delete from cursor to end of command, and "save" it.

C-y   Insert (yank) the last "saved" text here.

C-t   Transpose the character under the cursor with the next.

M-l   Change the rest of the word to lower case.

M-c   Change the rest of the word to upper case.

(RET)   Re-submit the command to R.

The final (RET) terminates the command line editing sequence.

Appendix D Function and variable index

Appendix D: Function and variable index   90

Appendix D: Function and variable index 91

Appendix E Concept index

Appendix E: Concept index 93

Appendix F References

D. M. Bates and D. G. Watts (1988), *Nonlinear Regression Analysis and Its Applications*. John Wiley & Sons, New York.

Richard A. Becker, John M. Chambers and Allan R. Wilks (1988), *The New S Language*. Chapman & Hall, New York. This book is often called the *"Blue Book"*.

John M. Chambers and Trevor J. Hastie eds. (1992), *Statistical Models in S*. Chapman & Hall, New York. This is also called the *"White Book"*.

John M. Chambers (1998) *Programming with Data*. Springer, New York. This is also called the *"Green Book"*.

A. C. Davison and D. V. Hinkley (1997), *Bootstrap Methods and Their Applications*, Cambridge University Press.

Annette J. Dobson (1990), *An Introduction to Generalized Linear Models*, Chapman and Hall, London.

Peter McCullagh and John A. Nelder (1989), *Generalized Linear Models*. Second edition, Chapman and Hall, London.

John A. Rice (1995), *Mathematical Statistics and Data Analysis*. Second edition. Duxbury Press, Belmont, CA.

S. D. Silvey (1970), *Statistical Inference*. Penguin, London.

R Language Definition

The following document is the official definition of the R language. The document is provided and reprinted verbatim with the permission of the R Development Core Team.

This document covers R version 2.5.1 released 6/27/2007. The release version is considered a draft release and is the latest available at the time of publication.

R Language Definition

Version 2.5.1 (2007-06-27) **DRAFT**

R Development Core Team

ISBN 3-900051-13-5

Table of Contents

1 Introduction

R is a system for statistical computation and graphics. It provides, among other things, a programming language, high level graphics, interfaces to other languages and debugging facilities. This manual details and defines the R language.

The R language is a dialect of S which was designed in the 1980s and has been in widespread use in the statistical community since. Its principal designer, John M. Chambers, was awarded the 1998 ACM Software Systems Award for S.

The language syntax has a superficial similarity with C, but the semantics are of the FPL (functional programming language) variety with stronger affinities with Lisp and APL. In particular, it allows "computing on the language", which in turn makes it possible to write functions that take expressions as input, something that is often useful for statistical modeling and graphics.

It is possible to get quite far using R interactively, executing simple expressions from the command line. Some users may never need to go beyond that level, others will want to write their own functions either in an ad hoc fashion to systematize repetitive work or with the perspective of writing add-on packages for new functionality.

The purpose of this manual is to document the language *per se*. That is, the objects that it works on, and the details of the expression evaluation process, which are useful to know when programming R functions. Major subsystems for specific tasks, such as graphics, are only briefly described in this manual and will be documented separately.

Although much of the text will equally apply to S, there are also some substantial differences, and in order not to confuse the issue we shall concentrate on describing R.

The design of the language contains a number of fine points and common pitfalls which may surprise the user. Most of these are due to consistency considerations at a deeper level, as we shall explain. There are also a number of useful shortcuts and idioms, which allow the user to express quite complicated operations succinctly. Many of these become natural once one is familiar with the underlying concepts. In some cases, there are multiple ways of performing a task, but some of the techniques will rely on the language implementation, and others work at a higher level of abstraction. In such cases we shall indicate the preferred usage.

Some familiarity with R is assumed. This is not an introduction to R but rather a programmers' reference manual. Other manuals provide complementary information: in particular section "Preface" in *R Introduction* provides an introduction to R and section "System and foreign language interfaces" in *Writing R Extensions* details how to extend R using compiled code.

2 Objects

In every computer language variables provide a means of accessing the data stored in memory. R does not provide direct access to the computer's memory but rather provides a number of specialized data structures we will refer to as objects. These objects are referred to through symbols or variables. In R, however, the symbols are themselves objects and can be manipulated in the same way as any other object. This is different from many other languages and has wide ranging effects.

In this chapter we provide preliminary descriptions of the various data structures provided in R. More detailed discussions of many of them will be found in the subsequent chapters. The R specific function `typeof` returns the *type* of an R object. Note that in the C code underlying R, all objects are pointers to a structure with typedef SEXPREC; the different R data types are represented in C by SEXPTYPE, which determines how the information in the various parts of the structure is used.

The following table describes the possible values returned by `typeof` and what they are.

`"NULL"`	NULL
`"symbol"`	a variable name
`"pairlist"`	a pairlist object (mainly internal)
`"closure"`	a function
`"environment"`	an environment
`"promise"`	an object used to implement lazy evaluation
`"language"`	an R language construct
`"special"`	an internal function that does not evaluate its arguments
`"builtin"`	an internal function that evaluates its arguments
`"char"`	a 'scalar' string object (internal only) ***
`"logical"`	a vector containing logical values
`"integer"`	a vector containing integer values
`"double"`	a vector containing real values
`"complex"`	a vector containing complex values
`"character"`	a vector containing character values
`"..."`	the special variable length argument ***
`"any"`	a special type that matches all types: there are no objects of this type
`"expression"`	an expression object
`"list"`	a list
`"bytecode"`	byte code (internal only) ***
`"externalptr"`	an external pointer object
`"weakref"`	a weak reference object
`"raw"`	a vector containing bytes
`"S4"`	an S4 object which is not a simple object

Users cannot easily get hold of objects of types marked with a '***'.

Function `mode` gives information about the *mode* of an object in the sense of Becker, Chambers & Wilks (1988), and is more compatible with other implementations of the S language. Finally, the function `storage.mode` returns the *storage mode* of its argument in the sense of Becker et al. (1988). It is generally used when calling functions written in another language, such as C or FORTRAN, to ensure that R objects have the data type expected by the routine being called. (In the S language, vectors with integer or real values are both of mode `"numeric"`, so their storage modes need to be distinguished.)

```
> x <- 1:3
> typeof(x)
```

Chapter 2: Objects   3

```
[1] "integer"
> mode(x)
[1] "numeric"
> storage.mode(x)
[1] "integer"
```

R objects are often coerced to different types during computations. There are also many functions available to perform explicit coercion. When programming in the R language the type of an object generally doesn't affect the computations, however, when dealing with foreign languages or the operating system it is often necessary to ensure that an object is of the correct type.

2.1 Basic types

2.1.1 Vectors

Vectors can be thought of as contiguous cells containing data. Cells are accessed through indexing operations such as `x[5]`. More details are given in Section 3.4 [Indexing], page 15.

R has six basic ('atomic') vector types: logical, integer, real, complex, string (or character) and raw. The modes and storage modes for the different vector types are listed in the following table.

typeof	mode	storage.mode
logical	logical	logical
integer	numeric	integer
double	numeric	double
complex	complex	complex
character	character	character
raw	raw	raw

Single numbers, such as `4.2`, and strings, such as `"four point two"` are still vectors, of length 1; there are no more basic types. Vectors with length zero are possible (and useful).

String vectors have mode and storage mode `"character"`. A single element of a character vector is often referred to as a *character string*.

2.1.2 Lists

Lists ("generic vectors") are another kind of data storage. Lists have elements, each of which can contain any type of R object, i.e. the elements of a list do not have to be of the same type. List elements are accessed through three different indexing operations. These are explained in detail in Section 3.4 [Indexing], page 15.

Lists are vectors, and the basic vector types are referred to as *atomic vectors* where it is necessary to exclude lists.

2.1.3 Language objects

There are three types of objects that constitute the R language. They are *calls, expressions*, and *names*. Since R has objects of type `"expression"` we will try to avoid the use of the word expression in other contexts. In particular syntactically correct expressions will be referred to as *statements*.

These objects have modes `"call"`, `"expression"`, and `"name"`, respectively.

They can be created directly from expressions using the `quote` mechanism and converted to and from lists by the `as.list` and `as.call` functions. Components of the parse tree can be extracted using the standard indexing operations.

2.1.3.1 Symbol objects

Symbols refer to R objects. The name of any R object is usually a symbol. Symbols can be created through the functions `as.name` and `quote`.

Symbol have mode `"name"`, storage mode `"symbol"`, and type `"symbol"`. They can be coerced to and from character strings using `as.character` and `as.name`. They naturally appear as atoms of parsed expressions, try e.g. `as.list(quote(x + y))`.

2.1.4 Expression objects

In R one can have objects of type `"expression"`. An *expression* contains one or more statements. A statement is a syntactically correct collection of tokens. Expression objects are special language objects which contain parsed but unevaluated R statements. The main difference is that an expression object can contain several such expressions. Another more subtle difference is that objects of type `"expression"` are only evaluated when explicitly passed to `eval`, whereas other language objects may get evaluated in some unexpected cases.

An expression object behaves much like a list and its components should be accessed in the same way as the components of a list.

2.1.5 Function objects

In R functions are objects and can be manipulated in much the same way as any other object. Functions (or more precisely, function closures) have three basic components: a formal argument list, a body and an environment. The argument list is a comma-separated list of arguments. An argument can be a symbol, or a '*symbol = default*' construct, or the special argument '...'. The second form of argument is used to specify a default value for an argument. This value will be used if the function is called without any value specified for that argument. The '...' argument is special and can contain any number of arguments. It is generally used if the number of arguments is unknown or in cases where the arguments will be passed on to another function.

The body is a parsed R statement. It is usually a collection of statements in braces but it can be a single statement, a symbol or even a constant.

A function's environment is the environment that was active at the time that the function was created. Any symbols bound in that environment are *captured* and available to the function. This combination of the code of the function and the bindings in its environment is called a 'function closure', a term from functional programming theory. In this document we generally use the term 'function', but use 'closure' to emphasize the importance of the attached environment.

It is possible to extract and manipulate the three parts of a closure object using `formals`, `body`, and `environment` constructs (all three can also be used on the left hand side of assignments). The last of these can be used to remove unwanted environment capture.

When a function is called, a new environment (called the *evaluation environment*) is created, whose enclosure (see Section 2.1.10 [Environment objects], page 5) is the environment from the function closure. This new environment is initially populated with the unevaluated arguments to the function; as evaluation proceeds, local variables are created within it.

There is also a facility for converting functions to and from list structures using `as.list` and `as.function`. These have been included to provide compatibility with S and their use is discouraged.

2.1.6 NULL

There is a special object called `NULL`. It is used whenever there is a need to indicate or specify that an object is absent. It should not be confused with a vector or list of zero length.

The `NULL` object has no type and no modifiable properties. There is only one `NULL` object in R, to which all instances refer. To test for `NULL` use `is.null`. You cannot set attributes on `NULL`.

2.1.7 Builtin objects and special forms

These two kinds of object contain the builtin functions of R, i.e., those that are displayed as
.Primitive in code listings (as well as those accessed via the .Internal function and hence not
user-visible as objects). The difference between the two lies in the argument handling. Builtin
functions have all their arguments evaluated and passed to the internal function, in accordance
with *call-by-value*, whereas special functions pass the unevaluated arguments to the internal
function.

From the R language, these objects are just another kind of function, except that their
definition cannot be listed. The typeof function can distinguish them from interpreted functions.

2.1.8 Promise objects

Promise objects are part of R's lazy evaluation mechanism. They contain three slots: a value,
an expression, and an environment. When a function is called the arguments are matched and
then each of the formal arguments is bound to a promise. The expression that was given for
that formal argument and a pointer to the environment the function was called from are stored
in the promise.

Until that argument is accessed there is no *value* associated with the promise. When the
argument is accessed, the stored expression is evaluated in the stored environment, and the result
is returned. The result is also saved by the promise. The substitute function will extract the
content of the expression slot. This allows the programmer to access either the value or the
expression associated with the promise.

Within the R language, promise objects are almost only seen implicitly. (In an upcoming
release they will never be visible to R code, as they will always be evaluated when accessed.)
Actual function arguments are of this type. There is also a delayedAssign function that will
make a promise out of an expression. There is generally no way in R code to check whether an
object is a promise or not, nor is there a way to use R code to determine the environment of a
promise.

2.1.9 Dot-dot-dot

The '...' object type is stored as a type of pairlist. The components of '...' can be accessed
in the usual pairlist manner from C code, but is not easily accessed as an object in interpreted
code. The object can be captured as a list, so for example in table one sees

```
    args <- list(...)
##  ....
    for (a in args) {
##  ....
```

If a function has '...' as a formal argument then any actual arguments that do not match a
formal argument are matched with '...'.

2.1.10 Environments

Environments can be thought of as consisting of two things. A *frame*, consisting of a set of
symbol-value pairs, and an *enclosure*, a pointer to an enclosing environment. When R looks
up the value for a symbol the frame is examined and if a matching symbol is found its value
will be returned. If not, the enclosing environment is then accessed and the process repeated.
Environments form a tree structure in which the enclosures play the role of parents. The tree
of environments is rooted in an empty environment, available through emptyenv(), which has
no parent. It is the direct parent of the environment of the base package (available through
the baseenv() function). Formerly baseenv() had the special value NULL, but as from version
2.4.0, the use of NULL as an environment is defunct.

Environments are created implicitly by function calls, as described in Section 2.1.5 [Function objects], page 4 and Section 3.5.2 [Lexical environment], page 19. In this case the environment contains the variables local to the function (including the arguments), and its enclosure is the environment of the currently called function. Environments may also be created directly by `new.env`. The frame content of an environment can be accessed and manipulated by use of `ls`, `get` and `assign` as well as `eval` and `evalq`.

The `parent.env` function may be used to access the enclosure of an environment.

Unlike most other R objects, environments are not copied when passed to functions or used in assignments. Thus, if you assign the same environment to several symbols and change one, the others will change too. In particular, assigning attributes to an environment can lead to surprises.

2.1.11 Pairlist objects

Pairlist objects are similar to Lisp's dotted-pair lists. They are used extensively in the internals of R, but are rarely visible in interpreted code, although they are returned by `formals`, and can be created by (e.g.) the `pairlist` function. A zero-length pairlist is `NULL`, as would be expected in Lisp but in contrast to a zero-length list. Each such object has three slots, a CAR value, a CDR value and a TAG value. The TAG value is a text string and CAR and CDR usually represent, respectively, a list item (head) and the remainder (tail) of the list with a NULL object as terminator (the CAR/CDR terminology is traditional Lisp and originally referred to the address and decrement registers on an early 60's IBM computer).

Pairlists are handled in the R language in exactly the same way as generic vectors ("lists"). In particular, elements are accessed using the same [[]] syntax. The use of pairlists is deprecated since generic vectors are usually more efficient to use. When an internal pairlist is accessed from R it is generally (including when subsetted) converted to a generic vector.

In a very few cases pairlists are user-visible: one is `.Options`.

2.1.12 The "Any" type

It is not really possible for an object to be of "Any" type, but it is nevertheless a valid type value. It gets used in certain (rather rare) circumstances, e.g. `as.vector(x, "any")`, indicating that type coercion should not be done.

2.2 Attributes

All objects except `NULL` can have one or more attributes attached to them. Attributes are stored as a pairlist where all elements are named, but should be thought of as a set of name=value pairs. A listing of the attributes can be obtained using `attributes` and set by `attributes<-`, individual components are accessed using `attr` and `attr<-`.

Some attributes have special accessor functions (e.g. `levels<-` for factors) and these should be used when available. In addition to hiding details of implementation they may perform additional operations. R attempts to intercept calls to `attr<-` and to `attributes<-` that involve the special attributes and enforces the consistency checks.

Matrices and arrays are simply vectors with the attribute `dim` and optionally `dimnames` attached to the vector.

Attributes are used to implement the class structure used in R. If an object has a `class` attribute then that attribute will be examined during evaluation. The class structure in R is described in detail in Chapter 5 [Object-oriented programming], page 26.

2.2.1 Names

A `names` attribute, when present, labels the individual elements of a vector or list. When an object is printed the `names` attribute, when present, is used to label the elements. The `names` attribute can also be used for indexing purposes, for example, `quantile(x)["25%"]`.

One may get and set the names using `names` and `names<-` constructions. The latter will perform the necessary consistency checks to ensure that the names attribute has the proper type and length.

Pairlists and one-dimensional arrays are treated specially. For pairlist objects, a virtual `names` attribute is used; the `names` attribute is really constructed from the tags of the list components. For one-dimensional arrays the `names` attribute really accesses `dimnames[[1]]`.

2.2.2 Dimensions

The `dim` attribute is used to implement arrays. The content of the array is stored in a vector in column-major order and the `dim` attribute is a vector of integers specifying the respective extents of the array. R ensures that the length of the vector is the product of the lengths of the dimensions. The length of one or more dimensions may be zero.

A vector is not the same as a one-dimensional array since the latter has a `dim` attribute of length one, whereas the former has no `dim` attribute.

2.2.3 Dimnames

Arrays may name each dimension separately using the `dimnames` attribute which is a list of character vectors. The `dimnames` list may itself have names which are then used for extent headings when printing arrays.

2.2.4 Classes

R has an elaborate class system, controlled via the `class` attribute. This attribute is a character vector containing the list of classes that an object inherits from. This forms the basis of the "generic methods" functionality in R.

This attribute can be accessed and manipulated virtually without restriction by users. There is no checking that an object actually contains the components that class methods expect. Thus, altering the `class` attribute should be done with caution, and when they are available specific creation and coercion functions should be preferred.

2.2.5 Time series attributes

The `tsp` attribute is used to hold parameters of time series, start, end, and frequency. This construction is mainly used to handle series with periodic substructure such as monthly or quarterly data.

2.2.6 Copying of attributes

Whether attributes should be copied when an object is altered is a complex area, but there are some general rules (Becker, Chambers & Wilks, 1988, pp. 144–6).

Scalar functions (those which operate element-by-element on a vector and whose output is similar to the input) should preserve attributes (except perhaps class).

Binary operations normally copy most attributes from the longer argument (and if they are of the same length from both, preferring the values on the first). Here 'most' means all except the `names`, `dim` and `dimnames` which are set appropriately by the code for the operator.

Subsetting (other than by an empty index) generally drops all attributes except `names`, `dim` and `dimnames` which are reset as appropriate. On the other hand, subassignment generally preserves attributes even if the length is changed. Coercion drops all attributes.

The default method for sorting drops all attributes except names, which are sorted along with the object.

2.3 Special compound objects

2.3.1 Factors

Factors are used to describe items that can have a finite number of values (gender, social class, etc.). A factor has a `levels` attribute and class `"factor"`. Optionally, it may also contain a `contrasts` attribute which controls the parametrisation used when the factor is used in a modeling functions.

A factor may be purely nominal or may have ordered categories. In the latter case, it should be defined as such and have a `class` vector `c("ordered"," factor")`.

Factors are currently implemented using an integer array to specify the actual levels and a second array of names that are mapped to the integers. Rather unfortunately users often make use of the implementation in order to make some calculations easier. This, however, is an implementation issue and is not guaranteed to hold in all implementations of R.

2.3.2 Data frame objects

Data frames are the R structures which most closely mimic the SAS or SPSS data set, i.e. a "cases by variables" matrix of data.

A data frame is a list of vectors, factors, and/or matrices all having the same length (number of rows in the case of matrices). In addition, a data frame generally has a `names` attribute labeling the variables and a `row.names` attribute for labeling the cases.

A data frame can contain a list that is the same length as the other components. The list can contain elements of differing lengths thereby providing a data structure for ragged arrays. However, as of this writing such arrays are not generally handled correctly.

3 Evaluation of expressions

When a user types a command at the prompt (or when an expression is read from a file) the first thing that happens to it is that the command is transformed by the parser into an internal representation. The evaluator executes parsed R expressions and returns the value of the expression. All expressions have a value. This is the core of the language.

This chapter describes the basic mechanisms of the evaluator, but avoids discussion of specific functions or groups of functions which are described in separate chapters later on or where the help pages should be sufficient documentation.

Users can construct expressions and invoke the evaluator on them.

3.1 Simple evaluation

3.1.1 Constants

Any number typed directly at the prompt is a constant and is evaluated.

```
> 1
[1] 1
```

Perhaps unexpectedly, the number returned from the expression 1 is a numeric. In most cases, the difference between an integer and a numeric value will be unimportant as R will do the right thing when using the numbers. There are, however, times when we would like to explicitly create an integer value for a constant. We can do this by calling the function `as.integer` or using various other techniques. But perhaps the simplest approach is to qualify our constant with the suffix character 'L'. For example, to create the integer value 1, we might use

```
> 1L
[1]
```

We can use the 'L' suffix to qualify any number with the intent of making it an explicit integer. So '0x10L' creates the integer value 16 from the hexadecimal representation. The constant `1e3L` gives 1000 as an integer rather than a numeric value and is equivalent to `1000L`. (Note that the 'L' is treated as qualifying the term `1e3` and not the 3.) If we qualify a value with 'L' that is not an integer value, e.g. `1e-3L`, we get a warning and the numeric value is created. A warning is also created if there is an unnecessary decimal point in the number, e.g. `1.L`.

We get a syntax error when using 'L' with complex numbers, e.g. `12iL` gives an error.

Constants are fairly boring and to do more we need symbols.

3.1.2 Symbol lookup

When a new variable is created it must have a name so it can be referenced and it usually has a value. The name itself is a symbol. When a symbol is evaluated its value is returned. Later we shall explain in detail how to determine the value associated with a symbol.

In this small example `y` is a symbol and its value is 4. A symbol is an R object too, but one rarely needs to deal with symbols directly, except when doing "programming on the language" (Chapter 6 [Computing on the language], page 32).

```
> y <- 4
> y
[1] 4
```

3.1.3 Function calls

Most of the computations carried out in R involve the evaluation of functions. We will also refer to this as function *invocation*. Functions are invoked by name with a list of arguments separated by commas.

```
> mean(1:10)
[1] 5.5
```

In this example the function `mean` was called with one argument, the vector of integers from 1 to 10.

R contains a huge number of functions with different purposes. Most are used for producing a result which is an R object, but others are used for their side effects, e.g., printing and plotting functions.

Function calls can have *tagged* (or *named*) arguments, as in `plot(x, y, pch = 3)` arguments without tags are known as *positional* since the function must distinguish their meaning from their sequential positions among the arguments of the call, e.g., that `x` denotes the abscissa variable and `y` the ordinate. The use of tags/names is an obvious convenience for functions with a large number of optional arguments.

A special type of function calls can appear on the left hand side of the assignment operator as in

```
> class(x) <- "foo"
```

What this construction really does is to call the function `class<-` with the original object and the right hand side. This function performs the modification of the object and returns the result which is then stored back into the original variable. (At least conceptually, this is what happens. Some additional effort is made to avoid unnecessary data duplication.)

3.1.4 Operators

R allows the use of arithmetic expressions using operators similar to those of the C programming language, for instance

```
> 1 + 2
[1] 3
```

Expressions can be grouped using parentheses, mixed with function calls, and assigned to variables in a straightforward manner

```
> y <- 2 * (a + log(x))
```

R contains a number of operators. They are listed in the table below.

−	Minus, can be unary or binary
+	Plus, can be unary or binary
!	Unary not
~	Tilde, used for model formulae, can be either unary or binary
?	Help
:	Sequence, binary (in model formulae: interaction)
*	Multiplication, binary
/	Division, binary
^	Exponentiation, binary
%x%	Special binary operators, x can be replaced by any valid name
%%	Modulus, binary
%/%	Integer divide, binary
%*%	Matrix product, binary
%o%	Outer product, binary
%x%	Kronecker product, binary
%in%	Matching operator, binary (in model formulae: nesting)
<	Less than, binary
>	Greater than, binary
==	Equal to, binary
>=	Greater than or equal to, binary

<=	Less than or equal to, binary
&	And, binary, vectorized
&&	And, binary, not vectorized
|	Or, binary, vectorized
||	Or, binary, not vectorized
<-	Left assignment, binary
->	Right assignment, binary
$	List subset, binary

Except for the syntax, there is no difference between applying an operator and calling a function. In fact, x + y can equivalently be written '+'(x, y). Notice that since '+' is a non-standard function name, it needs to be quoted.

R deals with entire vectors of data at a time, and most of the elementary operators and basic mathematical functions like `log` are vectorized (as indicated in the table above). This means that e.g. adding two vectors of the same length will create a vector containing the element-wise sums, implicitly looping over the vector index. This applies also to other operators like -, *, and / as well as to higher dimensional structures. Notice in particular that multiplying two matrices does not produce the usual matrix product (the %*% operator exists for that purpose). Some finer points relating to vectorized operations will be discussed in Section 3.3 [Elementary arithmetic operations], page 14.

To access individual elements of an atomic vector, one generally uses the x[i] construction.

```
> x <- rnorm(5)
> x
[1] -0.12526937 -0.27961154 -1.03718717 -0.08156527  1.37167090
> x[2]
[1] -0.2796115
```

List components are more commonly accessed using x$a or x[[i]].

```
> x <- options()
> x$prompt
[1] "> "
```

Indexing constructs can also appear on the right hand side of an assignment.

Like the other operators, indexing is really done by functions, and one could have used '['(x, 2) instead of x[2].

R's indexing operations contain many advanced features which are further described in Section 3.4 [Indexing], page 15.

3.2 Control structures

Computation in R consists of sequentially evaluating *statements*. Statements, such as x<-1:10 or mean(y), can be separated by either a semi-colon or a new line. Whenever the evaluator is presented with a syntactically complete statement that statement is evaluated and the *value* returned. The result of evaluating a statement can be referred to as the value of the statement[1] The value can always be assigned to a symbol.

Both semicolons and new lines can be used to separate statements. A semicolon always indicates the end of a statement while a new line *may* indicate the end of a statement. If the current statement is not syntactically complete new lines are simply ignored by the evaluator. If the session is interactive the prompt changes from '>' to '+'.

```
> x <- 0; x + 5
[1] 5
```

---

[1] Evaluation always takes place in an environment. See Section 3.5 [Scope of variables], page 19 for more details.

```
> y <- 1:10
> 1; 2
[1] 1
[1] 2
```

Statements can be grouped together using braces '{' and '}'. A group of statements is sometimes called a *block*. Single statements are evaluated when a new line is typed at the end of the syntactically complete statement. Blocks are not evaluated until a new line is entered after the closing brace. In the remainder of this section, *statement* refers to either a single statement or a block.

```
> { x <- 0
+ x + 5
+ }
[1] 5
```

3.2.1 if

The if/else statement conditionally evaluates two statements. There is a *condition* which is evaluated and if the *value* is TRUE then the first statement is evaluated; otherwise the second statement will be evaluated. The if/else statement returns, as its value, the value of the statement that was selected. The formal syntax is

```
if ( statement1 )
    statement2
else
    statement3
```

First, *statement1* is evaluated to yield *value1*. If *value1* is a logical vector with first element TRUE then *statement2* is evaluated. If the first element of *value1* is FALSE then *statement3* is evaluated. If *value1* is a numeric vector then *statement3* is evaluated when the first element of *value1* is zero and otherwise *statement2* is evaluated. Only the first element of *value1* is used. All other elements are ignored. If *value1* has any type other than a logical or a numeric vector an error is signalled.

If/else statements can be used to avoid numeric problems such as taking the logarithm of a negative number. Because if/else statements are the same as other statements you can assign the value of them. The two examples below are equivalent.

```
> if( any(x <= 0) ) y <- log(1+x) else y <- log(x)
> y <- if( any(x <= 0) ) log(1+x) else log(x)
```

The else clause is optional. The statement if(any(x <= 0)) x <- x[x <= 0] is valid. When the if statement is not in a block the else, if present, must appear on the same line as *statement1*. Otherwise the new line at the end of *statement1* yields a syntactically complete statement that is evaluated.

If/else statements can be nested.

```
if ( statement1 )
    statement2
else if ( statement3 )
    statement4
else if ( statement5 )
    statement6
else
    statement8
```

One of the even numbered statements will be evaluated and the resulting value returned. If the optional else clause is omitted and all the odd numbered *statement*'s evaluate to FALSE no statement will be evaluated and NULL is returned.

The odd numbered *statements* are evaluated, in order, until one evaluates to TRUE and then the associated even numbered *statement* is evaluated. In this example, *statement6* will only be evaluated if *statement1* is FALSE and *statement3* is FALSE and *statement5* is TRUE. There is no limit to the number of else if clauses that are permitted.

3.2.2 Looping

R has three statements that provide explicit looping.[2] They are for, while and repeat. The two built-in constructs, next and break, provide additional control over the evaluation. Each of the three statements returns the value of the last statement that was evaluated. It is possible, although uncommon, to assign the result of one of these statements to a symbol. R provides other functions for implicit looping such as tapply, apply, and lapply. In addition many operations, especially arithmetic ones, are vectorized so you may not need to use a loop.

There are two statements that can be used to explicitly control looping. They are break and next. The break statement causes an exit from the innermost loop that is currently being executed. The next statement immediately causes control to return to the start of the loop. The next iteration of the loop (if there is one) is then executed. No statement below next in the current loop is evaluated.

3.2.3 repeat

The repeat statement causes repeated evaluation of the body until a break is specifically requested. This means that you need to be careful when using repeat because of the danger of an infinite loop. The syntax of the repeat loop is

```
repeat statement
```

When using repeat, *statement* must be a block statement. You need to both perform some computation and test whether or not to break from the loop and usually this requires two statements.

3.2.4 while

The while statement is very similar to the repeat statement. The syntax of the while loop is

```
while ( statement1 ) statement2
```

where *statement1* is evaluated and if its value is TRUE then *statement2* is evaluated. This process continues until *statement1* evaluates to FALSE. If *statement2* is never evaluated then while returns NULL and otherwise it returns the value of the last evaluation of *statement2*.

3.2.5 for

The syntax of the for loop is

```
for ( name in vector )
    statement1
```

where *vector* can be either a vector or a list. For each element in *vector* the variable *name* is set to the value of that element and *statement1* is evaluated. A side effect is that the variable *name* still exists after the loop has concluded and it has the value of the last element of *vector* that the loop was evaluated for.

3.2.6 switch

Technically speaking, switch is just another function, but its semantics are close to those of control structures of other programming languages.

The syntax is

---

[2] Looping is the repeated evaluation of a statement or block of statements.

```
switch (statement, list)
```
where the elements of *list* may be named. First, *statement* is evaluated and the result, *value*, obtained. If *value* is a number between 1 and the length of *list* then the corresponding element *list* is evaluated and the result returned. If *value* is too large or too small NULL is returned.

```
> x <- 3
> switch(x, 2+2, mean(1:10), rnorm(5))
[1]  2.2903605  2.3271663 -0.7060073  1.3622045 -0.2892720
> switch(2, 2+2, mean(1:10), rnorm(5))
[1] 5.5
> switch(6, 2+2, mean(1:10), rnorm(5))
NULL
```

If *value* is a character vector then the element of '...' with a name that exactly matches *value* is evaluated. If there is no match NULL is returned.

```
> y <- "fruit"
> switch(y, fruit = "banana", vegetable = "broccoli", meat = "beef")
[1] "banana"
```

A common use of switch is to branch according to the character value of one of the arguments to a function.

```
> centre <- function(x, type) {
+ switch(type,
+        mean = mean(x),
+        median = median(x),
+        trimmed = mean(x, trim = .1))
+ }
> x <- rcauchy(10)
> centre(x, "mean")
[1] 0.8760325
> centre(x, "median")
[1] 0.5360891
> centre(x, "trimmed")
[1] 0.6086504
```

switch returns either the value of the statement that was evaluated or NULL if no statement was evaluated.

To choose from a list of alternatives that already exists switch may not be the best way to select one for evaluation. It is often better to use eval and the subset operator, [[, directly via eval(x[[condition]]).

3.3 Elementary arithmetic operations

In this section, we discuss the finer points of the rules that apply to basic operation like addition or multiplication of two vectors or matrices.

3.3.1 Recycling rules

If one tries to add two structures with a different number of elements, then the shortest is recycled to length of longest. That is, if for instance you add c(1, 2, 3) to a six-element vector then you will really add c(1, 2, 3, 1, 2, 3). If the length of the longer vector is not a multiple of the shorter one, a warning is given.

As from R 1.4.0, any arithmetic operation involving a zero-length vector has a zero-length result.

One exception is that when adding vectors to matrices, a warning is not given if the lengths are incompatible.

Chapter 3: Evaluation of expressions   15

3.3.2 Propagation of names

propagation of names (first one wins, I think - also if it has no names?? —- first one *with names* wins, recycling causes shortest to lose names)

3.3.3 Dimensional attributes

(matrix+matrix, dimensions must match. vector+matrix: first recycle, then check if dims fit, error if not)

3.3.4 NA handling

Missing values in the statistical sense, that is, variables whose value is not known, have the value NA. This should not be confused with the `missing` property for a function argument that has not been supplied (see Section 4.1.2 [Arguments], page 22).

As the elements of an atomic vector must be of the same type there are multiple types of NA values. There is one case where this is particularly important to the user. The default type of NA is `logical`, unless coerced to some other type, so the appearance of a missing value may trigger logical rather than numeric indexing (see Section 3.4 [Indexing], page 15 for details).

Numeric and logical calculations with NA generally return NA. In cases where the result of the operation would be the same for all possible values the NA could take, the operation may return this value. In particular, 'FALSE & NA' is FALSE, 'TRUE | NA' is TRUE. NA is not equal to any other value or to itself; testing for NA is done using `is.na`. However, an NA value will match another NA value in `match`.

Numeric calculations whose result is undefined, such as '0/0', produce the value NaN. This exists only in the `double` type and for real or imaginary components of the complex type. The function `is.nan` is provided to check specifically for NaN, `is.na` also returns TRUE for NaN. Coercing NaN to logical or integer type gives an NA of the appropriate type, but coercion to character gives the string "NaN". NaN values are incomparable so tests of equality or collation involving NaN will result in NA. They are regarded as matching any NaN value (and no other value, not even NA) by `match`.

The NA of character type is as from R 1.5.0 distinct from the string "NA". Programmers who need to specify an explicit string NA should use 'as.character(NA)' rather than "NA", or set elements to NA using `is.na<-`.

As from R 2.5.0 there are constants NA_integer_, NA_real_, NA_complex_ and NA_character_ which will generate (in the parser) an NA value of the appropriate type, and will be used in deparsing when it is not otherwise possible to identify the type of an NA (and the `control` options ask for this to be done).

There is no NA value for raw vectors.

3.4 Indexing

R contains several constructs which allow access to individual elements or subsets through indexing operations. In the case of the basic vector types one can access the i-th element using `x[i]`, but there is also indexing of lists, matrices, and multi-dimensional arrays. There are several forms of indexing in addition to indexing with a single integer. Indexing can be used both to extract part of an object and to replace parts of an object (or to add parts).

R has three basic indexing operators, with syntax displayed by the following examples

```
x[i]
x[i, j]
x[[i]]
x[[i, j]]
x$a
```

```
x$"a"
```

For vectors and matrices the [[forms are rarely used, although they have some slight semantic differences from the [form (e.g. it drops any `names` or `dimnames` attribute, and that partial matching is used for character indices). When indexing multi-dimensional structures with a single index, x[[i]] or x[i] will return the ith sequential element of x.

For lists, one generally uses [[to select any single element, whereas [returns a list of the selected elements.

The [[form allows only a single element to be selected using integer or character indices, whereas [allows indexing by vectors. Note though that for a list, the index can be a vector and each element of the vector is applied in turn to the list, the selected component, the selected component of that component, and so on. The result is still a single element.

The form using $ applies to recursive objects such as lists and pairlists. It allows only a literal character string or a symbol as the index. That is, the index is not computable: for cases where you need to evaluate an expression to find the index, use x[[expr]]. When $ is applied to a non-recursive object the result is always NULL: as from R 2.5.0 this is deprecated and will give a warning.

3.4.1 Indexing by vectors

R allows some powerful constructions using vectors as indices. We shall discuss indexing of simple vectors first. For simplicity, assume that the expression is x[i]. Then the following possibilities exist according to the type of i.

- **Integer**. All elements of i must have the same sign. If they are positive, the elements of x with those index numbers are selected. If i contains negative elements, all elements except those indicated are selected.

  If i is positive and exceeds `length(x)` then the corresponding selection is NA. A negative out of bounds value for i causes an error.

  A special case is the zero index, which has null effects: x[0] is an empty vector and otherwise including zeros among positive or negative indices has the same effect as if they were omitted.

- **Other numeric**. Non-integer values are converted to integer (by truncation towards zero) before use.

- **Logical**. The indexing i should generally have the same length as x. If it is shorter, then its elements will be recycled as discussed in Section 3.3 [Elementary arithmetic operations], page 14. If it is longer, then x is conceptually extended with NAs. The selected values of x are those for which i is TRUE.

- **Character**. The strings in i are matched against the names attribute of x and the resulting integers are used. For [[and $ partial matching is used if exact matching fails, so x$aa will match x$aabb if x does not a component named "aa" and "aabb" is the first name which has prefix "aa". However, [requires an exact match. The string "" is treated specially: it indicates 'no name' and matches no element (not even those without a name). Note that partial matching is only used when extracting and not when replacing.

- **Factor**. The result is identical to x[as.integer(i)]. The factor levels are never used. If so desired, use x[as.character(i)] or a similar construction.

- **Empty**. The expression x[] returns x, but drops "irrelevant" attributes from the result. Only `names` and in multi-dimensional arrays `dim` and `dimnames` attributes are retained.

- **NULL**. This is treated as if it were `integer(0)`.

Indexing with a missing (i.e. NA) value gives an NA result. This rule applies also to the case of logical indexing, i.e. the elements of x that have an NA selector in i get included in the result, but their value will be NA.

Notice however, that there are different modes of NA—the literal constant is of mode "logical", but it is frequently automatically coerced to other types. One effect of this is that x[NA] has the length of x, but x[c(1, NA)] has length 2. That is because the rules for logical indices apply in the former case, but those for integer indices in the latter.

Indexing with [will also carry out the relevant subsetting of any names attributes.

3.4.2 Indexing matrices and arrays

Subsetting multi-dimensional structures generally follows the same rules as single-dimensional indexing for each index variable, with the relevant component of dimnames taking the place of names. A couple of special rules apply, though:

Normally, a structure is accessed using the number of indices corresponding to its dimension. It is however also possible to use a single index in which case the dim and dimnames attributes are disregarded and the result is effectively that of c(m)[i]. Notice that m[1] is usually very different from m[1,] or m[, 1].

It is possible to use a matrix of integers as an index. In this case, the number of columns of the matrix should match the number of dimensions of the structure, and the result will be a vector with length as the number of rows of the matrix. The following example shows how to extract the elements m[1, 1] and m[2, 2] in one operation.

```
> m <- matrix(1:4, 2)
> m
     [,1] [,2]
[1,]    1    3
[2,]    2    4
> i <- matrix(c(1, 1, 2, 2), 2, byrow = TRUE)
> i
     [,1] [,2]
[1,]    1    1
[2,]    2    2
> m[i]
[1] 1 4
```

Negative indices are not allowed in indexing matrices. NA and zero values are allowed: rows in an index matrix containing a zero are ignored, whereas rows containing an NA produce an NA in the result.

Both in the case of using a single index and in matrix indexing, a names attribute is used if present, as had the structure been one-dimensional.

If an indexing operation causes the result to have one of its extents of length one, as in selecting a single slice of a three-dimensional matrix with (say) m[2, ,], the corresponding dimension is generally dropped from the result. If a single-dimensional structure results, a vector is obtained. This is occasionally undesirable and can be turned off by adding the 'drop = FALSE' to the indexing operation. Notice that this is an additional argument to the [function and doesn't add to the index count. Hence the correct way of selecting the first row of a matrix as a 1 by *n* matrix is m[1, , drop = FALSE]. Forgetting to disable the dropping feature is a common cause of failure in general subroutines where an index occasionally, but not usually has length one. This rule still applies to a one-dimensional array, where any subsetting will give a vector result unless 'drop = FALSE' is used.

Notice that vectors are distinct from one-dimensional arrays in that the latter have dim and dimnames attributes (both of length one). One-dimensional arrays are not easily obtained from subsetting operations but they can be constructed explicitly and are returned by table. This is sometimes useful because the elements of the dimnames list may themselves be named, which is not the case for the names attribute.

Some operations such as `m[FALSE, ]` result in structures in which a dimension has zero extent. R generally tries to handle these structures sensibly.

3.4.3 Indexing other structures

The operator `[` is a generic function which allows class methods to be added, and the `$` and `[[` operators likewise. Thus, it is possible to have user-defined indexing operations for any structure. Such a function, say `[.foo` is called with a set of arguments of which the first is the structure being indexed and the rest are the indices. In the case of `$`, the index argument is of mode `"symbol"` even when using the `x$"abc"` form. It is important to be aware that class methods do not necessarily behave in the same way as the basic methods, for example with respect to partial matching.

The most important example of a class method for `[` is that used for data frames. It is not be described in detail here (see the help page for `[.data.frame`, but in broad terms, if two indices are supplied (even if one is empty) it creates matrix-like indexing for a structure that is basically a list of vectors of the same length. If a single index is supplied, it is interpreted as indexing the list of columns—in that case the `drop` argument is ignored, with a warning.

The basic operators `$` and `[[` can be applied to environments. Only character indices are allowed and no partial matching is done.

3.4.4 Subset assignment

Assignment to subsets of a structure is a special case of a general mechanism for complex assignment:

```
x[3:5] <- 13:15
```

The result of this commands is as if the following had been executed

```
'*tmp*' <- x
x <- "[<-"('*tmp*',3:5, value=13:15)
```

The same mechanism can be applied to other functions than `[`. The assignment function has the same name with `<-` pasted on. Its last argument, which must be called `value`, is the new value to be assigned.

```
names(x) <- c("a","b")
```

is equivalent to

```
'*tmp*' <- x
x <- "names<-"('*tmp*', value=c("a","b"))
```

Nesting of complex assignments is evaluated recursively

```
names(x)[3] <- "Three"
```

is equivalent to

```
'*tmp*' <- x
x <- "names<-"('*tmp*', value="[<-"(names('*tmp*'), 3, value="Three"))
```

Complex assignments in the enclosing environment (using `<<-`) are also permitted:

```
names(x)[3] <<- "Three"
```

is equivalent to

```
'*tmp*' <<- get(x, envir=parent.env(), inherits=TRUE)
names('*tmp*')[3] <- "Three"
x <<- '*tmp*'
```

and also to

```
'*tmp*' <- get(x,envir=parent.env(), inherits=TRUE)
x <<- "names<-"('*tmp*', value="[<-"(names('*tmp*'), 3, value="Three"))
```

Only the target variable is evaluated in the enclosing environment, so

```
e<-c(a=1,b=2)
i<-1
local({
    e <- c(A=10,B=11)
    i <-2
    e[i] <<- e[i]+1
})
```

uses the local value of i on both the LHS and RHS, and the local value of e on the RHS of the superassignment statement. It sets e in the outer environment to

```
a  b
1 12
```

That is, the superassignment is equivalent to the three lines

```
'*tmp*' <- get(x,envir=parent.env(), inherits=TRUE)
'*tmp*'[i] <- e[i]+1
x <<- '*tmp*'
```

Similarly

```
x[is.na(x)] <<- 0
```

is equivalent to

```
'*tmp*' <- get(x,envir=parent.env(), inherits=TRUE)
'*tmp*'[is.na(x)] <- 0
x <<- '*tmp*'
```

and not to

```
'*tmp*' <- get(x,envir=parent.env(), inherits=TRUE)
'*tmp*'[is.na('*tmp*')] <- 0
x <<- '*tmp*'
```

These two candidate interpretations differ only if there is also a local variable x. It is a good idea to avoid having a local variable with the same name as the target variable of a superassignment. As this case was handled incorrectly in versions 1.9.1 and earlier there must not be a serious need for such code.

3.5 Scope of variables

Almost every programming language has a set of scoping rules, allowing the same name to be used for different objects. This allows, e.g., a local variable in a function to have the same name as a global object.

R uses a *lexical scoping* model, similar to languages like Pascal. However, R is a *functional programming language* and allows dynamic creation and manipulation of functions and language objects, and has additional features reflecting this fact.

3.5.1 Global environment

The global environment is the root of the user workspace. An assignment operation from the command line will cause the relevant object to belong to the global environment. Its enclosing environment is the next environment on the search path, and so on back to the empty environment that is the enclosure of the base environment.

3.5.2 Lexical environment

Every call to a function creates a *frame* which contains the local variables created in the function, and is evaluated in an environment, which in combination creates a new environment.

Notice the terminology: A frame is a set of variables, an environment is a nesting of frames (or equivalently: the innermost frame plus the enclosing environment).

Environments may be assigned to variables or be contained in other objects. However, notice that they are not standard objects—in particular, they are not copied on assignment.

A closure (mode `"function"`) object will contain the environment in which it is created as part of its definition (By default. The environment can be manipulated using `environment<-`). When the function is subsequently called, its evaluation environment is created with the closure's environment as enclosure. Notice that this is not necessarily the environment of the caller!

Thus, when a variable is requested inside a function, it is first sought in the evaluation environment, then in the enclosure, the enclosure of the enclosure, etc.; once the global environment or the environment of a package is reached, the search continues up the search path to the environment of the base package. If the variable is not found there, the search will proceed next to the empty environment, and will fail.

3.5.3 The call stack

Every time a function is invoked a new evaluation frame is created. At any point in time during the computation the currently active environments are accessible through the *call stack*. Each time a function is invoked a special construct called a context is created internally and is placed on a list of contexts. When a function has finished evaluating its context is removed from the call stack.

Making variables defined higher up the call stack available is called dynamic scope. The binding for a variable is then determined by the most recent (in time) definition of the variable. This contradicts the default scoping rules in R, which use the bindings in the environment in which the function was defined (lexical scope). Some functions, particularly those that use and manipulate model formulas, need to simulate dynamic scope by directly accessing the call stack.

Access to the call stack is provided through a family of functions which have names that start with '`sys.`'. They are listed briefly below.

`sys.call`   Get the call for the specified context.

`sys.frame`
> Get the evaluation frame for the specified context.

`sys.nframe`
> Get the environment frame for all active contexts.

`sys.function`
> Get the function being invoked in the specified context.

`sys.parent`
> Get the parent of the current function invocation.

`sys.calls`
> Get the calls for all the active contexts.

`sys.frames`
> Get the evaluation frames for all the active contexts.

`sys.parents`
> Get the numeric labels for all active contexts.

`sys.on.exit`
> Set a function to be executed when the specified context is exited.

`sys.status`
> Calls `sys.frames`, `sys.parents` and `sys.calls`.

`parent.frame`
> Get the evaluation frame for the specified parent context.

3.5.4 Search path

In addition to the evaluation environment structure, R has a search path of environments which are searched for variables not found elsewhere. This is used for two things: packages of functions and attached user data.

The first element of the search path is the global environment and the last is the base package. An `Autoloads` environment is used for holding proxy objects that may be loaded on demand. Other environments are inserted in the path using `attach` or `library`.

Packages which have a *namespace* have a different search path. When a search for an R object is started from an object in such a package, the package itself is searched first, then its imports, then the base namespace and finally the global environment and the rest of the regular search path. The effect is that references to other objects in the same package will be resolved to the package, and objects cannot be masked by objects of the same name in the global environment or in other packages.

4 Functions

4.1 Writing functions

While R can be very useful as a data analysis tool most users very quickly find themselves wanting to write their own functions. This is one of the real advantages of R. Users can program it and they can, if they want to, change the system level functions to functions that they find more appropriate.

R also provides facilities that make it easy to document any functions that you have created. See section "Writing R documentation" in *Writing R Extensions*.

4.1.1 Syntax and examples

The syntax for writing a function is

    function (arglist) body

The first component of the function declaration is the keyword `function` which indicates to R that you want to create a function.

An argument list is a comma separated list of formal arguments. A formal argument can be a symbol, a statement of the form '`symbol = expression`', or the special formal argument '`...`'.

The *body* can be any valid R expression. Generally, the body is a group of expressions contained in curly braces ('{' and '}').

Generally functions are assigned to symbols but they don't need to be. The value returned by the call to `function` is a function. If this is not given a name it is referred to as an anonymous function. Anonymous functions are most frequently used as arguments other functions such as the `apply` family or `outer`.

Here is a simple function: `echo <- function(x) print(x)`. So `echo` is a function that takes a single argument and when `echo` is invoked it prints its argument.

4.1.2 Arguments

The formal arguments to the function define the variables whose values will be supplied at the time the function is invoked. The names of these arguments can be used within the function body where they obtain the value supplied at the time of function invocation.

Default values for arguments can be specified using the special form '`name = expression`'. In this case, if the user does not specify a value for the argument when the function is invoked the expression will be associated with the corresponding symbol. When a value is needed the *expression* is evaluated in the evaluation frame of the function.

Default behaviours can also be specified by using the function `missing`. When `missing` is called with the name of a formal argument it returns `TRUE` if the formal argument was not matched with any actual argument and has not been subsequently modified in the body of the function. An argument that is `missing` will thus have its default value, if any. The `missing` function does not force evaluation of the argument.

The special type of argument '`...`' can contain any number of supplied arguments. It is used for a variety of purposes. It allows you to write a function that takes an arbitrary number of arguments. It can be used to absorb some arguments into an intermediate function which can then be extracted by functions called subsequently.

4.2 Functions as objects

Functions are first class objects in R. They can be used anywhere that an R object is required. In particular they can be passed as arguments to functions and returned as values from functions. See Section 2.1.5 [Function objects], page 4 for the details.

4.3 Evaluation

4.3.1 Evaluation environment

When a function is called or invoked a new evaluation frame is created. In this frame the formal arguments are matched with the supplied arguments according to the rules given in Section 4.3.2 [Argument matching], page 23. The statements in the body of the function are evaluated sequentially in this environment frame.

The enclosing frame of the evaluation frame is the environment frame associated with the function being invoked. This may be different from S. While many functions have `.GlobalEnv` as their environment this does not have to be true and functions defined in packages with namespaces (normally) have the package namespace as their environment.

4.3.2 Argument matching

The first thing that occurs in a function evaluation is the matching of formal to the actual or supplied arguments. This is done by a three-pass process:

1. **Exact matching on tags.** For each named supplied argument the list of formal arguments is searched for an item whose name matches exactly. It is an error to have the same formal argument match several actuals or vice versa.

2. **Partial matching on tags.** Each remaining named supplied argument is compared to the remaining formal arguments using partial matching. If the name of the supplied argument matches exactly with the first part of a formal argument then the two arguments are considered to be matched. It is an error to have multiple partial matches. Notice that if `f <- function(fumble, fooey) fbody`, then `f(f = 1, fo = 2)` is illegal, even though the 2nd actual argument only matches `fooey`. `f(f = 1, fooey = 2)` *is* legal though since the second argument matches exactly and is removed from consideration for partial matching. If the formal arguments contain '...' then partial matching is only applied to arguments that precede it.

3. **Positional matching.** Any unmatched formal arguments are bound to *unnamed* supplied arguments, in order. If there is a '...' argument, it will take up the remaining arguments, tagged or not.

If any arguments remain unmatched an error is declared.

Argument matching is augmented by the functions `match.arg`, `match.call` and `match.fun`. Access to the partial matching algorithm used by R is via `pmatch`.

4.3.3 Argument evaluation

One of the most important things to know about the evaluation of arguments to a function is that supplied arguments and default arguments are treated differently. The supplied arguments to a function are evaluated in the evaluation frame of the calling function. The default arguments to a function are evaluated in the evaluation frame of the function.

The semantics of invoking a function in R argument are *call-by-value*. In general, supplied arguments behave as if they are local variables initialized with the value supplied and the name of the corresponding formal argument. Changing the value of a supplied argument within a function will not affect the value of the variable in the calling frame.

R has a form of lazy evaluation of function arguments. Arguments are not evaluated until needed. It is important to realize that in some cases the argument will never be evaluated. Thus, it is bad style to use arguments to functions to cause side-effects. While in **C** it is common to use the form, `foo(x = y)` to invoke `foo` with the value of `y` and simultaneously to assign the value of `y` to `x` this same style should not be used in R. There is no guarantee that the argument will ever be evaluated and hence the assignment may not take place.

It is also worth noting that the effect of foo(x <- y) if the argument is evaluated is to change the value of x in the calling environment and not in the evaluation environment of foo.

It is possible to access the actual (not default) expressions used as arguments inside the function. The mechanism is implemented via promises. When a function is being evaluated the actual expression used as an argument is stored in the promise together with a pointer to the environment the function was called from. When (if) the argument is evaluated the stored expression is evaluated in the environment that the function was called from. Since only a pointer to the environment is used any changes made to that environment will be in effect during this evaluation. The resulting value is then also stored in a separate spot in the promise. Subsequent evaluations retrieve this stored value (a second evaluation is not carried out). Access to the unevaluated expression is also available using `substitute`.

When a function is called, each formal argument is assigned a promise in the local environment of the call with the expression slot containing the actual argument (if it exists) and the environment slot containing the environment of the caller. If no actual argument for a formal argument is given in the call and there is a default expression, it is similarly assigned to the expression slot of the formal argument, but with the environment set to the local environment.

The process of filling the value slot of a promise by evaluating the contents of the expression slot in the promises environment is called *forcing* the promise. A promise will only be forced once, the value slot content being used directly later on.

A promise is forced when its value is needed. This usually happens inside internal functions, but a promise can also be forced by direct evaluation of the promise itself. This is occasionally useful when a default expression depends on the value of another formal argument or other variable in the local environment. This is seen in the following example where the lone `label` ensures that the label is based on the value of x before it is changed in the next line.

```
function(x, label = deparse(x)) {
    label
    x <- x + 1
    print(label)
}
```

The expression slot of a promise can itself involve other promises. This happens whenever an unevaluated argument is passed as an argument to another function. When forcing a promise, other promises in its expression will also be forced recursively as they are evaluated.

4.3.4 Scope

Scope or the scoping rules are simply the set of rules used by the evaluator to find a value for a symbol. Every computer language has a set of such rules. In R the rules are fairly simple but there do exist mechanisms for subverting the usual, or default rules.

R adheres to a set of rules that are called *lexical scope*. This means the variable bindings in effect at the time the expression was created are used to provide values for any unbound symbols in the expression.

Most of the interesting properties of scope are involved with evaluating functions and we concentrate on this issue. A symbol can be either bound or unbound. All of the formal arguments to a function provide bound symbols in the body of the function. Any other symbols in the body of the function are either local variables or unbound variables. A local variable is one that is defined within the function. Because R has no formal definition of variables, they are simply used as needed, it can be difficult to determine whether a variable is local or not. Local variables must first be defined, this is typically done by having them on the left-hand side of an assignment.

Chapter 4: Functions   25

During the evaluation process if an unbound symbol is detected then R attempts to find a value for it. The scoping rules determine how this process proceeds. In R the environment of the function is searched first, then its enclosure and so on until the global environment is reached.

The global environment heads a search list of environments that are searched sequentially for a matching symbol. The value of the first match is then used.

When this set of rules is combined with the fact that functions can be returned as values from other functions then some rather nice, but at first glance peculiar, properties obtain.

A simple example:

```
f <- function() {
    y <- 10
    g <- function(x) x + y
    return(g)
}
h <- f()
h(3)
```

A rather interesting question is what happens when h is evaluated. To describe this we need a bit more notation. Within a function body variables can be bound, local or unbound. The bound variables are those that match the formal arguments to the function. The local variables are those that were created or defined within the function body. The unbound variables are those that are neither local nor bound. When a function body is evaluated there is no problem determining values for local variables or for bound variables. Scoping rules determine how the language will find values for the unbound variables.

When h(3) is evaluated we see that its body is that of g. Within that body x is bound to the formal argument and y is unbound. In a language with lexical scope x will be associated with the value 3 and y with the value 10 local to f so h(3) should return the value 13. In R this is indeed what happens.

In S, because of the different scoping rules one will get an error indicating that y is not found, unless there is a variable y in your workspace in which case its value will be used.

5 Object-oriented programming

Object-oriented programming is a style of programming that has become popular in recent years. Much of the popularity comes from the fact that it makes it easier to write and maintain complicated systems. It does this through several different mechanisms.

Central to any object-oriented language are the concepts of class and of methods. A *class* is a definition of an object. Typically a class contains several *slots* that are used to hold class-specific information. An object in the language must be an instance of some class. Programming is based on objects or instances of classes.

Computations are carried out via *methods*. Methods are basically functions that are specialized to carry out specific calculations on objects, usually of a specific class. This is what makes the language object oriented. In R, *generic functions* are used to determine the appropriate method. The generic function is responsible for determining the class of its argument(s) and uses that information to select the appropriate method.

Another feature of most object-oriented languages is the concept of inheritance. In most programming problems there are usually many objects that are related to one another. The programming is considerably simplified if some components can be reused.

If a class inherits from another class then generally it gets all the slots in the parent class and can extend it by adding new slots. On method dispatching (via the generic functions) if a method for the class does not exist then a method for the parent is sought.

In this chapter we discuss how this general strategy has been implemented in R and discuss some of the limitations within the current design. One of the advantages that most object systems impart is greater consistency. This is achieved via the rules that are checked by the compiler or interpretor. Unfortunately because of the way that the object system is incorporated into R this advantage does not obtain. Users are cautioned to use the object system in a straightforward manner. While it is possible to perform some rather interesting feats these tend to lead to obfuscated code and may depend on implementation details that will not be carried forward.

The greatest use of object oriented programming in R is through `print` methods, `summary` methods and `plot` methods. These methods allow us to have one generic function call, `plot` say, that dispatches on the type of its argument and calls a plotting function that is specific to the data supplied.

In order to make the concepts clear we will consider the implementation of a small system designed to teach students about probability. In this system the objects are probability functions and the methods we will consider are methods for finding moments and for plotting. Probabilities can always be represented in terms of the cumulative distribution function but can often be represented in other ways. For example as a density, when it exists or as a moment generating function when it exists.

5.1 Definition

Rather than having a full-fledged object-oriented system R has a class system and a mechanism for dispatching based on the class of an object. The dispatch mechanism for interpreted code relies on four special objects that are stored in the evaluation frame. These special objects are `.Generic`, `.Class`, `.Method` and `.Group`. There is a separate dispatch mechanism used for internal functions and types that will be discussed elsewhere.

The class system is facilitated through the `class` attribute. This attribute is a list of class names. So to create an object of class `"foo"` one simply attaches a class attribute with the string '`"foo"`' in it. Thus, virtually anything can be turned in to an object of class `"foo"`.

The object system makes use of *generic functions* via two dispatching functions, `UseMethod` and `NextMethod`. The typical use of the object system is to begin by calling a generic function.

Chapter 5: Object-oriented programming 27

This is typically a function is very simple and consists of a single line of code. The system function `mean` is just such a function,

```
> mean
function (x, ...)
UseMethod("mean")
```

When `mean` is called it can have any number of arguments but its first argument is special and the class of that first argument is used to determine which method should be called. The variable `.Class` is set to the class attribute of `x`, `.Generic` is set to the string `"mean"` and a search is made for the correct method to invoke. The class attributes of any other arguments to `mean` are ignored.

Suppose that `x` had a class attribute that contained `"foo"` and `"bar"`, in that order. Then R would first search for a function called `mean.foo` and if it did not find one it would then search for a function `mean.bar` and if that search was also unsuccessful then a final search for `mean.default` would be made. If the last search is unsuccessful R reports an error. It is a good idea to always write a default method. Note that the functions `mean.foo` etc. are referred to, in this context, as methods.

`NextMethod` provides another mechanism for dispatching. A function may have a call to `NextMethod` anywhere in it. The determination of which method should then be invoked is based primarily on the current values of `.Class` and `.Generic`. This is somewhat problematic since the method is really an ordinary function and users may call it directly. If they do so then there will be no values for `.Generic` or `.Class`.

If a method is invoked directly and it contains a call to `NextMethod` then the first argument to `NextMethod` is used to determine the generic function. An error is signalled if this argument has not been supplied; it is therefore a good idea to always supply this argument.

In the case that a method is invoked directly the class attribute of the first argument to the method is used as the value of `.Class`.

Methods themselves employ `NextMethod` to provide a form of inheritance. Commonly a specific method performs a few operations to set up the data and then it calls the next appropriate method through a call to `NextMethod`.

Consider the following simple example. A point in two-dimensional Euclidean space can be specified by its Cartesian (x-y) or polar (r-theta) coordinates. Hence, to store information about the location of the point, we could define two classes, `"xypoint"` and `"rthetapoint"`. All the 'xypoint' data structures are lists with an x-component and a y-component. All 'rthetapoint' objects are lists with an r-component and a theta-component.

Now, suppose we want to get the x-position from either type of object. This can easily be achieved through generic functions. We define the generic function `xpos` as follows.

```
xpos <- function(x, ...)
    UseMethod("xpos")
```

Now we can define methods:

```
xpos.xypoint <- function(x) x$x
xpos.rthetapoint <- function(x) x$r * cos(x$theta)
```

The user simply calls the function `xpos` with either representation as the argument. The internal dispatching method finds the class of the object and calls the appropriate methods.

It is pretty easy to add other representations. One need not write a new generic function only the methods. This makes it easy to add to existing systems since the user is only responsible for dealing with the new representation and not with any of the existing representations.

The bulk of the uses of this methodology are to provided specialized printing for objects of different types; there are about 40 methods for `print`.

5.2 Inheritance

The class attribute of an object can have several elements. When a generic function is called the first inheritance is mainly handled through `NextMethod`. `NextMethod` determines the method currently being evaluated, finds the next class from th

FIXME: something is missing here

5.3 Method dispatching

Generic functions should consist of a single statement. They should always be of the form `foo <- function(x, ...) UseMethod("foo", x)`. The semantics of `UseMethod` are an appropriate method is determined and then that method is invoked with the same arguments, in the same order as the call to the generic as if the call had been made directly to the method.

In order to determine the correct method the class attribute of the first argument to the generic is obtained and used to find the correct method. The name of the generic function is combined with the first element of the class attribute into the form, *generic.class* and a function with that name is sought. If the function is found then it is used. If no such function is found then the second element of the class attribute is used, and so on until all the elements of the class attribute have been exhausted. If no method has been found at that point then the method *generic.default* is used. If the first argument to the generic function has no class attribute then *generic.default* is used. Since the introduction of namespaces the methods may not be accessible by their names (i.e. `get("generic.class")` may fail), but they will be accessible by `getS3method("generic","class")`.

Any object can have a `class` attribute. This attribute can have any number of elements. Each of these is a string that defines a class. When a generic function is invoked the class of its first argument is examined.

5.4 UseMethod

`UseMethod` is a special function and it behaves differently from other function calls. The syntax of a call to it is `UseMethod(generic, object)`, where *generic* is the name of the generic function, *object* is the object used to determine which method should be chosen. `UseMethod` can only be called from inside a function. The S definition of `UseMethod` contains an additional argument of '...' that can affect the default values for subsequent methods. R produces a warning if there are more than two arguments to `UseMethod` and ignores these additional arguments.

`UseMethod` changes the evaluation model in two ways. First, when it is invoked it determines the next method (function) to be called. It then invokes that function using the current evaluation environment; this process will be described shortly. The second way in which `UseMethod` changes the evaluation environment is that it does not return control to the calling function. This means, that any statements after a call to `UseMethod` are guaranteed not to be executed.

When `UseMethod` is invoked the generic function is the specified value in the call to `UseMethod`. The object to dispatch on is either the supplied second argument or the first argument to the current function. The class of the argument is determined and the first element of it is combined with the name of the generic to determine the appropriate method. So, if the generic had name `foo` and the class of the object is `"bar"`, then R will search for a method named `foo.bar`. If no such method exists then the inheritance mechanism described above is used to locate an appropriate method.

Once a method has been determined R invokes it in a special way. Rather than creating a new evaluation environment R uses the environment of the current function call (the call to the generic). Any assignments or evaluations that were made before the call to `UseMethod` will be in effect. The arguments that were used in the call to the generic are rematched to the formal arguments of the selected method.

When the method is invoked it is called with arguments that are the same in number and have the same names as in the call to the generic. They are matched to the arguments of the method according to the standard R rules for argument matching. However the object, i.e. the first argument has been evaluated.

The call to `UseMethod` has the effect of placing some special objects in the evaluation frame. They are `.Class`, `.Generic` and `.Method`. These special objects are used to by R to handle the method dispatch and inheritance. `.Class` is the class of the object, `.Generic` is the name of the generic function and `.Method` is the name of the method currently being invoked. If the method was invoked through one of the internal interfaces then there may also be an object called `.Group`. This will be described in Section Section 5.6 [Group methods], page 30. After the initial call to `UseMethod` these special variables, not the object itself, control the selection of subsequent methods.

The body of the method is then evaluated in the standard fashion. In particular variable look-up in the body follows the rules for the method. So if the method has an associated environment then that is used. In effect we have replaced the call to the generic by a call to the method. Any local assignments in the frame of the generic will be carried forward into the call to the method. Use of this *feature* is discouraged. It is important to realize that control will never return to the generic and hence any expressions after a call to `UseMethod` will never be executed.

Any arguments to the generic that were evaluated prior to the call to `UseMethod` remain evaluated.

The arguments in the call to the generic are rematched with the arguments for the method using the standard argument matching mechanism. The first argument, i.e. the object, will have been evaluated.

If the first argument to `UseMethod` is not supplied it is assumed to be the name of the current function. If two arguments are supplied to `UseMethod` then the first is the name of the method and the second is assumed to be the object that will be dispatched on. It is evaluated so that the required method can be determined. In this case the first argument in the call to the generic is not evaluated and is discarded. There is no way to change the other arguments in the call to the method these remain as they were in the call to the generic. This is in contrast to `NextMethod` where the arguments in the call to the next method can be altered.

5.5 NextMethod

`NextMethod` is used to provide a simple inheritance mechanism.

Methods invoked as a result of a call to `NextMethod` behave as if they had been invoked from the previous method. The arguments to the inherited method are in the same order and have the same names as the call to the current method. This means that they are the same as for the call to the generic. However, the expressions for the arguments are the names of the corresponding formal arguments of the current method. Thus the arguments will have values that correspond to their value at the time NextMethod was invoked.

Unevaluated arguments remain unevaluated. Missing arguments remain missing.

The syntax for a call to `NextMethod` is `NextMethod(generic, object, ...)`. If the `generic` is not supplied the value of `.Generic` is used. If the `object` is not supplied the first argument in the call to the current method is used. Values in the '`...`' argument are used to modify the arguments of the next method.

It is important to realize that the choice of the next method depends on the current values of `.Generic` and `.Class` and not on the object. So changing the object in a call to `NextMethod` affects the arguments received by the next method but does not affect the choice of the next method.

Methods can be called directly. If they are then there will be no `.Generic`, `.Class` or `.Method`. In this case the `generic` argument of `NextMethod` must be specified. The value of `.Class` is taken to be the class attribute of the object which is the first argument to the current function. The value of `.Method` is the name of the current function. These choices for default values ensure that the behaviour of a method doesn't change depending on whether it is called directly or via a call to a generic.

An issue for discussion is the behaviour of the '...' argument to `NextMethod`. The White Book describes the behaviour as follows:

- named arguments replace the corresponding arguments in the call to the current method. Unnamed arguments go at the start of the argument list.

What I would like to do is:

-first do the argument matching for NextMethod; -if the object or generic are changed fine -first if a named list element matches an argument (named or not) the list value replaces the argument value. - the first unnamed list element

Values for lookup: Class: comes first from .Class, second from the first argument to the method and last from the object specified in the call to NextMethod

Generic: comes first from .Generic, if nothing then from the first argument to the method and if it's still missing from the call to NextMethod

Method: this should just be the current function name.

5.6 Group methods

For several types of internal functions R provides a dispatching mechanism for operators. This means that operators such as `==` or `<` can have their behaviour modified for members of special classes. The functions and operators have been grouped into three categories and group methods can be written for each of these categories. There is currently no mechanism to add groups. It is possible to write methods specific to any function within a group.

The following table lists the functions for the different Groups.

'Math'	abs, acos, acosh, asin, asinh, atan, atanh, ceiling, cos, cosh, cumsum, exp, floor, gamma, lgamma, log, log10, round, signif, sin, sinh, tan, tanh, trunc
'Summary'	all, any, max, min, prod, range, sum
'Ops'	+, -, *, /, ^, < , >, <=, >=, !=, ==, %%, %/%, &, |, !

For operators in the Ops group a special method is invoked if the two operands taken together suggest a single method. Specifically, if both operands correspond to the same method or if one operand corresponds to a method that takes precedence over that of the other operand. If they do not suggest a single method then the default method is used. Either a group method or a class method dominates if the other operand has no corresponding method. A class method dominates a group method.

When the group is Ops the special variable `.Method` is a string vector with two elements. The elements of `.Method` are set to the name of the method if the corresponding argument is a member of the class that was used to determine the method. Otherwise the corresponding element of `.Method` is set to the zero length string, `""`.

5.7 Writing methods

Users can easily write their own methods and generic functions. A generic function is simply a function with a call to `UseMethod`. A method is simply a function that has been invoked via method dispatch. This can be as a result of a call to either `UseMethod` or `NextMethod`.

Chapter 5: Object-oriented programming   31

It is worth remembering that methods can be called directly. That means that they can be entered without a call to `UseMethod` having been made and hence the special variables `.Generic`, `.Class` and `.Method` will not have been instantiated. In that case the default rules detailed above will be used to determine these.

The most common use of generic functions is to provide `print` and `summary` methods for statistical objects, generally the output of some model fitting process. To do this, each model attaches a class attribute to its output and then provides a special method that takes that output and provides a nice readable version of it. The user then needs only remember that `print` or `summary` will provide nice output for the results of any analysis.

6 Computing on the language

R belongs to a class of programming languages in which subroutines have the ability to modify or construct other subroutines and evaluate the result as an integral part of the language itself. This is similar to Lisp and Scheme and other languages of the "functional programming" variety, but in contrast to FORTRAN and the ALGOL family. The Lisp family takes this feature to the extreme by the "everything is a list" paradigm in which there is no distinction between programs and data.

R presents a friendlier interface to programming than Lisp does, at least to someone used to mathematical formulas and C-like control structures, but the engine is really very Lisp-like. R allows direct access to parsed expressions and functions and allows you to alter and subsequently execute them, or create entirely new functions from scratch.

There is a number of standard applications of this facility, such as calculation of analytical derivatives of expressions, or the generation of polynomial functions from a vector of coefficients. However, there are also uses that are much more fundamental to the workings of the interpreted part of R. Some of these are essential to the reuse of functions as components in other functions, as the (admittedly not very pretty) calls to `model.frame` that are constructed in several modeling and plotting routines. Other uses simply allow elegant interfaces to useful functionality. As an example, consider the `curve` function, which allows you to draw the graph of a function given as an expression like `sin(x)` or the facilities for plotting mathematical expressions.

In this chapter, we give an introduction to the set of facilities that are available for computing on the language.

6.1 Direct manipulation of language objects

There are three kinds of language objects that are available for modification, calls, expressions, and functions. At this point, we shall concentrate on the call objects. These are sometimes referred to as "unevaluated expressions", although this terminology is somewhat confusing. The most direct method of obtaining a call object is to use `quote` with an expression argument, e.g.,

```
> e1 <- quote(2 + 2)
> e2 <- quote(plot(x, y))
```

The arguments are not evaluated, the result is simply the parsed argument. The objects `e1` and `e2` may be evaluated later using `eval`, or simply manipulated as data. It is perhaps most immediately obvious why the `e2` object has mode `"call"`, since it involves a call to the `plot` function with some arguments. However, `e1` actually has exactly the same structure as a call to the binary operator + with two arguments, a fact that gets clearly displayed by the following

```
> quote("+"(2, 2))
2 + 2
```

The components of a call object are accessed using a list-like syntax, and may in fact be converted to and from lists using `as.list` and `as.call`

```
> e2[[1]]
plot
> e2[[2]]
x
> e2[[3]]
y
```

When keyword argument matching is used, the keywords can be used as list tags:

```
> e3 <- quote(plot(x = age, y = weight))
> e3$x
age
```

Chapter 6: Computing on the language   33

```
> e3$y
weight
```

All the components of the call object have mode `"name"` in the preceding examples. This is true for identifiers in calls, but the components of a call can also be constants—which can be of any type, although the first component had better be a function if the call is to be evaluated successfully—or other call objects, corresponding to subexpressions. Objects of mode name can be constructed from character strings using `as.name`, so one might modify the e2 object as follows

```
> e2[[1]] <- as.name("+")
> e2
x + y
```

To illustrate the fact that subexpressions are simply components that are themselves calls, consider

```
> e1[[2]] <- e2
> e1
x + y + 2
```

All grouping parentheses in input are preserved in parsed expressions. They are represented as a function call with one argument, so that 4 - (2 - 2) becomes `"-"(4, "(" ("-"(2, 2)))` in prefix notation. In evaluations, the '(' operator just returns its argument.

This is a bit unfortunate, but it is not easy to write a parser/deparser combination that both preserves user input, stores it in minimal form and ensures that parsing a deparsed expression gives the same expression back.

As it happens, R's parser is not perfectly invertible, nor is its deparser, as the following examples show

```
> deparse(quote(c(1, 2)))
[1] "c(1, 2)"
> deparse(1:2)
[1] "c(1, 2)"
> quote("-"(2, 2))
2 - 2
> quote(2 - 2)
2 - 2
```

Deparsed expressions should, however, evaluate to an equivalent value to the original expression (up to rounding error).

...internal storage of flow control constructs...note Splus incompatibility...

6.2 Substitutions

It is in fact not often that one wants to modify the innards of an expression like in the previous section. More frequently, one wants to simply get at an expression in order to deparse it and use it for labeling plots, for instance. An example of this is seen at the beginning of `plot.default`:

```
xlabel <- if (!missing(x))
    deparse(substitute(x))
```

This causes the variable or expression given as the x argument to `plot` to be used for labeling the x-axis later on.

The function used to achieve this is `substitute` which takes the expression x and substitutes the expression that was passed through the formal argument x. Notice that for this to happen, x must carry information about the expression that creates its value. This is related to the

Chapter 6: Computing on the language   34

lazy evaluation scheme of R (see Section 2.1.8 [Promise objects], page 5). A formal argument is really a *promise*, an object with three slots, one for the expression that defines it, one for the environment in which to evaluate that expression, and one for the value of that expression once evaluated. `substitute` will recognize a promise variable and substitute the value of its expression slot. If `substitute` is invoked inside a function, the local variables of the function are also subject to substitution.

The argument to `substitute` does not have to be a simple identifier, it can be an expression involving several variables and substitution will occur for each of these. Also, `substitute` has an additional argument which can be an environment or a list in which the variables are looked up. For example:

```
> substitute(a + b, list(a = 1, b = quote(x)))
1 + x
```

Notice that quoting was necessary to substitute the `x`. This kind of construction comes in handy in connection with the facilities for putting math expression in graphs, as the following case shows

```
> plot(0)
> for (i in 1:4)
+    text(1, 0.2 * i,
+        substitute(x[ix] == y, list(ix = i, y = pnorm(i))))
```

It is important to realize that the substitutions are purely lexical; there is no checking that the resulting call objects make sense if they are evaluated. `substitute(x <- x + 1, list(x = 2))` will happily return `2 <- 2 + 1`. However, some parts of R make up their own rules for what makes sense and what does not and might actually have a use for such ill-formed expressions. For example, using the "math in graphs" feature often involves constructions that are syntactically correct, but which would be meaningless to evaluate, like '{}>=40*" years"'.

Substitute will not evaluate its first argument. This leads to the puzzle of how to do substitutions on an object that is contained in a variable. The solution is to use `substitute` once more, like this

```
> expr <- quote(x + y)
> substitute(substitute(e, list(x = 3)), list(e = expr))
substitute(x + y, list(x = 3))
> eval(substitute(substitute(e, list(x = 3)), list(e = expr)))
3 + y
```

The exact rules for substitutions are as follows: Each symbol in the parse tree for the first is matched against the second argument, which can be a tagged list or an environment frame. If it is a simple local object, its value is inserted, *except* if matching against the global environment. If it is a promise (usually a function argument), the promise expression is substituted. If the symbol is not matched, it is left untouched. The special exception for substituting at the top level is admittedly peculiar. It has been inherited from S and the rationale is most likely that there is no control over which variables might be bound at that level so that it would be better to just make substitute act as `quote`.

The rule of promise substitution is slightly different from that of S if the local variable is modified before `substitute` is used. R will then use the new value of the variable, whereas S will unconditionally use the argument expression—unless it was a constant, which has the curious consequence that `f((1))` may be very different from `f(1)` in S. The R rule is considerably cleaner, although it does have consequences in connection with lazy evaluation that comes as a surprise to some. Consider

```
logplot <- function(y, ylab = deparse(substitute(y))) {
    y <- log(y)
    plot(y, ylab = ylab)
```

Chapter 6: Computing on the language   35

```
    }
```

This looks straightforward, but one will discover that the y label becomes an ugly c(...) expression. It happens because the rules of lazy evaluation causes the evaluation of the `ylab` expression to happen *after* y has been modified. The solution is to force `ylab` to be evaluated first, i.e.,

```
    logplot <- function(y, ylab = deparse(substitute(y))) {
        ylab
        y <- log(y)
        plot(y, ylab = ylab)
    }
```

Notice that one should not use `eval(ylab)` in this situation. If `ylab` is a language or expression object, then that would cause the object to be evaluated as well, which would not at all be desirable if a math expression like `quote(log[e](y))` was being passed.

A variant on `substitute` is `bquote`, which is used to replace some subexpressions with their values. The example from above

```
    > plot(0)
    > for (i in 1:4)
    +     text(1, 0.2 * i,
    +          substitute(x[ix] == y, list(ix = i, y = pnorm(i))))
```

could be written more compactly as

```
    plot(0)
    for(i in 1:4)
        text(1, 0.2*i, bquote( x[.(i)] == .(pnorm(i)) ))
```

The expression is quoted except for the contents of `.()` subexpressions, which are replaced with their values. There is an optional argument to compute the values in a different environment. The syntax for `bquote` is borrowed from the LISP backquote macro.

6.3 More on evaluation

The `eval` function was introduced earlier in this chapter as a means of evaluating call objects. However, this is not the full story. It is also possible to specify the environment in which the evaluation is to take place. By default this is the evaluation frame from which `eval` is called, but quite frequently it needs to be set to something else.

Very often, the relevant evaluation frame is that of the parent of the current frame (cf. ???). In particular, when the object to evaluate is the result of a `substitute` operation of the function arguments, it will contain variables that make sense to the caller only (notice that there is no reason to expect that the variables of the caller are in the lexical scope of the callee). Since evaluation in the parent frame occurs frequently, an `eval.parent` function exists as a shorthand for `eval(expr, sys.frame(sys.parent()))`.

Another case that occurs frequently is evaluation in a list or a data frame. For instance, this happens in connection with the `model.frame` function when a `data` argument is given. Generally, the terms of the model formula need to be evaluated in `data`, but they may occasionally also contain references to items in the caller of `model.frame`. This is sometimes useful in connection with simulation studies. So for this purpose one needs not only to evaluate an expression in a list, but also to specify an enclosure into which the search continues if the variable is not in the list. Hence, the call has the form

```
    eval(expr, data, sys.frame(sys.parent()))
```

Notice that evaluation in a given environment may actually change that environment, most obviously in cases involving the assignment operator, such as

```
eval(quote(total <- 0), environment(robert$balance)) # rob Rob
```

This is also true when evaluating in lists, but the original list does not change because one is really working on a copy.

6.4 Evaluation of expression objects

Objects of mode "expression" are defined in Section 2.1.4 [Expression objects], page 4. They are very similar to lists of call objects.

```
> ex <- expression(2 + 2, 3 + 4)
> ex[[1]]
2 + 2
> ex[[2]]
3 + 4
> eval(ex)
[1] 7
```

Notice that evaluating an expression object evaluates each call in turn, but the final value is that of the last call. In this respect it behaves almost identically to the compound language object quote({2 + 2; 3 + 4}). However, there is a subtle difference: Call objects are indistinguishable from subexpressions in a parse tree. This means that they are automatically evaluated in the same way a subexpression would be. Expression objects can be recognized during evaluation and in a sense retain their quotedness. The evaluator will not evaluate an expression object recursively, only when it is passed directly to **eval** function as above. The difference can be seen like this:

```
> eval(substitute(mode(x), list(x = quote(2 + 2))))
[1] "numeric"
> eval(substitute(mode(x), list(x = expression(2 + 2))))
[1] "expression"
```

The deparser represents an expression object by the call that creates it. This is similar to the way it handles numerical vectors and several other objects that do not have a specific external representation. However, it does lead to the following bit of confusion:

```
> e <- quote(expression(2 + 2))
> e
expression(2 + 2)
> mode(e)
[1] "call"
> ee <- expression(2 + 2)
> ee
expression(2 + 2)
> mode(ee)
[1] "expression"
```

I.e., e and ee look identical when printed, but one is a call that generates an expression object and the other is the object itself.

6.5 Manipulation of function calls

It is possible for a function to find out how it has been called by looking at the result of sys.call as in the following example of a function that simply returns its own call:

```
> f <- function(x, y, ...) sys.call()
> f(y = 1, 2, z = 3, 4)
f(y = 1, 2, z = 3, 4)
```

Chapter 6: Computing on the language   37

However, this is not really useful except for debugging because it requires the function to keep track of argument matching in order to interpret the call. For instance, it must be able to see that the 2nd actual argument gets matched to the first formal one (x in the above example).

More often one requires the call with all actual arguments bound to the corresponding formals. To this end, the function `match.call` is used. Here's a variant of the preceding example, a function that returns its own call with arguments matched

```
> f <- function(x, y, ...) match.call()
> f(y = 1, 2, z = 3, 4)
f(x = 2, y = 1, z = 3, 4)
```

Notice that the second argument now gets matched to x and appears in the corresponding position in the result.

The primary use of this technique is to call another function with the same arguments, possibly deleting some and adding others. A typical application is seen at the start of the lm function:

```
mf <- cl <- match.call()
mf$singular.ok <- mf$model <- mf$method <- NULL
mf$x <- mf$y <- mf$qr <- mf$contrasts <- NULL
mf$drop.unused.levels <- TRUE
mf[[1]] <- as.name("model.frame")
mf <- eval(mf, sys.frame(sys.parent()))
```

Notice that the resulting call is evaluated in the parent frame, in which one can be certain that the involved expressions make sense. The call can be treated as a list object where the first element is the name of the function and the remaining elements are the actual argument expressions, with the corresponding formal argument names as tags. Thus, the technique to eliminate undesired arguments is to assign NULL, as seen in lines 2 and 3, and to add an argument one uses tagged list assignment (here to pass `drop.unused.levels = TRUE`) as in line 4. To change the name of the function called, assign to the first element of the list and make sure that the value is a name, either using the `as.name("model.frame")` construction here or `quote(model.frame)`.

The `match.call` function has an `expand.dots` argument which is a switch which if set to FALSE lets all '...' arguments be collected as a single argument with the tag '...'.

```
> f <- function(x, y, ...) match.call(expand.dots = FALSE)
> f(y = 1, 2, z = 3, 4)
f(x = 2, y = 1, ... = list(z = 3, 4))
```

The '...' argument is a list (a pairlist to be precise), not a call to `list` like it is in S:

```
> e1 <- f(y = 1, 2, z = 3, 4)$...
> e1
$z
[1] 3

[[2]]
[1] 4
```

One reason for using this form of `match.call` is simply to get rid of any '...' arguments in order not to be passing unspecified arguments on to functions that may not know them. Here's an example paraphrased from `plot.formula`:

```
m <- match.call(expand.dots = FALSE)
m$... <- NULL
m[[1]] <- "model.frame"
```

A more elaborate application is in `update.default` where a set of optional extra arguments can add to, replace, or cancel those of the original call:

```
extras <- match.call(expand.dots = FALSE)$...
if (length(extras) > 0) {
    existing <- !is.na(match(names(extras), names(call)))
    for (a in names(extras)[existing]) call[[a]] <- extras[[a]]
    if (any(!existing)) {
        call <- c(as.list(call), extras[!existing])
        call <- as.call(call)
    }
}
```

Notice that care is taken to modify existing arguments individually in case `extras[[a]]` == NULL. Concatenation does not work on call objects without the coercion as shown; this is arguably a bug.

Two further functions exist for the construction of function calls, namely `call` and `do.call`.

The function `call` allows creation of a call object from the function name and the list of arguments

```
> x <- 10.5
> call("round", x)
round(10.5)
```

As seen, the value of x rather than the symbol is inserted in the call, so it is distinctly different from `round(x)`. The form is used rather rarely, but is occasionally useful where the name of a function is available as a character variable.

The function `do.call` is related, but evaluates the call immediate and takes the arguments from an object of mode `"list"` containing all the arguments. A natural use of this is when one wants to apply a function like `cbind` to all elements of a list or data frame.

```
is.na.data.frame <- function (x) {
    y <- do.call("cbind", lapply(x, "is.na"))
    rownames(y) <- row.names(x)
    y
}
```

Other uses include variations over constructions like `do.call("f", list(...))`. However, one should be aware that this involves evaluation of the arguments before the actual function call, which may defeat aspects of lazy evaluation and argument substitution in the function itself. A similar remark applies to the `call` function.

6.6 Manipulation of functions

It is often useful to be able to manipulate the components of a function or closure. R provides a set of interface functions for this purpose.

`body`   Returns the expression that is the body of the function.

`formals`   Returns a list of the formal arguments to the function. This is a `pairlist`.

`environment`
               Returns the environment associated with the function.

`body<-`   This sets the body of the function to the supplied expression.

`formals<-`
               Sets the formal arguments of the function to the supplied list.

`environment<-`
               Sets the environment of the function to the specified environment.

Chapter 6: Computing on the language   39

It is also possible to alter the bindings of different variables in the environment of the function, using code along the lines of `evalq(x <- 5, environment(f))`.

It is also possible to convert a function to a list using `as.list`. The result is the concatenation of the list of formal arguments with the function body. Conversely such a list can be converted to a function using `as.function`. This functionality is mainly included for S compatibility. Notice that environment information is lost when `as.list` is used, whereas `as.function` has an argument that allows the environment to be set.

7 System and foreign language interfaces

7.1 Operating system access

Access to the operating system shell is via the R function **system**. The details will differ by platform (see the on-line help), and about all that can safely be assumed is that the first argument will be a string **command** that will be passed for execution (not necessarily by a shell) and the second argument will be **internal** which if true will collect the output of the command into an R character vector.

The functions **system.time** and **proc.time** are available for timing (although the information available may be limited on non-Unix-like platforms).

Information from the operating system environment can be accessed and manipulated with

Sys.getenv	OS environment variables
Sys.putenv	
Sys.getlocale	System locale
Sys.putlocale	
Sys.localeconv	
Sys.time	Current time
Sys.timezone	Time zone

A uniform set of file access functions is provided on all platforms:

file.access	Ascertain File Accessibility
file.append	Concatenate files
file.choose	Prompt user for file name
file.copy	Copy files
file.create	Create or truncate a files
file.exists	Test for existence
file.info	Miscellaneous file information
file.remove	remove files
file.rename	rename files
file.show	Display a text file
unlink	Remove files or directories.

There are also functions for manipulating file names and paths in a platform-independent way.

basename	File name without directory
dirname	Directory name
file.path	Construct path to file
path.expand	Expand ~ in Unix path

7.2 Foreign language interfaces

See section "System and foreign language interfaces" in *Writing R Extensions* for the details of adding functionality to R via compiled code.

Functions **.C** and **.Fortran** provide a standard interface to compiled code that has been linked into R, either at build time or via **dyn.load**. They are primarily intended for compiled **C** and FORTRAN code respectively, but the **.C** function can be used with other languages which can generate C interfaces, for example C++.

Functions **.Call** and **.External** provide interfaces which allow compiled code (primarily compiled **C** code) to manipulate R objects.

Chapter 7: System and foreign language interfaces   41

7.3 .Internal and .Primitive

The `.Internal` and `.Primitive` interfaces are used to call C code compiled into R at build time. See section ".Internal and .Primitive" in *Writing R Extensions*.

8 Exception handling

The exception handling facilities in R are provided through two mechanisms. Functions such as `stop` or `warning` can be called directly or options such as `"warn"` can be used to control the handling of problems.

8.1 stop

A call to `stop` halts the evaluation of the current expression, prints the message argument and returns execution to top-level.

8.2 warning

The function `warning` takes a single argument that is a character string. The behaviour of a call to `warning` depends on the value of the option `"warn"`. If `"warn"` is negative warnings are ignored. If it is zero, they are stored and printed after the top-level function has completed. If it is one, they are printed as they occur and if it is 2 (or larger) warnings are turned into errors.

If `"warn"` is zero (the default), a variable `last.warning` is created and the messages associated with each call to `warning` are stored, sequentially, in this vector. If there are fewer than 10 warnings they are printed after the function has finished evaluating. If there are more than 10 then a message indicating how many warnings occurred is printed. In either case `last.warning` contains the vector of messages, and `warnings` provides a way to access and print it.

8.3 on.exit

A function can insert a call to `on.exit` at any point in the body of a function. The effect of a call to `on.exit` is to store the value of the body so that it will be executed when the function exits. This allows the function to change some system parameters and to ensure that they are reset to appropriate values when the function is finished. The `on.exit` is guaranteed to be executed when the function exits either directly or as the result of a warning.

An error in the evaluation of the `on.exit` code causes an immediate jump to top-level without further processing of the `on.exit` code.

`on.exit` takes a single argument which is an expression to be evaluated when the function is exited.

8.4 Error options

There are a number of `options` variables that can be used to control how R handles errors and warnings. The are listed in the table below.

'warn'   Controls the printing of warnings.

'warning.expression'

        Sets an expression that is to be evaluated when a warning occurs. The normal printing of warnings is suppressed if this option is set.

'error'   Installs an expression that will be evaluated when an error occurs. The normal printing of error messages and warning messages precedes the evaluation of the expression.

Expressions installed by `options("error")` are evaluated before calls to `on.exit` are carried out.

One can use `options(error = expression(q("yes")))` to get R to quit when an error has been signalled. In this case an error will cause R to shut down and the global environment will be saved.

9 Debugging

Debugging code has always been a bit of an art. R provides several tools that help users find problems in their code. These tools halt execution at particular points in the code and the current state of the computation can be inspected.

Most debugging takes place either through calls to `browser` or `debug`. Both of these functions rely on the same internal mechanism and both provide the user with a special prompt. Any command can be typed at the prompt. The evaluation environment for the command is the currently active environment. This allows you to examine the current state of any variables etc.

There are five special commands that R interprets differently. They are,

'(RET)' Go to the next statement if the function is being debugged. Continue execution if the browser was invoked.

'c'
'cont' Continue the execution.

'n' Execute the next statement in the function. This works from the browser as well.

'where' Show the call stack

'Q' Halt execution and jump to the top-level immediately.

If there is a local variable with the same name as one of the special commands listed above then its value can be accessed by using `get`. A call to `get` with the name in quotes will retrieve the value in the current environment.

The debugger provides access only to interpreted expressions. If a function calls a foreign language (such as **C**) then no access to the statements in that language is provided. Execution will halt on the next statement that is evaluated in R. A symbolic debugger such as `gdb` can be used to debug compiled code.

9.1 browser

A call to the function `browser` causes R to halt execution at that point and to provide the user with a special prompt. Arguments to `browser` are ignored.

```
> foo <- function(s) {
+ c <- 3
+ browser()
+ }
> foo(4)
Called from: foo(4)
Browse[1]> s
[1] 4
Browse[1]> get("c")
[1] 3
Browse[1]>
```

9.2 debug/undebug

The debugger can be invoked on any function by using the command `debug(fun)`. Subsequently, each time that function is evaluated the debugger is invoked. The debugger allows you to control the evaluation of the statements in the body of the function. Before each statement is executed the statement is printed out and a special prompt provided. Any command can be given, those in the table above have special meaning.

Debugging is turned off by a call to `undebug` with the function as an argument.

```
> debug(mean.default)
> mean(1:10)
debugging in: mean.default(1:10)
debug: {
    if (na.rm)
        x <- x[!is.na(x)]
    trim <- trim[1]
    n <- length(c(x, recursive = TRUE))
    if (trim > 0) {
        if (trim >= 0.5)
            return(median(x, na.rm = FALSE))
        lo <- floor(n * trim) + 1
        hi <- n + 1 - lo
        x <- sort(x, partial = unique(c(lo, hi)))[lo:hi]
        n <- hi - lo + 1
    }
    sum(x)/n
}
Browse[1]>
debug: if (na.rm) x <- x[!is.na(x)]
Browse[1]>
debug: trim <- trim[1]
Browse[1]>
debug: n <- length(c(x, recursive = TRUE))
Browse[1]> c
exiting from: mean.default(1:10)
[1] 5.5
```

9.3 trace/untrace

Another way of monitoring the behaviour of R is through the `trace` mechanism. `trace` is called with a single argument that is the name of the function you want to trace. The name does not need to be quoted but for some functions you will need to quote the name in order to avoid a syntax error.

When `trace` has been invoked on a function then every time that function is evaluated the call to it is printed out. This mechanism is removed by calling `untrace` with the function as an argument.

```
> get("[<-")
.Primitive("[<-")
> trace("[<-")
> x <- 1:10
> x[3] <- 4
trace: "[<-"(*tmp*, 3, value = 4)
```

9.4 traceback

When an error has caused a jump to top-level a special variable called `.Traceback` is placed into the base environment. `.Traceback` is a character vector with one entry for each function call that was active at the time the error occurred. An examination of `.Traceback` can be carried out by a call to `traceback`.

10 Parser

The parser is what converts the textual representation of R code into an internal form which may then be passed to the R evaluator which causes the specified instructions to be carried out. The internal form is itself an R object and can be saved and otherwise manipulated within the R system.

10.1 The parsing process

10.1.1 Modes of parsing

Parsing in R occurs in three different variants:

- The read-eval-print loop
- Parsing of text files
- Parsing of character strings

The read-eval-print loop forms the basic command line interface to R. Textual input is read until a complete R expression is available. Expressions may be split over several input lines. The primary prompt (by default '> ') indicates that the parser is ready for a new expression, and a continuation prompt (by default '+ ') indicates that the parser expects the remainder of an incomplete expression. The expression is converted to internal form during input and the parsed expression is passed to the evaluator and the result is printed (unless specifically made invisible). If the parser finds itself in a state which is incompatible with the language syntax, a "Syntax Error" is flagged and the parser resets itself and resumes input at the beginning of the next input line.

Text files can be parsed using the `parse` function. In particular, this is done during execution of the `source` function, which allows commands to be stored in an external file and executed as if they had been typed at the keyboard. Note, though, that the entire file is parsed and syntax checked before any evaluation takes place.

Character strings, or vectors thereof, can be parsed using the `text=` argument to `parse`. The strings are treated exactly as if they were the lines of an input file.

10.1.2 Internal representation

Parsed expressions are stored in an R object containing the parse tree. A fuller description of such objects can be found in Section 2.1.3 [Language objects], page 3 and Section 2.1.4 [Expression objects], page 4. Briefly, every elementary R expression is stored in function call form, as a list with the first element containing the function name and the remainder containing the arguments, which may in turn be further R expressions. The list elements can be named, corresponding to tagged matching of formal and actual arguments. Note that *all* R syntax elements are treated in this way, e.g. the assignment `x <- 1` is encoded as `"<-"(x, 1)`.

10.1.3 Deparsing

Any R object can be converted to an R expression using `deparse`. This is frequently used in connection with output of results, e.g. for labeling plots. Notice that only objects of mode `"expression"` can be expected to be unchanged by reparsing the output of deparsing. For instance, the numeric vector `1:5` will deparse as `"c(1, 2, 3, 4, 5)"`, which will reparse as a call to the function `c`. As far as possible, evaluating the deparsed and reparsed expression gives the same result as evaluating the original, but there are a couple of awkward exceptions, mostly involving expressions that weren't generated from a textual representation in the first place.

10.2 Comments

Comments in R are ignored by the parser. Any text from a # character to the end of the line is taken to be a comment, unless the # character is inside a quoted string. For example,

```
> x <- 1  # This is a comment...
> y <- "  #... but this is not."
```

10.3 Tokens

Tokens are the elementary building blocks of a programming language. They are recognised during *lexical analysis* which (conceptually, at least) takes place prior to the syntactic analysis performed by the parser itself.

10.3.1 Constants

There are five types of constants: integer, logical, numeric, complex and string.

In addition, there are four special constants, NULL, NA, Inf, and NaN.

NULL is used to indicate the empty object. NA is used for absent ("Not Available") data values. Inf denotes infinity and NaN is not-a-number in the IEEE floating point calculus (results of the operations respectively $1/0$ and $0/0$, for instance).

Logical constants are either TRUE or FALSE.

Numeric constants follow a similar syntax to that of the **C** language. They consist of an integer part consisting of zero or more digits, followed optionally by '.' and a fractional part of zero or more digits optionally followed by an exponent part consisting of an 'E' or an 'e', an optional sign and a string of zero or more digits. Either the fractional or the decimal part can be empty, but not both at once.

Valid numeric constants: 1 10 0.1 .2 1e-7 1.2e+7 2e 3e+

The two latter examples are hardly useful in practice, but they are accepted and treated as '2' and '3', respectively.

Numeric constants can also be hexadecimal, starting with '0x' or '0x' followed by zero or more digits, 'a-f' or 'A-F'.

There is now a separate class of integer constants. They are created by using the qualifier L at the end of the number. For example, 123L gives an integer value rather than a numeric value. The suffix L can be used to qualify any non-complex number with the intent of creating an integer. So it can be used with numbers given by hexadecimal or scientific notation. However, if the value is not a valid integer, a warning is emitted and the numeric value created. The following shows examples of valid integer constants, values which will generate a warning and give numeric constants and syntax errors.

Valid integer constants: 1L, 0x10L, 1000000L, 1e6L
Valid numeric constants: 1.1L, 1e-3L
Syntax error: 12iL

A warning is emitted for values that contain an unnecessary decimal point, e.g. 1.L.

Note also that a preceding sign (+ or -) is treated as a unary operator, not as part of the constant.

Complex constants have the form of a decimal numeric constant followed by 'i'. Notice that only purely imaginary numbers are actual constants, other complex numbers are parsed a unary or binary operations on numeric and imaginary numbers.

Valid complex constants: 2i 4.1i 1e-2i

String constants are delimited by a pair of single (' ') or double ("") quotes and can contain all other printable characters. Quotes and other special characters within strings are specified using *escape sequences*:

Chapter 10: Parser   47

\'	single quote
\"	double quote
\n	newline
\r	carriage return
\t	tab character
\b	backspace
\a	bell
\f	form feed
\v	vertical tab
\\	backslash itself

\nnn   character with given octal code – sequences of one, two or three digits in the range 0 ... 8 are accepted.

\xnn   character with given hex code – sequences of one or two hex digits (with entries 0 ... 9 A ... F a ... f).

\unnnn \u{nnnn}
      (where multibyte locales are supported, otherwise an error). Unicode character with given hex code – sequences of up to four hex digits. The character needs to be valid in the current locale.

\Unnnnnnnn \U{nnnnnnnn}
      (where multibyte locales are supported and not on Windows, otherwise an error). Unicode character with given hex code – sequences of up to eight hex digits.

A single quote may also be embedded directly in a double-quote delimited string and vice versa.

10.3.2 Identifiers

Identifiers consist of a sequence of letters, digits, the period ('.') and the underscore. They must not start with a digit nor underscore, nor with a period followed by a digit.

The definition of a letter depends on the current locale: the precise set of characters allowed is given by the C expression (isalnum(c) || c == '.' || c == '_') and will include accented letters in many Western European locales.

Notice that identifiers starting with a period are not by default listed by the ls function and that '...' and '..1', '..2', etc. are special.

Notice also that objects can have names that are not identifiers. These are generally accessed via get and assign, although they can also be represented by text strings in some limited circumstances when there is no ambiguity (e.g. "x" <- 1). As get and assign are not restricted to names that are identifiers they do not recognise subscripting operators or assignment functions. The following pairs are *not* equivalent

```
x$a<-1        assign("x$a",1)
x[[1]]        get("x[[1]]")
names(x)<-nm  assign("names(x)",nm)
```

10.3.3 Reserved words

The following identifiers have a special meaning and cannot be used for object names

```
if else repeat while function for in next break
TRUE FALSE NULL Inf NaN
NA NA_integer_ NA_real_ NA_complex_ NA_character_
... ..1 ..2 etc.
```

10.3.4 Special operators

R allows user-defined infix operators. These have the form of a string of characters delimited by the '%' character. The string can contain any printable character except '%'. The escape sequences for strings do not apply here.

Note that the following operators are predefined

```
%% %*% %/% %in% %o% %x%
```

10.3.5 Separators

Although not strictly tokens, stretches of whitespace characters (spaces and tabs) serve to delimit tokens in case of ambiguity, (compare x<-5 and x < -5).

Newlines have a function which is a combination of token separator and expression terminator. If an expression can terminate at the end of the line the parser will assume it does so, otherwise the newline is treated as whitespace. Semicolons (';') may be used to separate elementary expressions on the same line.

Special rules apply to the else keyword: inside a compound expression, a newline before else is discarded, whereas at the outermost level, the newline terminates the if construction and a subsequent else causes a syntax error. This somewhat anomalous behaviour occurs because R should be usable in interactive mode and then it must decide whether the input expression is complete, incomplete, or invalid as soon as the user presses (RET).

The comma (',') is used to separate function arguments and multiple indices.

10.3.6 Operator tokens

R uses the following operator tokens

+ - * / %% ^	arithmetic
> >= < <= == !=	relational
! & |	logical
~	model formulae
-> <-	assignment
$	list indexing
:	sequence

(Several of the operators have different meaning inside model formulas)

10.3.7 Grouping

Ordinary parentheses—'(' and ')'—are used for explicit grouping within expressions and to delimit the argument lists for function definitions and function calls.

Braces—'{' and '}'—delimit blocks of expressions in function definitions, conditional expressions, and iterative constructs.

10.3.8 Indexing tokens

Indexing of arrays and vectors performed using the single and double brackets, '[]' and '[[]]'. Also, indexing tagged lists may be done using the '$' operator.

10.4 Expressions

An R program consists of a sequence of R expressions. An expression can be a simple expression consisting of only a constant or an identifier, or it can be a compound expression constructed from other parts (which may themselves be expressions).

The following sections detail the various syntactical constructs that are available.

10.4.1 Function calls

A function call takes the form of a function reference followed by a comma-separated list of arguments within a set of parentheses.

> `function_reference ( arg1, arg2, ...... , argn )`

The function reference can be either

- an identifier (the name of the function)
- a text string (ditto, but handy if the function has a name which is not a valid identifier)
- an expression (which should evaluate to a function object)

Each argument can be tagged (`tag=expr`), or just be a simple expression. It can also be empty or it can be one of the special tokens '`...`', '`..2`', etc.

A tag can be an identifier or a text string.

Examples:

```
f(x)
g(tag = value, , 5)
"odd name"("strange tag" = 5, y)
(function(x) x^2)(5)
```

10.4.2 Infix and prefix operators

The order of precedence (highest first) of the operators are

```
::
$ @
^
- +                    (unary)
:
%xyz%
* /
+ -                    (binary)
> >= < <= == !=
!
& &&
| ||
~                      (unary and binary)
-> ->>
=                      (as assignment)
<- <<-
```

The exponentiation operator '`^`' and the left assignment operators '`<- - = <<-`' group right to left, all other operators group left to right. That is, $2 \verb|^| 2 \verb|^| 3$ is 2^8, not 4^3, whereas $1 - 1 - 1$ is -1, not 1.

Notice that the operators `%%` and `%/%` for integer remainder and divide have higher precedence than multiply and divide.

Although it is not strictly an operator, it also needs mentioning that the '`=`' sign is used for tagging arguments in function calls and for assigning default values in function definitions.

The '`$`' sign is in some sense an operator, but does not allow arbitrary right hand sides and is discussed under Section 10.4.3 [Index constructions], page 50. It has higher precedence than any of the other operators.

The parsed form of a unary or binary operation is completely equivalent to a function call with the operator as the function name and the operands as the function arguments.

Chapter 10: Parser

Parentheses are recorded as equivalent to a unary operator, with name "(", even in cases where the parentheses could be inferred from operator precedence (e.g., a * (b + c)).

Notice that the assignment symbols are operators just like the arithmetic, relational, and logical ones. Any expressions is allowed also on the target side of an assignment, as far as the parser is concerned (2 + 2 <- 5 is a valid expression as far as the parser is concerned. The evaluator will object, though). Similar comments apply to the model formula operator.

10.4.3 Index constructions

R has three indexing constructs, two of which are syntactically similar although with somewhat different semantics:

```
object [ arg1, ...... , argn ]
object [[ arg1, ...... , argn ]]
```

The *object* can formally be any valid expression, but it is understood to denote or evaluate to a subsettable object. The arguments generally evaluate to numerical or character indices, but other kinds of arguments are possible (notably drop = FALSE).

Internally, these index constructs are stored as function calls with function name "[" respectively "[[".

The third index construction is

```
object $ tag
```

Here, *object* is as above, whereas *tag* is an identifier or a text string. Internally, it is stored as a function call with name "$"

10.4.4 Compound expressions

A compound expression is of the form

```
{ expr1 ; expr2 ; ...... ; exprn }
```

The semicolons may be replaced by newlines. Internally, this is stored as a function call with "{" as the function name and the expressions as arguments.

10.4.5 Flow control elements

R contains the following control structures as special syntactic constructs

```
if ( cond ) expr
if ( cond ) expr1 else expr2
while ( cond ) expr
repeat expr
for ( var in list ) expr
```

The expressions in these constructs will typically be compound expressions.

Within the loop constructs (while, repeat, for), one may use break (to terminate the loop) and next (to skip to the next iteration).

Internally, the constructs are stored as function calls:

```
"if"(cond, expr)
"if"(cond, expr1, expr2)
"while"(cond, expr)
"repeat"(expr)
"for"(var, list, expr)
"break"()
"next"()
```

Chapter 10: Parser   51

10.4.6 Function definitions

A function definition is of the form

> function (*arglist*) *body*

The function body is an expression, often a compound expression. The *arglist* is a comma-separated list of items each of which can be an identifier, or of the form '*identifier = default*', or the special token '...'. The *default* can be any valid expression.

Notice that function arguments unlike list tags, etc., cannot have "strange names" given as text strings.

Internally, a function definition is stored as a function call with function name function and two arguments, the *arglist* and the *body*. The *arglist* is stored as a tagged pairlist where the tags are the argument names and the values are the default expressions.

Function and Variable Index

Function and Variable Index 53

Concept Index

Appendix A References

Richard A. Becker, John M. Chambers and Allan R. Wilks (1988), *The New S Language*. Chapman & Hall, New York. This book is often called the *"Blue Book"*.

Index

adverse selection, 108
alpha, 44, 111
  persistence of, 46
arbitrage pricing theory,
  2, 10
Arrow, Kenneth, 83
Ask, 7
author's motto, 20
auto regression, 22
autocorrelation, 99
average true range, 63

Bachelier, Louis, 3–4
Beat the Dealer, 78
bell shaped curve, 15
Bernoulli, Daniel, 37, 82–83
  proposed log utility, 37
Bernoulli, Nicolas, 37
beta, 44, 111
  persistence of, 46
bid, 7
bid-ask bounce, 24
Black Scholes model, 115
Black, Fisher, 10
Brownian Motion, 4
Burgi, Joost, 82

calls, similar to stop loss, 65
Capital Asset Pricing Model,
  45, 46, 95–96
CAPM, *see* Capital Asset
  Pricing Model
cdf normal, 18
CD-ROM, 11
Churchill, Winston, 51–52

compensation, manager
  behavior at thresholds,
  120
correlation, 76, 96, 99
  coefficient, definition, 42
  lagged, 99
  non-linear, 99
  of squared returns, 118
Covariance, defined, 42
  effect on variance, 95
Cramer, Gabriel, 82
cumulative density function,
  16
  normal, 17

data adjustments, 109
  adjusting for holidays, 111
  mining, 64
  net changes, 103
  price levels, 103
  quality, 102
  round off errors in, 109
  sample bias, 106
  synchronization, 103
  time stamping, 106
Debreu, G., 83
distribution
  advantages of empirical,
  69, 70
  binomial, 14
  choice of, 114
  continuous theoretical, 94
  definition, 14
  empirical, 23–24, 75, 96,
  114–115

empirical advantages of,
  114–115
empirical disadvantages
  of, 114
empirical disadvantages
  of, 116
empirical probability
  density function
  (pdf), 24
log normal, 19–20
lognormal as multiplicative
  model, 19, 61
non-parametric, 24
normal, 15–16
normal, as additive model,
  61
parametric, 24
probability, 14
Student, 40
tails, fat tails, 22, 114
theoretical advantages of,
  114
theoretical disadvantages,
  114
theoretical, 114
diversification, effect of, 81
drawdown, 78
drift, 6

e, 33, 37
Efficient frontier, 46–47
efficient market hypothesis,
  2–5, 9
EGARCH, 23
Einstein, Albert, 3–4

295